SOUTHERN COMFORT

SOUTHERN COMFORT

THE HISTORY OF BORDERS RUGBY

NEIL DRYSDALE

BIRLINN

First published in 2011 by
Birlinn Limited
West Newington House
10 Newington Road
Edinburgh
EH9 1QS

www.birlinn.co.uk

In association with the Bill McLaren Foundation

Visit www.billmclarenfoundation.co.uk for more information.

ISBN: 978 1 84158 997 8
eBook ISBN: 978 0 85790 097 5

British Library Cataloguing-in-Publication Data
A catalogue record for this book is available from the British Library

Typeset by Iolaire Typesetting, Newtonmore
Printed and bound by MPG Books Limited, Bodmin

CONTENTS

CONTENTS

FOREWORD

WHEN I TRAVELLED to Britain in 1984, as part of the Australian team which went on to win the Grand Slam, I already knew that rugby was popular in the Borders, and that Bill McLaren was the voice of the game. But I wasn't aware just how fanatically the sport was followed in the South of Scotland until I had bumped into many, many fans after we had been beaten 9–6 by the Borderers in Hawick. These supporters didn't just want to bask in their victory; instead, they wanted to talk to us, explore our shared love for rugby, and we chatted for so long that I ended up getting a lift in a police car back to the team hotel at three o'clock on the Sunday morning. It was a truly memorable experience.

The following week, in advance of our meeting with Scotland at Murrayfield, our squad was gathered together in a team meeting and, when it finished, this dapper gentleman walked up to me and politely asked if I could provide him with a few details of my career at that stage. He wasn't intrusive, nor did he seem to want any attention focused on himself. Instead, this was the peerless Bill McLaren going about his craft, working tirelessly behind the scenes, researching facts and checking statistics, to make sure that when the time came for him to pick up the microphone, he could make it all sound easy.

Already, as a youngster growing up in Australia, I had grown transfixed by listening to Bill painting pictures of Tests from places I had never visited, and it was fascinating to witness him at close quarters going about his business, quietly, unfussily, but with a genuine interest in the young players to whom he was speaking. I could tell that he must have been a terrific teacher. He was also the commentator who could best convey what was happening on a rugby field and did so without screaming, or trying to whip up arguments and being controversial for the sake of it. The love for – and knowledge of – rugby were there in the words, the fluency with which he described the action, and that was due to the hours of preparation which Bill had expended on getting it right in advance. He came to see us during our 1988 tour of Britain, and also attended our training sessions in Australia in 1992 before the Scots played us in two Test matches. Bill knew so much about us already, but, in his eyes, there was always something new to discover and that dedication left a positive impression with everybody he met.

For me, and I can't express it any other way, Bill *was* rugby. Nobody else will ever compare to him. He was a great man, a great mate, and he was Hawick through and through. He and his home town were inseparable and they always will be.

As the years passed, I returned to the Borders on a fairly regular basis and developed an affinity with the obvious passion which existed in that region for everything to do with rugby, and which ensured that they kept producing a string of world-class players, men in the mould of John Rutherford, Roy Laidlaw, Colin Deans and Jim Renwick. Personally, I think we have lost something in the modern era, where touring teams follow a relentless schedule of airport to hotel and training pitch to Test match, then it's on to the same routine the next week, and the same the week after that, and that is all the players get to see of the countries they are visiting. In 1984 we had 18 fixtures on our trip to Britain and Ireland and although our main focus was obviously rugby, we also had time to explore the communities and learn about the customs in the different places, as well as forging a connection with the supporters, which for me was very important.

This meant I had the chance to go out and take a look around the various towns and talk to people in the South of Scotland and, whether developing my fondness for Hawick Balls – the delicious minty sweets which the ubiquitous Bill used to hand out to friends, colleagues and players on his travels – or subsequently participating at the Melrose Sevens, which was one of the great events on the rugby calendar, I gradually started to understand how rugby was close to being a religion in that part of the world.

I was part of the Randwick team which visited Melrose in 1990, along with team-mates such as Glen Ella, John Maxwell and Michael Cheika, the latter of whom now coaches Stade Français, and it soon became pretty obvious that, while Borders people will extend a warm greeting to visitors, that friendliness stopped as soon as we had walked out on to the pitch. It was a fantastic tournament but it was also a real test of endurance, because you gained so little time to recover between matches, and I can remember the sense of relief when I dived over in the corner to score a try at the end of our match with Melrose, which obviously didn't please the locals or Craig Chalmers too much! That was another aspect of the Borders which fascinated me: the way in which they pulled together and, whether you went to Hawick or Melrose or Galashiels, they all had their own identities and yet could pool their resources together in a bigger cause when it was required.

The upshot has clearly benefited Scottish rugby, and I feel privileged to have known Bill – the two of us were inducted into the IRB Hall of Fame in the same year – and although many things have changed in the sport, I genuinely believe that the values which Bill cherished, such as the camaraderie which existed between teams, and a sense of adventure and desire to entertain being encouraged by coaches, will not be sacrificed in the pursuit of winning at all costs. So too, I hope that the qualities which have brought so much success to the Borders will continue to thrive in the future. It is a special part of the world and one which rugby enthusiasts everywhere should cherish.

David Campese,
July 2011

INTRODUCTION

JONI MITCHELL had it right. Sometimes you don't know what you've got till it's gone. Year in, year out, those of us who were born and grew up in the Central Belt used to take it for granted that, while football was the number one sport in Scotland, there would always be a part of our country where a volunteer army of Stakhanovite souls could be relied upon to expend countless hours of energy into developing excellence in rugby union.

That place was the Scottish Borders and their part in the story of the oval ball has been immense. Indeed, without the tireless endeavours of generations of players and coaches, officials and supporters, there would probably have been no Grand Slam in 1984 or 1990, because the contribution of those who emerged from the likes of Melrose and Hawick, Gala and Jed-Forest, Selkirk and Kelso was crucial to the eventual triumphs of Jim Aitken and David Sole's teams. And when one casts one's gaze over the litany of world-class performers who have emerged from those little communities in the South — where no town has a population of more than 20,000 — and examines the influence on the global game of individuals such as Jim Telfer, Derrick Grant, Hugh McLeod, Bill McLaren and Ned Haig, allied to the status of such maestri as John Rutherford, Colin Deans, Gary Armstrong, John Jeffrey, Jim Renwick, Roy Laidlaw, Alan Tait, Keith Robertson, Craig Chalmers, Alan Tomes, Doddie Weir and, continuing into the present day with the most-capped

Scot to have played the game, Chris Paterson, it should be evident that those who have been the catalysts for sustained success in Borders rugby, whether in the limelight or toiling assiduously behind the scenes, deserve to have their exploits from the last 140-plus years celebrated with gratitude from the outside world.

In recent seasons, the sport throughout Scotland has been buffeted by negative headlines, protracted internecine warfare, endless club versus district arguments and howls of anguish from many traditional rugby aficionados about what they perceive to be the pernicious consequences of professionalism during the last 15 years. Indeed, just a few weeks before these words were written, the SRU chief executive, Gordon McKie, exited his post at Murrayfield, amid reports of committee unrest, and accusations that he was a bean-counter with more interest in balancing the books than drafting a vision for the future. To many of us, who feel as if we have been inescapably caught up in the sporting equivalent of a war zone, these stramashes, which have usually been conducted by people without the courage to stick their heads above the parapet, have been deeply damaging to the Scottish game. And while it would be pleasant to imagine that common sense might finally break out, once the majority of people realise that the sport has been drinking in the last-chance saloon for far too long, that is probably about as likely as Brian Moore doing an entire commentary shift with a smile on his face and a song in his heart.

In which light, it seemed like the right time to highlight one of the truly uplifting stories in Scottish rugby and nowhere merits richer plaudits than the Borders, whether in the region's radical creation of the Border League, or their invention of Sevens (which will shortly be included in the Olympic Games, and which has recently surged in popularity among countries in Africa, Europe and Australasia), or the astonishing exploits of clubs such as Hawick and Melrose, both of which have punched far above their weights in the sport, with a giddying spirit of enterprise and energy.

On my regular visits to these two locales during the last 20 years, the qualities which have constantly shone like beacons have been the dedication, selfless commitment and sheer unfettered enthusiasm of those who live and breathe to spread the rugby gospel. Some people still maintain that the sport has suffered since the arrival of professionalism, with too much attention focused on a small, elite band of players, while Scotland's clubs have plummeted into steep decline. But anybody who tried to convey that message to the thousands of fans who roared their approval when Melrose surged to victory in the Premiership, the Border League and their own Sevens this spring would have received a pretty sharp retort to the suggestion that their pursuit was in the doldrums.

Instead, they were part of an ongoing tale which encompasses local heroes, stalwart servants who seek neither recognition nor riches, but remain happy to work tirelessly behind the scenes; and the exertions of this volunteer army have been the catalyst for the development of a gifted ensemble of virtuoso players, many of whom shone for the South, then with Scotland and the British and Irish Lions, without ever forgetting about their roots. This book is a tribute to them and also a commemoration of one or two special individuals, men such as Bill McLaren, whose voice first left me enthralled by the whole pageantry of rugby in the 1970s, and Jim Telfer, whose gruff tones have occasionally reduced towering hulks to quivering jellyfish, but whose contribution, as a player and a coach – but, sadly, not an administrator – have been invaluable in nurturing generations of youngsters in his native Borders and spreading the game's gospel from such hamlets as Earlston and Melrose to the rugby enclaves of the southern hemisphere.

The publication of this work would not have been possible without contributions from many of the most illustrious names in Scotland's history and I am grateful for the input of such childhood heroes of mine as Jim Telfer, Colin Deans, Alan Tomes, Jim Renwick, John Rutherford, Ian Barnes, Norman Pender, Keith Robertson and George Fairbairn. From a more contemporary vintage, I was privileged to speak to an array of such estimable characters as Craig Chalmers, John Jeffrey, Iain Paxton, Doddie Weir, Gary Armstrong, Rowen Shepherd, Alan Tait, Ross Ford, Craig Redpath and Chris Paterson. The latter man, in my opinion, encapsulates the qualities which have been shared by many of his illustrious predecessors: an unstinting effort and consummate team ethic in every performance, allied to an unfailing modesty in dealing with his celebrity. I am probably not the only person to believe that if Scotland could send out 15 Patersons on to the pitch, we would win many more international matches than we would lose.

The Borders' consistent exploits have depended, of course, on a string of other dedicated club men and women, whose labours have ensured Border League success for their own communities and these people have been the heart and the pulse of the sport in the South of Scotland. I talked to many of these individuals and would particularly like to thank Gala's John Gray and Colin Playfair, Melrose's Jack Dun, Langholm's John Smith, Kelso's Ewan Brewis and Norman Anderson, Hawick's John Thorburn, Jed-Forest's Heather Smith, Peebles' Jim Currie and Selkirk's Donald Macleod and Ross Thomson. I am also grateful for the insight of the Scotland Rugby League historian, Gavin Willacy, and the RFL's Tony Collins. In terms of analysing the Borders professional structure, and why it suffered so grievously at the hands of the SRU, I am also appreciative of the back-ground information provided by the former Scotland centre,

Alastair Cranston, and two other officials, who requested anonymity. It would have been a merciful release if I had been able to avoid the tristesse-laden saga of the Border Reivers during that professional organisation's troubled incarnations, but the failure of Scotland to respond to professionalism is central to what has gone wrong in the country's rugby since the high points of the Grand Slam in 1990 and World Cup semi-final appearance in 1991 and I felt that it was necessary to explore the reasons why the issue became so problematic.

I was keen to gather as many reminiscences as possible and this task has been made easier by the assistance of a number of my journalistic colleagues. Thanks are due (in no particular order) to Alasdair Reid, William Paul, David Ferguson, Bill Lothian, Kevin Ferrie, Bill Johnstone, Peter Donald, John Dawson, Alex Gordon and John Beattie. Others who have made my task easier include the always-illuminating secretary of Glasgow Hawks, Hugh Barrow, the SRU's Dominic McKay and Graham Law, and the historian and journalist Laing Speirs, while the insightful rugby columnist and proud Souter, Allan Massie, obviously shares the same reverence for the aforementioned Rutherford as myself. I am also indebted to the fashion in which the late Walter Thomson and Sandy Thorburn covered the earlier chapters of Scotland's rugby development, while the staff at Airyhall Library in Aberdeen were exemplars of patience in dealing with the reams of material which I printed out during a storm-tossed winter.

As usual, I would like to thank my agent, Mark Stanton, and Peter Burns, the sports editor at Birlinn, while, yet again, paying tribute to my wife, Dianne, who was a tower of strength (and technical know-how), whether driving me to and from the Borders or instructing me in such essential tools of the trade as cutting and pasting!

It has all added up to a cherishable experience and I have

made the acquaintance of a rich array of characters, whose names may be unknown outside the Borders, but whose devotion to rugby was – and is – compelling. Very few of us can ever hope to dazzle in the style of John Rutherford and Keith Robertson or scare the life out of opposition packs in the fashion of Colin Deans and Alan Tomes, but the sport in the South of Scotland also depends on such unheralded stalwarts as Jim Currie, the Peebles farmer whose labours have been instrumental in the progression of his club into the Border League. Similarly, when Philiphaugh, the charming home of Selkirk RFC, fell victim to a deluge of rain, thunderstorms and a freak hailstorm in the spring of 2003, which cumulatively caused serious damage to its facilities and the surrounding areas, it was not just the rugby community which helped in the restoration, but the rest of the townsfolk as well. That shared pride in preserving rugby, whatever the circumstances, is humbling.

In any venture of this nature, one has to cover both positive and negative aspects, but I have generally attempted to favour the former and pay due homage to a small area of Scotland which has provided the nation with more than a sixth of its international players. Ultimately, it will be up to others to decide, but I hope that Borders people believe me when I tell them that I regard their litany of achievements, ever since Langholm came into existence in 1871, as a genuine sporting wonder.

Neil Drysdale,
June 2011

Chapter One

THE DEATH OF AN ICONIC FIGURE

WHEN THE NEWS first surfaced that Bill McLaren had passed away in his beloved Borders in January 2010, it was one of those moments when millions of people, who had never met the man, but heard his mellifluous tones, stopped for an instant, enveloped by a wave of sadness. McLaren, one of a small band of commentators who could enthral those with little or no interest in rugby union, was a genuinely iconic figure; a self-effacing Scot who never allowed fame to transcend his innate courtesy to everybody he encountered, and was as famous in the wider world as when he walked round his native Hawick.

On one occasion, while travelling to a Scotland press conference in Dunedin in 1996, I only had to mention my origins for my taxi driver to start chatting about the people he regarded as the three sages of the Caledonian game; namely, Jim Telfer, John Rutherford and Bill McLaren. It was a triumvirate of contrasting personalities, to be sure, but with one common bond in that they were all born and bred in the Scottish Borders, and had stamped their imprint on the sport through their addiction to, and expertise with, the oval ball. And if you can please the rugby faithful in the Land of the Long White Cloud, you can do it anywhere else on the planet. This driver had never visited Scotland, but he had ample tales to relate about listening to Bill on his rickety old wireless as a teenager.

Hence the sorrow at the news of McLaren's death, even if he had, by his own admission, enjoyed a good innings in living until he was 86, and particularly when one recalled how close he came to succumbing to tuberculosis more than 60 years earlier. In that sense, Bill was very much of his time and place: he recognised that, in the grand scheme, rugby was only a game and should never be regarded as a matter of life or death, especially in light of the dreadful carnage which McLaren witnessed while fighting at the Battle of Monte Cassino during the Second World War. And yet, for all that he returned from the conflict with some awful tableaux etched on his mind, you would rarely have guessed it from the instinctive good humour which he brought to any conversation. So too, if sport was a lifelong passion, it was also a bedrock for the qualities which he cherished as a teacher, a journalist and 'the Voice of Rugby' – a term which he never used himself, and which caused him some embarrassment when he was feted on his travels.

Understandably enough, his funeral provoked debate about some aspects of McLaren's career, such as his perceived disenchantment with the introduction of professionalism in the union code in 1995. Yet, on the evidence of the interview which I carried out at his Hawick home in 2003, his love for rugby never wavered as he advanced into the winter of his life. On the contrary, Bill both confessed he could hardly wait for that year's World Cup, and even admitted – he was always a prescient fellow – that he believed England had a decent chance of winning the tournament in Australia. But what struck me most was his response to my question about why rugby had appealed to him so much.

I suppose it is the fact it gives everybody a chance to play their part on the field, whether they are wee fellows or big hulking brutes of boys. The worst thing, when you are a PE teacher, is to hear children telling you that there is no place for them on a sports pitch, and that was one of the positive things about rugby and the way it was organised in the Borders, where we were all encouraged to enjoy ourselves first and worry about the technical details later on. It allowed everyone an opportunity to find a position which they could try to make their own, and I always had the idea that if you made youngsters feel wanted, they would enjoy being part of a team. The skinny ones could go to the wing if they wanted to run with the ball, the more muscular ones could learn about working together at the scrum, and the wee ones could be scrum-half or test themselves at fly-half. I remember watching a football match in Glasgow, way back in the mists of time, where this giant lad kept scoring goals for fun against these tiny wee defenders and I thought to myself: 'That's not a fair contest'. I am not criticising football, for the sake of it, but it just always struck me that rugby had a lot more going for it, in terms of making everyone feel that they could contribute to the game and work for the benefit of their team.

The Borders has thrived on this conviction for the last 150 years and longer, and there are worse philosophies than making everybody believe they have a role to play in sport, as in society. At McLaren's funeral, there were tears in the January chill, but there was also laughter, respect, camaraderie, and an overwhelming sense that Bill had made a difference, not only to the thousands of Hawick children he had taught throughout his career, but to the close-knit little communities such as Melrose, Selkirk, Jedburgh, Kelso, Langholm, Galashiels and the rest of the places which comprise the Borders, an area which has produced a disproportionate number of international rugby stars since the sport came into existence. Indeed, even the bare statistic that a region with a population of roughly one-fortieth of that of Scotland has generated over

170 internationalists – around a sixth of the total number of men who have ever pulled on a blue jersey – demonstrates the efficacy of the work at the grass roots, the unpaid years of service from battalions of volunteers around Mansfield Park and the Greenyards, Netherdale and Philiphaugh, and the pride in their roots which encompasses the attitude of those who preach the rugby gospel. McLaren was one of the chief evangelists and enjoyed the ability to communicate technical details to the cognoscenti without ever losing touch with those who only watched one match a year to discover whether the Scots might beat the English.

In short, as his grandson, Gregor Lawson, declared, during a commemoration which amply celebrated the myriad ingredients of McLaren's appeal: 'To Nana [his wife, Bette], he was a hot water bottle, hooverer, dance partner, her golden boy, the love of her life and soulmate of 62 years. He was a modern dad, when dads weren't very modern, a great mate and role model, and, to his grandchildren, he was everything a Papa should be. He was a great storyteller, and he was always great fun.' Ultimately, in Lawson's words, Bill was 'a great Hawick man, a great rugby man, a great family man'. If anything, I would go further and assert that McLaren possessed all the diverse qualities which have explained and defined the rise and continuing success of rugby in the Borders.

Certainly, the faces in the crowd at his funeral testified to one simple truth: that his commentaries had coincided with most of the golden moments in the history of the game in Scotland, from the triumphs of the 1984 and 1990 Grand Slams to the brace of victories over England within the space of a week in 1971, and onwards to his country's success in the last Five Nations Championship in 1999, as McLaren edged towards retirement, on his own terms, with his reputation wholly intact. Borderers were pivotal performers in all these achievements, whether as coaches, tough-tackling centres, mercurial half-backs or redoubtable props, and many came to pay their respects at Teviot Parish Church.

Alasdair Reid, a long-term colleague of mine, summed up the atmosphere superbly in the *Herald* when he a painted a vivid picture of the valediction to a nonpareil.

They came from the worlds of sport, and politics, and broadcasting. But they came in their greatest numbers from the tight-knit community of Borders rugby, determined to say a respectful farewell to one of their own. Big-boned men in club blazers sat, shoulder to burly shoulder, along the packed pews. Bill McLaren's family had asked the mourners to wear their club blazers and they responded in huge numbers, sporting the crests and badges of the handful of sides which, between them, have earned the area global renown. A good number of them were in the congregation – John Jeffrey of Kelso, the White Shark himself, with John Rutherford of Selkirk, so dapper you would swear he could still do a shift for Scotland. There was Jed-Forest's Gary Armstrong, Melrose's Doddie Weir, and Gregor Townsend of Gala; great players and names that resonate far beyond the Tweed Valley. And, of course, we had the Hawick contingent too. McLaren's nearest and dearest – not that you would have known it when he was commentating on their games – 58 players, who graduated from the green of Hawick to the blue of Scotland.

Had tuberculosis not struck him down in 1948, McLaren would almost certainly have added to their number. But the holy trinity were there: Jim Renwick, Colin Deans and Tony Stanger, 52 caps apiece, and a shared background in the primary school teams which McLaren coached. And Hugh McLeod, the teak-tough prop they called the Hawick Hardman when he was in his prime half a century ago. McLaren's coffin was borne into and carried from the church on the shoulders of members of the current [Mansfield Park] team. It was the most fitting farewell for a thoroughly local hero.

By exploring some of the characteristics which McLaren shared with his Borders brethren, we can perhaps begin to comprehend why such a small region has proved instrumental in moulding Scotland's rugby past, present and, hopefully, future. Bill, first and foremost, was a student of methodical preparation, with a keen eye for minutiae, and shared Jim Telfer's approach that genius is an infinite capacity for taking pains. In the Murrayfield media centre, there is an example of the detailed, pre-match research which he carried out and, even in his 70s, on that sojourn to New Zealand 15 years ago, he still devoted hours to the task of unearthing as many nuggets of information and career statistics as he possibly could about the All Blacks prior to joining up with his Scottish colleagues for the tourists' briefing, oblivious to the fact that he was already steeped in knowledge about his compatriots. This was reminiscent of the thirst for new ideas and innovative tactics, which were so beloved of Telfer, a man who once digressed from an interview about the Five Nations in his office at Murrayfield by speaking about his regard for Marshal Tito, the old partisan leader in Yugoslavia. On many occasions, Telfer has been portrayed as a Victor Meldrewesque figure, and he certainly knew how to put the fear of God into those he regarded as abusing their talent, but it is more sensible to view him as one of those Borders individuals with a fiercely independent streak, who reckoned that Scotland would always be struggling in the numbers game, compared to the likes of France, England and, further afield, South Africa and Australia, so he and his colleagues had to act as guerrilla commanders, making a virtue of necessity, burrowing away at the grass roots, and creating the pathways for the next generation and the one after that. Almost from the day he picked up a rugby ball, Telfer was involved with teams, whether at club or district level, who had far fewer participants than were available to the coaches and selectors in Glasgow and Edinburgh, but he and McLaren shared the perspective that if you make a convert soon enough, you will have them for life. Essentially, it was a policy of 'Education, Education, Education' before the phrase was hijacked by Tony Blair, and it paid a rich dividend, both in Telfer's ability to transform the British and Irish Lions into slayers of the Springboks in 1997, and McLaren's ability to reel off names, caps, locations and trivia, as if it was the easiest thing in the world. It wasn't, but this capacity for thriving on their teaching background and imparting the sheer, unalloyed joy of participating in rugby has served the Borders proud throughout its history.

Understandably, therefore, Telfer paid a rich tribute to McLaren when he learned of the latter's passing. 'Bill was always around when I was involved in rugby and, to me, he was like Robert Burns; an ordinary man, who was universally known. He was one in a million and unique as far as commentary was concerned,' said the Melrosian. 'He had a real feeling for the game and understood completely what it was all about. Coming from the Borders and with his innate knowledge, he could suss out players and talk to them until the cows came home. His biggest contribution was to non-rugby people, who used to listen to him, and Bill educated the world about rugby. He was a genuine rugby person, who loved speaking about the game to anybody that wanted to listen. He was also eager to learn the thoughts of [New Zealand's peerless flanker] Richie McCaw and [the Australian winger] David Campese on the technical side, just as much as he would talk with the coaches. And, obviously, there was the voice, which was special.'

Ah yes, the voice. Which was as distinctive in its own milieu as Sinatra was in Las Vegas or Richie Benaud commentating from Australia during a dank Scottish winter. Even now, more than a year after his demise, McLaren's broadcasts remain peerless examples of their craft; he never used 20 words where four or five would suffice and blended his pawky humour with enough technical information to carry out the job of instructing *and* entertaining in the same sentence. It was not a trick as such, but a skill which he perfected while recovering from the TB which nearly killed him. Yet although McLaren was fortunate to be born with such a richly evocative lilt, the words would have counted for nothing if he had been spouting gibberish or running up blind alleys.

Instead, he possessed a singular knack for taking a sidestep in an unexpected direction, or thinking on his feet, with descriptions of players which ideally suited the circumstances. A bedraggled scrum-half on a sodden afternoon in Selkirk might resemble 'a drookit rat', another was 'as slippery as a baggy in a Borders burn', a kick might 'hirple' through the posts, or two battling packs might indulge in 'a bit of argy-bargy in the scrum'. Some players were 'rampant stags', others 'ran like mad giraffes', and his favourites, whether they hailed from Dundee, Durban or Dunedin – Bill was never biased in his life – were accorded their due with his almost limitless vocabulary. He was to the English language what John Rutherford was to Scotland; a master of any situation, who never forgot that he was there to serve others, and yet possessed so many adroit qualities that rugby was often elevated from a mere sport into a work of art. When one looks back to the 1980s and recalls the number of Borders stars who emerged in the same period, whether it was Rutherford at Selkirk, John Jeffrey at Kelso, Peter Dods at Gala or Roy Laidlaw at Jed-Forest, it was clear this was a halcyon period for the sport in the South of Scotland and the whole country benefited from the process. And if there were men and women toiling tirelessly behind the scenes at these organisations, another part of the attraction, which explained the spread in rugby's appeal, was how these players seemed so down-to-earth and decent, especially compared with their football counterparts, who had not only made Scotland an international laughing stock at the 1978 World Cup in Argentina, but had become associated with drunken loutishness and a petulant prima-donnaism.

McLaren hated this 'Look-at-me' ostentation. He genuinely believed that rugby gained immensely from the fact that characters such as Laidlaw, Renwick and Jeffrey returned to their jobs in the Borders, whether working on farms or earning a living from their trades in plumbing and joinery, or as roofers, lorry drivers and mechanics. Jeffrey, one of the most redoubtable flankers of his generation, told me the story of how, after the Scots had thrashed Zimbabwe 51–12 in the 1991 World Cup – and this was a period of almost unprecedented riches for the Murrayfield brigade – he was not commended for the quality of his performance when he headed back to the Borders the next morning, but chided and derided for spilling the ball with the try line at his mercy! Yet, if this was being unduly nit-picking, such remarks kept the leading lights grounded and one of the reasons behind the South's constant success lay in how quickly any perceived swollen heads had their egos deflated by their townsfolk. McLaren, himself, was regularly offered opportunities to spread his wings beyond rugby by the BBC and one suspects that he would have been equally adept at commentating on state occasions as sporting events, given his talent for plucking an apt phrase from the ether without resorting to mere cliché. But, as another son of the South, Allan Massie, the author and journalist, declared in *The Scotsman*, that would have interfered with Bill's teaching and it was not to be countenanced.

He was a schoolmaster all his working life and though he became one of the most famous, and certainly best-loved, of sporting commentators and journalists, he resisted invitations and inducements to become a full-time broadcaster. It would have thrown his life out of balance and while he enjoyed the respect and affection which he had earned, he had no taste for celebrity. Bill was modest and regarded himself as the servant of rugby rather than its voice. He loved the game and that came through in all of his commentaries, but he loved his wife, Bette, and his family more, and maybe his home town of Hawick, too, though I suspect that he would never have managed to disassociate the idea of Hawick from the idea of rugby.

Listening to him was like attending a match with a very knowledgeable friend. He also did the simple things that some commentators forget because they are too busy expressing their own opinions; making sure he identified the man with the ball or the tackler, for instance. He was also wonderfully fair and generous. Though a proud Scot, I doubt if anyone ever detected bias in his commentary – even when his son-in-law, Alan Lawson, scored a brilliant try against England in 1976. He never forgot that all sorts of people were listening to him, some who knew a lot about rugby, others who knew very little, and he had to cater for all of them. To do this satisfactorily is difficult and many good commentators in all sports can't bring it off. Bill always could.

The advent of professionalism saddened him, though you would never have known it from his commentaries. He recognised the high quality of the professional game at its best, but he knew how much had been lost and regretted that international players were now cut off from the clubs and communities that had bred them. But he retired at a time of his own choosing [after the Melrose Sevens in 2002], before, so he said, someone tapped him on the shoulder and talked of a replacement. This was in character.

So was the thrill which McLaren derived from Scotland's displays throughout the 1999 Five Nations Championship when it briefly appeared that another glorious ensemble might be taking shape. I met him at the Stade de France in Paris, on a glorious sun-drenched afternoon in April, prior to the tussle with Les Bleus and despite his advancing years, Bill was still distributing his Hawick Balls, the boiled sweets which seemed to accompany him around the globe. He was optimistic about the visitors' chances, albeit combined with a note of caution about how the conditions might suit the hosts, but, as it transpired, it was the Scots who produced a scintillating exhibition of power and panache, while scoring five first-half tries with a breathtaking *joie de vivre*. Once or twice, I glanced over at the BBC box, and there he was, revelling in the spectacle, but also concerned about the severity of the injury which saw the mercurial Thomas Castaignède stretchered off in the second minute of the contest. One would never have guessed that this, in his opinion, was one of his country's finest ever displays, nor that much of their success was down to the magnificent contributions of the Borderers in the ranks.

Yet it would be hard to overstate the importance of three of that XV, in the guise of Gary Armstrong, Alan Tait and Gregor Townsend, who combined with a rare symbiosis, which reflected the diverse strands of Borders tradition from the early days. Armstrong, the terrier-like scrum-half, was following in a distinguished line of previous No 9s, but if anybody had ever put in more tackles and flung their body into the fray more often for their country than this little Jed knight, it was difficult to recall their name. Even when the Scots led 33–22 at the interval, Armstrong knew there would be a response from the French, if only to stifle the chorus of boos inside the stadium, and he urged his team to be ready for the onslaught. However, such was his unstinting commitment and relentless industry that it often felt as if there were two or three Armstrong clones on the pitch. But nobody was surprised: wee Gary had done this since the outset of his career, transcending all manner of setbacks in the process.

He had also suffered more injuries than the majority of his contemporaries and the IRB's sanctioning of professionalism at least allowed him to make the move from the Borders to Newcastle and set himself and his family up with something more substantial than back-slapping congratulations and a pint behind every bar in Jedburgh. To a significant extent, this was where McLaren's argument broke down, because it was all very well for the doctors, accountants, property developers and lawyers to rejoice in amateurism; they knew they were secure once they had packed away their boots. Armstrong, a working-class man from a rugby-daft family, was not so fortunate, in which light the arrival of the pay-for-play era provided him with an element of security for the future.

Tait, his fellow Borderer and Newcastle team-mate, was an even starker example of the choices which had confronted many of the lower-paid sports stars in the South of Scotland. He had switched codes to rugby league in the late 1980s and, for a while at least, was treated as something of a pariah figure in Scottish circles, as if it was a dreadful crime to be paid for excelling on the sporting stage. (And this paled in comparison to some of his predecessors, who were shunned by their former friends after moving to the league circuit in the 1950s and 1960s). Eventually, just as Jonathan Davies did in Wales, the so-called prodigal son returned to the union environment and duly showed his compatriots what they had been missing for the best part of a decade. Indeed, Tait was one of the linchpins of Scotland's success in that 1999 championship and it was noticeable that when he retired at the conclusion of the World Cup a few months later, his country fell into a slough of despond from which, in truth, they have never really recovered.

If Armstrong and Tait were the hard-as-nails, bristling bulwarks at the heart of that Caledonian line-up, Townsend was the fellow with the artistic temperament and a sprinkling of magic in his repertoire. Throughout Borders history, there had been other instances of this amalgam of silk and steel and, invariably, it required both properties to prosper. Yet, when the disparate elements clicked together, it frequently offered glimpses of genius, and the fashion in which Townsend, bolstered by the reassuring presence of Tait in the centre and Armstrong watching his back, controlled the proceedings in Paris was as masterly as it was mesmerising. The following morning, a crowd of us bumped into McLaren at Charles de Gaulle airport and he was still purring at the fashion in which the Scots had performed out of their skins. On most other weekends, their win would only have been good enough to earn them the runners-up berth in the campaign, but Sunday brought another shock when Wales, outpunched and out-fought for the majority of the proceedings against England, somehow managed to stay on their feet and snatch victory with a Scott Gibbs try and Neil Jenkins conversion in the dying seconds of the match. In the Borders, Telfer remarked that it might have been raining outside, but the sun was shining radiantly inside his house. McLaren, too, was en-thralled by the manner in which his compatriots had soared to the Five Nations title during a dramatic denouement. Neither of them had any personal antipathy towards the RFU's finest, far from it. This was pride in Scotland's derring-do rather than *Schadenfreude*. But it was a success which would not have been possible without the Borders influence.

Why should this have happened? Why did football exert a grip everywhere else in Scotland when rugby held sway in the Borders? There was one straightforward reason: the zeal shown by the Victorian devotees, who had established thriv-ing 15-a-side organisations in their towns and villages before the Old Firm were even in existence. Next, there was the size and shape issue: the South had a major agricultural base and many of the farmers had more bulk and muscle than pace – in short (and tall), they were better suited to rugby than any other pursuit. There again, one cannot ignore the influence of men such as Ned Haig, the butcher who dreamt up the idea of Sevens, which has now become a global pursuit, allied to the development work carried out at the likes of Hawick and Gala, whose founders realised that they had to provide opportunities to more than 20 or 30 players, and they could not simply cater for the elite. This, in turn, filtered down to the schools, and generations of children grew up with the game in their blood. As McLaren, one of those who was an integral part of the process, told me, while we were watching the Hawick Sevens on a frozen April afternoon at Mansfield Park: 'It seemed like the most natural thing in the world to be playing rugby from an early age. And once you have success, and you have your own [Borders] league, that gives the youngsters something else to aim at.' He always feared that the collapse of the traditional industries and subsequent migration of many in the Borders to the cities in the late 1980s and 1990s might weaken the standard in his region – and Bill was uncharacteristically gloomy about the SRU's messing around with the Borders professional team, which came and went, and lived and died, almost on a whim – and, to some extent, that pessimism was justified. Nonetheless, when one examines the sheer numbers who came through the ranks from the Borders, it was a testimony to the link between the schools and their local clubs.

That same process never happened in Edinburgh and Glasgow, where the private schools created their rugby structures without bothering to look beyond their own enclaves for players and coaches. It might be simplistic to claim that the sport flourished in the South, because it was run on egalitarian principles, but if there is truth in the adage that if you catch a kid young, you capture him forever, the Borders recognised the best means of setting up a conveyor belt of talent. In Glasgow, on the other hand, the likes of Queen's Park dedicated themselves to spreading the football gospel, while the likes of Clydesdale Cricket Club organised a winter team, from which eventually emerged Rangers FC. (Mind you, it should not be ignored that this is also how Hawick RFC came into being, when their cricketers decided that, in order to keep fit when the nights drew in, they should begin playing football. Both the association and the rugby varieties were considered before they elected for the latter and it has to be wondered how different the history of Scottish rugby might have been if they had gone in the other direction!)

Success, of course, breeds popularity and the trophy-winning exploits of McLaren's beloved club in the halcyon period between 1945 and 1972, when they won eight un-official championships and 15 Border League titles, was the catalyst for players flocking to the sport in ever-greater numbers. But this brings us to another important factor, whereby these clubs built up momentum in rugby, at the same time as football was king everywhere else. Expressed bluntly, the Borderers liked a scrap, and there was scope for some genuine physical confrontations in their favourite sport, which differed from the football ethos, which revolved more around individual skill than collective might.

This led to a polarisation between the South and the cities. Duggie Middleton, the Heriot's historian, pointed out to me the fashion in which the Borders fans would denigrate their capital opponents as a 'bunch of pen-pushers', whilst some of the central-belt teams made cheap gibes about the 'brainless' mentality of the farming fraternity. Much of this was good-natured banter, but a greater truth lurked under the surface. Namely that when the going got tough, whether at club or district level, it was the men from the South of Scotland who would invariably do whatever was required to seize the initiative, leading to a situation where even the likes of John Beattie – one of the meanest hombres ever to represent Scotland and the Lions – spoke of his apprehension about embarking on trips to places such as Langholm, where there was a genuinely hostile reception for visitors.

This aggressive quality meant that the city slickers frequently came a cropper on their trips down to the Borders even when they were of equal ability to, or marginally better than, their Southern counterparts. It was not so much that the likes of Heriot's and Glasgow Accies were in the habit of producing players with a soft centre, but rather that clubs in the mould of Hawick, Gala and Kelso knew what it took to get over the line, and also had experience of the flak they would face from their peers if they came up short. The late Brian Gilbert, a man who coached in Glasgow for most of his career, spelled out the different mentalities which existed between the two areas with the memorable phrase: 'When the going gets tough, our guys go skiing.' But the astute Gilbert made several other telling observations about why the Borders was such a hotbed of rugby.

Down in Hawick, they pin up the team for the following Saturday's match on the notice board in the town centre and there is no place to hide once your name is on that list. The locals know everybody, they argue about the selections, there is an incredible amount of competition for places, and it all adds up to a situation where rugby is at the heart of the community. Up here in Glasgow – and it is much the same in Edinburgh – you can have a bad game and slip off quietly into the night and you can pretty much guarantee that you won't bump into anybody who was at the match, which means there isn't the same pressure on you to perform at your best, week in, week out. I have tried to get the message through to our youngsters that the success of the Borders sides hasn't happened by accident and that we are never going to reach the same standards if we don't care as much as they do. But, in the final analysis, if you have the attitude that it is only a bit of fun and that it doesn't matter that much whether you win or lose, you are going to be struggling when you come up against guys who are playing for their whole town.

For the most part, this Borders obsession had positive consequences, but, occasionally, there was justified criticism of the 'Aye-Been' attitude to any new developments in the sport, whereby the traditionalists stuck to rigid conventions and rituals which were past their sell-by date, when they needed to be more forward-thinking. By the early 1990s, it was clear to most of us that rugby was destined to become a professional sport sooner rather than later – though many were surprised at how rapidly the transition occurred – and when the New Zealanders arrived in Britain for their winter tour in 1993, it was obvious that, to all intents and purposes, their squad was packed with players whose livelihoods amounted to the full-time pursuit of rugby excellence. The evidence of the gulf in standards between their second-string team and the hapless South of Scotland side, which lined up against the All Blacks on a Wednesday afternoon in November, could hardly have been more cruelly exposed than by the eventual 84–5 margin of defeat: an outcome which not only led to an unprecedented amount of soul-searching among players, fans and the media, but also prompted jokes to the effect that somebody should have told the Scots that they were allowed to move once the haka was finished! McLaren was there that day, and even the master found it a tough assignment to gloss over the deficiencies of his compatriots. He eventually reached the stage where he stopped saying 'and x or y will be disappointed with that . . .' and replaced it with lavish praise for the Kiwis.

However, many other Borderers were less inclined to paper over the cracks. Craig Chalmers, one of the new breed of hard-nosed Scots with a professional approach to rugby, even if he was not earning a wage for participating in the sport, warned his compatriots that they had to wake up and appreciate that the talent in the national game was spread a foot wide and an inch deep. Iwan Tukalo also voiced his concerns: 'Those who have claimed that if the full Scottish side is okay, then there can't be much wrong with the system, will have had this myth shattered by Wednesday's debacle.'

It was a clash between conflicting philosophies, and an argument which raged on behind the scenes for the best part of the next decade, yet, just as they had done so many times before, the Scots regrouped and were involved in a Borders-inspired revival when a Scottish Districts Select, coached by John Rutherford and captained by Gary Armstrong, produced a morale-boosting victory over Auckland in the same month as the South's slaughter. And while this particular Kiwi provincial line-up was not remotely of the same quality as the one which had beaten the British and Irish Lions a few months earlier – bearing in mind that ten of their front-line personnel were absent, otherwise engaged on New Zealand duty – the Scots, too, were a relatively inexperienced collective, yet managed to inflict the only defeat which Auckland suffered on their tour.

The win was notable for a number of reasons, not least the pre-match speeches which were made by both the afore-mentioned Border heroes. Rutherford, so urbane and genial in his normal day-to-day existence, knew that his troops would need to get down and dirty to have any chance and he duly fired them up with a piece of Telfer-style rhetoric. 'You are playing against Auckland. They are a top New

Zealand province. They are ruthless. You might be the nicest guy in the world off the pitch, you might be a great sportsman on it, but against these people, you have to be an out-and-out c★★★.'

That was the cue for Armstrong to follow with his own exhortation to his confrères, before finishing his address with the words: 'And just remember what Rudd told you . . . when you go out against boys like these, you have got to play like c★★★s!'

Once the contest had started, however, Armstrong was at the heart of everything good in his side's endeavours, acting as one of the catalysts for a win which demonstrated that reports of the demise of Scottish rugby had been exaggerated. And that incident might have served as a microcosm of the diverse brands of people that visitors will encounter in the Borders. There are the silent types, the lads who do their talking through their actions and make a resounding impression on rugby fields across the globe. And if you needed words, there was always Bill McLaren. No wonder there were so many mourners packed into the pews of Teviot Parish Church that cold January day.

Chapter Two

THE BIRTH OF BORDERS RUGBY

THERE WAS NO 'eureka' moment about the fashion in which rugby union became as inextricably linked with the Borders as Sir Walter Scott. Instead, as the Victorians assiduously developed the basics of many athletic pursuits, fuelled by their desire for self-improvement and nurturing a healthy workforce, the sport arrived in Scotland, initially in the public schools of the country's two major cities. Edinburgh Academy adopted the 'Rules of Play' formulated at Rugby in 1851, before Merchiston followed suit seven years later, and these establishments came together in December 1858 to lock horns in what is now accepted as the oldest regular fixture in the global game.

Yet, if this was the beginning of an organised pastime, there had already been signs that rugby would capture the imagination of those who dwelled in the Borders. For hundreds of years previously, the community of Duns had staged the Fastern's E'en Ba Festival, and such was the popularity of this extravaganza – which is coming soon, in a revised format, to Sky One or Channel 5, if they ever get to hear about it! – that scores of Borderers flocked to Duns whenever it was staged. Essentially, three young males – called 'Ba-Men' – were chosen by their townspeople to make the arrangements on the Wednesday evening, prior to the festival, whereupon they would convene for the 'Shaping of the Ba', accompanied by a drummer and fiddler, while they sang: 'Never let the gree gang doon, For the good o'oor toon.' Thereafter, they prepared four balls: the first was gilt and called 'the golden ball'; the second was the 'silver ball'; and the third was spotted. The fourth was presented to the most important member of the community and either he, or a member of his family, or his baron Baillie, threw the first ball to commence the action in what quickly developed into a giant scrum. All the shops were shut, their windows and doors firmly shuttered up, and the proceedings started with the ball being thrown up in the Mercat Square. The objective for the married men was to 'Kirk the ba'' by putting it into the pulpit of the parish church, which was situated in a lane off the Square, and to proclaim their triumph by giving the church bells an almighty ring. In contrast, their rivals, the bachelors, had the thornier task of placing the ball in the hopper of any of the grinding mills in the district, the nearest of which was over a mile away. If an unmarried man succeeded in this ambition, the miller would dust his cap and coat, before offering him a meal of pork and dumplings, which was the standard fare of the day. If this all sounds arcane, or more suitable for the cloisters of Hogwarts than a forerunner to the Five or Six Nations Championship, it was taken very seriously by those who strained their sinews throughout the event, and the individual who 'kirked' or 'milled' that first ball would receive a prize of one shilling and sixpence, which was a small fortune in the 19th century, while those coming in second and third would gain a shilling and sixpence respectively. Once they had finished their labours, the 'Ba-Men' retired to one of the taverns in Duns and slaked their thirsts on the balance of the subscribed money.

There were similar muscular pageants held annually in Kirkwall in Orkney – the tradition continues to this day – and the Borders locale of Jedburgh still plays host to a battle between the Uppies and Doonies, with both sides striving to get the ball to the top or bottom end of the playing area, which pretty much covers everything in the town. Hugh Hornby, the author of a book on 'extraordinary football games of Britain', has witnessed many of these pastimes and believes the Borders had a special role in their creation.

'I just had an interest in these early games and started to visit one or two of them,' declared Hornby, who was impressed by the clamorous scenes in Jedburgh. 'Most of the games that died out were very popular and actually had no problem with people turning out to take part in them. In fact, that was the very problem, the damage done to property and disruption to traffic were the main factors in authorities and magistrates and do-gooders – you might say – stamping them out. Of course, one or two of the games in this area were victims of that, but others have survived and are still keenly followed.'

One of the first historians of the sport in Scotland, Sandy Thorburn, even speculated on whether rugby owed its origins in the Borders to the game of 'harpastum', which had been played by Roman legionaries. And although that notion might be fanciful, there were myriad indications that the farming communities in the South relished their involvement in mass participation pursuits, with similarities to what would subsequently develop into the 15-a-side pastime. For instance, in 1815, Sir Walter Scott, the author of *Ivanhoe*, *The Heart of Midlothian* and other famous novels, was the guiding light for a match between the men of Selkirk, with some assistance from their peers in Gala and Hawick, and the men of the Valleys. The contest, in the meadow lying between the Yarrow and Ettrick Waters, was staged in front of the Duke and Duchess of Buccleuch, and featured up to 750 players on a field which was one mile long by three-quarters wide, making it appear less like a sporting tussle and more akin to a battle royal. The first score was made by one of the Selkirk representatives, Rab Hall, who, according to the contemporaneous reports, 'seized hold of the ball, succeeded in eluding the clutches of his desperate opponents, and, rushing into the stream, held the ball aloft in a token of victory.' This was no-holds-barred confrontation, scarcely for the faint-hearted, as was illustrated when William Riddell, who was apparently a Scottish antecedent of Usain Bolt, broke away from the scrum and would have scored, but for the slight problem that he was impeded by a mounted spectator when striving to finish off his attack!

These activities may have been harum-scarum in nature, but there again, rugby, as it was conducted in the early years, would scarcely be understood by a modern-day viewer if he or she was transported back to the 1850s and 1860s. At the outset, it featured 20 players (or more) on both sides and the majority of these participants were concentrated in and around the scrum, with many contests being dominated by ferocious and often indiscriminate mauling. Fisticuffs often broke out – and private feuds would occasionally be settled behind the clubhouse later on – while 'hacking', the deliberate tripping of an opponent who did not have the ball, was permitted until the 1870s. By then, Scotland and England had met in the first ever rugby international, at Raeburn Place, in 1871, with the hosts winning by a goal and a try to a try. And, more pertinently to the Borders, clubs began springing up all through the region as the sport gained in popularity.

Rugby was not the first recreation to arrive in the Borders. Kelso Cricket Club was founded in 1820 and the likes of Hawick and Selkirk soon followed them, without the union code dominating matters, as eventually proved the case. Football did not hog the limelight either, as it did throughout the rest of Scotland from the 1870s onwards, possibly because none of the small communities in the South was large enough to accommodate a senior club, while the mill owners, who held sway over their employees, were often former public schoolboys who preferred cricket and rugby to the association version, which they brusquely branded 'soccer'. At any rate,

Langholm sprung into existence in 1871, Hawick were born in 1873, with Gala, Kelso, Melrose and Duns arriving in 1875, 1876, 1877 and 1878 respectively, as the prelude to Peebles and Jed-Forest joining them in 1881 and 1885. (Selkirk were not founded until 1907).

Soon enough, these organisations were involved in regular fixtures against one another, and although the early (anonymous) newspaper reports are frustratingly short of detail, the nascent rivalry between the competing clubs was fuelled by such incidents as the famous row which erupted between Gala and Melrose, when the former turned up at their ground one morning only to discover that the goalposts had been moved to Melrose, sparking a rivalry which still burns brightly. As Laing Speirs, the renowned Scottish journalist and historian, recounted in his *Border League Story*, what their initial tussles lacked in sophistication, they more than made up for in aggression and local pride.

Nothing could have summed up the approach that was to mark out the character of the Border League better than the first match between Langholm and Hawick in 1873. There was a lengthy discussion before the match about the laws, most of the argument being over whether a goal should be kicked over the bar, which was Hawick's favoured option, or under it, which Langholm preferred. They won that argument, but the game ended in a draw, with the ironic point being that they had forced a touchdown, but [their kicker] sent the conversion over the bar. It was, of course, a classic example of the sort of on-field incident that was going to liven up Border games for the next century and more.

Langholm, Hawick and Gala were in action against the others 25 years before the [20th] century dawned and Melrose and Jed-Forest, or Jedburgh, as they were known in the early days, were soon regular opponents. [Eventually] representatives from the South clubs convened in 1890 to pick a side to play Edinburgh. There must have been some teething problems, because another meeting was called, at St Boswells, to discuss some contentious issues towards the close of the following season. One of them was 'the great dissatisfaction, which exists in the South with the present state of affairs, and the best way to secure redress of grievances and the further-ance [sic] of rugby would be easier promoted through the formation of a South of Scotland Rugby Union'.

Basically, this statement encapsulated the simmering resent-ment which festered between the private schools in the major cities and their counterparts in the Borders. Much of it revolved around class, with the likes of Edinburgh and Glasgow Accies restricting their membership to former pupils and making no effort to spread the rugby gospel beyond those (narrow) confines, whereas Langholm, Hawick and the rest were simply interested in promoting the sport, without worrying unduly about old school ties and other pieces of flummery. This is not the place for a diatribe on the impact which the latter have played in cementing the perception of rugby as a purely middle- and upper-class pursuit. Suffice to say that the Borders were prepared to embrace radical new ideas and, akin to what was happening in the Welsh valleys during the same period, operated on the basis that the best means of pursuing success lay in encouraging everybody in their area to pick up a rugby ball and gain the opportunity to play with it as soon as possible. The former pupils' (FP) clubs did the opposite, and sparked a situation where the majority of people in their communities were specifically excluded.

The consequence was that the SRU was branded an elitist body by many people in the South, sparking a division which intensified as the years rolled by. Yet the Borders clubs were blessed with sufficient ambition and prescience to flourish on their own terms, as was obvious when a young Borders butcher, called Ned Haig, introduced Sevens to the world in 1883. At this distance, it is easy to forget how often the best ideas spring from necessity, but the reality was that Melrose RFC were suffering serious financial problems and needed something which would assist them in raising funds. Enter Haig, who was born in Jedburgh in 1858, and was clearly an ingenious fellow, whose appetite for rugby had been whetted by his early involvement with the Fastern's E'en Ba festival.

Consequently, with his brethren and their organisation in the toils, Haig devised the basic template for a game which has now become a global phenomenon. 'Want of money made us rack our brains as to what was to be done to keep the club from going to the wall,' he later wrote in *An Old Melrose Player's Recollections*. 'The idea struck me that a [rugby] football tournament might prove attractive, but, as it was hopeless to think of having several games in one afternoon, with 15 players on each side, the teams were reduced to seven men.' At a stroke, Haig had hit upon a successful formula, and all that remained was for the structure and regulations to be thrashed out by the committee at Melrose, who have always been one of the most progressive clubs in their homeland.

Since when, their members have taken pains to enshrine Haig's name for posterity and the *Border Advertiser* related how the Sevens concept was an instant hit:

Haig's contribution, according to that statement by himself, was the idea of a football tournament. The wording suggests that the reduction to seven players per side was the outcome of discussion between some or probably all of the club's officials of the mechanics of running such a tournament. It is not now possible to say whether a football tournament with athletics events, or vice versa, was the original idea. Whatever the truth of the matter might be, generations of spectators and players have been grateful that the Melrose Sports started and included a football tournament. Originally, the 'seven men' comprised a full back, two quarter-backs and four forwards, but, with the introduction of the passing game, the forwards were reduced to three and an extra half-back played.

Initially, the programme [of events] included foot races, drop kicks, dribbling races and place kicking. However, the 'Football Competition' was the main attraction and a cup was presented for it by the ladies of Melrose. On 29th April, 1883, the first Melrose Sports were held at the Greenyards, beginning at 12.30 and concluding at 7.30. The day was not very favourable, being cold in the morning and wet long before the close.

But by the time this event [the Sevens] commenced, an enormous crowd of spectators had assembled, special trains having been run from Galashiels and Hawick and about 1,600 tickets had been taken at Melrose during the day. From the former place alone, there were 862 tickets booked, of whom 509 came by special train, and the other 353 by ordinary train. Among these was a number of manufacturers and Melrose itself was represented by many of the gentry of the district. As [rugby] football has been the popular game of the season in the district, perhaps because its nature corresponds with the spirit of the hardy Borderer, the competition had been looked forward to with great interest, as most of the clubs of the district were expected to compete for the prize. The excitement during the games was thus great and that portion of the spectators, belonging to the various townships, did all they could to encourage their clubs and players. This was especially the case with the Galashiels people, who leaped the barrier at critical points of play on several occasions and mixed among the players. To their credit, let it be said that no portion of spectators, however warm their feelings, interfered with any of the clubs. The competition was played under rugby rules, fifteen minutes of play being allowed in each heat, and seven members of every club competing. The regulations were that, in the first heat, if two clubs tied, they would both be allowed to play in the second; if two clubs tied in the second round, they would play on until one scored, when that one was declared the winner. [Gala Forest, a junior team, had a bye, because Kelso didn't turn up].

Melrose and Gala were left to decide the result of the final. The ground by this time was soft and slippery, owing to the rain, and the Gala team were pretty well knocked up [exhausted] after a tough contest with St Cuthbert's. After a short interval, however, they were forced to begin again, or run the risk of being disqualified. The Melrose team had had a long rest and the two clubs they had played previously were both light and they were therefore much fresher than their opponents. They played for fifteen minutes, a fast and rough game, but as nothing was scored, it was agreed by the captains to play another quarter of an hour. After ten minutes, Melrose obtained a try and left the field without either trying to kick their goal [conversion] or finish the game, claiming the cup. But they were challenged by Gala on the ground that the game had not been finished. The proceedings were then brought to an abrupt conclusion, and the spectators left the ground, amid much confusion. It is said the referee decided the tie in favour of Melrose, but they should have played the quarter of an hour before they claimed the cup.

That version of events seems to have been written, through clenched teeth, by a non-Melrose reporter, but the success of the whole festival spoke for itself and Haig, as one of the participants, was delighted at the sizeable crowd's response. In later seasons the format was tinkered with and guest sides were gradually invited from all over the globe, bringing some wonderfully gifted performers from Australia, New Zealand

and South Africa to the Borders. Yet the beautiful simplicity of Haig's original vision has not been diminished in the process of transforming Sevens into an Olympic sport. Some rugby aficionados have mixed feelings about the abbreviated version of the sport – just as many cricket enthusiasts shudder at the recent invention of the Twenty20 game – but Melrose pioneered something special, something which both thrilled most of the cognoscenti and appealed to the unconverted, and rugby owed a significant debt to Ned Haig.

Perhaps, predictably, there was not any overwhelming enthusiasm for Sevens from the school-based entities in the Central Belt. (*Plus ca change!*) But, in all these dealings, it should be borne in mind that the Scottish Rugby Union was resolutely committed to amateurism and preserving what it viewed as the essential ethos of rugby. There is scant value in bemoaning this attitude with the benefit of hindsight; it was simply a reflection of the times and the conservative conviction of most SRU officials, whose autocratic secretary, J Aikman Smith, a chap whose default setting was 'No' to any suggestion which might tamper with the sanctity of the existing laws or, heaven forbid, persuade more supporters to attend matches. In his opinion – and it was an attitude shared by many of his contemporaries and those who followed – rugby existed as a game for players, not spectators, and he was aghast at the notion that the former should have their jerseys numbered to improve recognition. 'It is a rugby match, not a cattle show,' he is reported to have said to King George V on one occasion, and he meant it. But there again, he was merely sticking to his principles. What stuck in the craws of so many Borderers was that these tenets seemed to imply the South was wrong for encouraging competition.

All of this ensured that an atmosphere of mutual suspicion consistently existed between the Edinburgh elite and their counterparts to the South. Yet, amid the tensions, the establishment of a string of clubs in the Borders swiftly led to their derby matches developing a genuine edge, with the crowds at these fixtures adding a raucous amount of partisan bias to the proceedings. These matters can sometimes be overstated, but if there is a prevailing theme from the accounts of the Borderers' early tussles, it lies in the uncompromising hardness of those involved, both on and off the field. There were numerous instances of supporters spilling on to the pitch, while disagreements between players were often the prelude to impromptu boxing matches, sparking a situation where, in the words of Borders historian Laing Speirs: 'The simple rule was that if one player annoyed another – and the players made a habit of annoying one another – they retired behind the pavilion to settle their differences with fists. Sometimes as many as four or five fights were in progress at the same time. But the game carried on regardless.'

It may be asked why the sport immediately gained a widespread audience while other games, such as cricket, continued to dwell in sedate anonymity in the South from decade to decade, even though they had laid down roots before rugby was even invented. But the historians of the time seemed in agreement that the physicality of the oval-ball pursuit tapped into the Borderers' consciousness. One of their number, R J Phillips, summed up this argument with the words: 'It wasn't that the Scot was rougher than the Saxon, but he was hardier, partly by racial inheritance and partly by his football upbringing.'

There may be a sprinkling of merit in this assertion, but I sought out Jim Telfer for his perspective and the former Scotland centre and national coach, who masterminded the British and Irish Lions' successful tour of South Africa in 1997, was typically prescient. That came as no surprise because, in many respects, Telfer is *the* living, breathing embodiment of rugby in the raw, as practised in his backyard. During the past

25 years, I have witnessed some of the most redoubtable customers in the Caledonian game almost visibly shrink with apprehension at the prospect of crossing swords with Telfer – and there have been instances where he has made Sir Alex Ferguson seem like an oasis of calm by comparison – but though he can be combative, curmudgeonly, cantankerous and cussed to the point of blind obstinacy, the bottom line is that this fellow has forgotten more about the game he loves than the majority of us will ever know. Hence, his characteristically forthright answer to my original question.

There have always been a lot of people who work outdoors in the Borders, with their hands, men who have to be big and strong, and whether they are working on farms or in other aspects of the agricultural business, or they are labouring or involved in stonemasonry, they have wanted a game which would play to their strengths and where they could go out and use that power to their best advantage. Soccer wasn't for most of them, but rugby suited them down to the ground. And once you had the formation of so many clubs in such a short time frame, it created a climate where every town wanted to get the better of their nearest rivals, a few miles away. It also suited the way people worked in the 19th century, where they didn't have whole days they could devote to sport. With rugby, right from the outset, they could use a horse and cart and get from Gala to Melrose quickly. And of course, once Langholm were up and running, that guaranteed that the other communities in the region would knuckle down and get their act together.

Of course, there is local rivalry and passions occasionally run high in the heat of battle. I know from my time with Melrose that there is a real hunger and burning desire amongst the others to beat us. And it was the same whenever we took on Hawick in my playing days. But that is healthy competition and there is no malice attached to it, or not from my experience. Sometimes, the rivalry becomes very parochial, narrow-minded and introverted, and you will find clubs judging whether a season has been a success or not by whether they won their derby fixtures, not where they finished in the league.

But, for me, the success of the Borders has actually been a very positive development and it is something that we should be proud about in Scottish sport. There is no religious aspect, we have established a pastime where the minister's son is playing alongside the plumber's son, and the doctor's boy is in the same team as the joiner's lad. So it is all very democratic and egalitarian and I honestly believe that if you travel to Gala or Hawick, or Melrose or Kelso, you will be given a warm welcome by their members and, if you want to play rugby or watch rugby, you will be made to feel very welcome.

Rugby is still a snobby sport in some areas, but certainly not down here. When I was growing up [in the 1950s], you never questioned whether or not you should be playing rugby, you just went out and did it. (And the only alternative was cross-country running.) Every club did its best to set up development programmes to search for talent and I think we have made a virtue of necessity, because we have such a small population down here, compared to the rest of the country, that we can never afford to be complacent.

Some of our most talented guys have gone to the fee-paying schools in the cities, but most of them return to their roots after they have finished their education. John Jeffrey, for instance [the Scotland and Lions flanker], went to Merchiston [in Edinburgh], but you wouldn't associate JJ with anywhere other than Kelso. And that is one of the strengths of the sport in these parts. There is a continuity, a sense that we are carrying on a tradition, and while more youngsters are playing soccer these days, the link between the [nine] secondary schools in the region and the rugby clubs is still strong and we still have lots of promising kids who are as dedicated to their rugby as anybody could be. We need that attitude and that determination from the young generation if we are to build on the successes of the past. And nobody can afford to rest on their laurels.

Jeffrey's progress was in the opposite direction, to some extent, from one of the first superstars of Scottish rugby. Back in the 1880s, Charles Reid, the towering Edinburgh Academical forward with the nickname 'Hippo', was first capped for his country when he was only 17 years and 36 days old and still at school. In those days there were no Jonah Lomus or Va'aiga Tuigamalas – or not in the British game at any rate – but Reid, who weighed in at over 15 stone and stood 6ft 3in tall, was as close to a man-mountain as his contemporaries had ever witnessed. He was a formidable presence for Scotland in the second row in many of the early international tussles with the Home Nations – he made 20 appearances against England, Wales and Ireland between 1881 and 1888 – and although it may be a fruitless exercise trying to compare the talents of luminaries from different generations, the universal praise which has been accorded to this fellow indicates that he possessed prodigious gifts. Certainly R J Phillips considered him 'Scotland's greatest forward', yet all the recognition meant little to Reid, who moved to the Borders after graduating as a doctor, and subsequently turned out for the junior club, Selkirk Union, where he must have looked like an avenging angel to those unfortunate opponents, who were tasked with attempting to halt his progress.

Indeed, although he was not a Borderer, he thrived after making the journey to the South of Scotland. And as Walter Thomson, one of, if not the greatest, of the Scottish rugby historian fraternity (and the famous 'Fly-Half' of the *Sunday*

Post) – later wrote: 'If Selkirk had been as deft as some of their neighbours in claiming caps on somewhat tenuous grounds, they might have bragged, right till the time of Hawick's Jock Beattie in the 1930s, that they held the Border record in international appearances.'

By the end of the 19th century, the efforts of characters such as Reid had yielded some significant success for Scotland. He led them to their maiden Home Championship triumph in 1887, following victories over Wales (by a substantial margin of four goals and eight tries to nil) and Ireland (by one goal, one goal from a mark and two tries to nil) with a draw (one try apiece) against England at Whalley Range in Manchester. The fact that his Test career finished at the age of 24 only seems extraordinary if we overlook the fact that individuals in his mould viewed sport as play; his vocation was medicine. And, according to the testimony of those who covered rugby at the time, Reid derived an equal amount of pleasure from marauding round the paddock in Selkirk as he did anywhere else.

By this stage, the Borders had established the Sevens version of rugby, most of their clubs were thriving, and they were blazing their own trail, on their own terms, often without the approval of the governing body. But there was to be no immediate cessation of hostilities between the two parties as the South embarked on an ambitious plan.

Chapter Three

A LEAGUE APART IN THE BORDERS

W HENEVER SPORTING teams spring into existence in any
region or country, the next logical development is for
them to forge an alliance and arrange to meet each
other in a formalised league structure. It happened in football, in
cricket, in most pursuits where there was any element of rivalry
and genuine competition and, therefore, it must have seemed a
natural progression for the likes of Hawick, Gala and Melrose to
advance from locking horns on a sporadic basis to devising a
tournament which would benefit them all. Yet, when these
Borders organisations duly took that action at the start of the
20th century, implementing radical proposals for a structured
new event, the response to their endeavours in some quarters
suggested they were committing a treasonable act.

However, perhaps it was not surprising that the SRU and
their colleagues who presided over rugby in Scotland looked
askance at the news from the South of the country, when it was
revealed that their near neighbours were engaged in establishing
a Border League, at a time when such innovation ran contrary to
the normal practice of clubs meeting in the equivalent of friendly
contests. Such tournaments may be commonplace across the
rugby spectrum today, but they were unheard of in the union
code back in 1902, which helped explain the suspicion with
which the Edinburgh administrators regarded the notion. So
too, there had already been a schism in England, where the
Northern Union clubs had split from the RFU over the issue of

paying players for what was called 'broken time', in what, inevitably, led to the creation of rugby league. In which light, it was maybe understandable that talk of a Border League carried the whiff of professionalism, which was, of course, a dirty word in the 15-a-side game for nearly another 100 years.

Nonetheless, for all their frosty glances, there was little, if anything, that the SRU could do to prevent the idea coming to fruition. At the outset, the event featured just five clubs – Langholm, Hawick, Melrose, Gala and Jed-Forest – but these organisations had both strong local roots and a keen rivalry between their respective communities which made their association appear an eminently practical solution. In any case, Murrayfield could ill afford to be overly heavy-handed with the Borders, lest these clubs decamped to the rival code, so the tutting and tsking ultimately added up to a lot of sound and fury signifying precious little. Indeed, in the long run, the officials responsible for orchestrating the Border League were sporting revolutionaries, whose brainchild led to the creation of a tournament which was not merely the first of its kind in the rugby world, but the third-oldest union competition – following on from the Varsity match (which was launched in 1872) and the Calcutta Cup (which commenced seven years later) – of any variety.

All of which makes it doubly frustrating that there should be such limited documentation, explaining the mechanics of how exactly the Border League came into existence. As it is, the original minute books have vanished forever, while the first official records of league fixtures do not start until a decade after the initial competition. Even the beetle-browed historians, who have delved into these matters with the diligence of a Holmes or a Poirot, have invariably been forced to conclude that these early years are something of a mystery. Perhaps, as some people claimed, the clubs involved did not wish to antagonise those who ran the sport any further than they could – and certainly not before the SRU had granted their blessing to the Border structure – but it seems peculiar that the details of one of Scottish sport's more treasured concepts should be shrouded in fog. Yet that is undoubtedly the case, as explained by Border chronicler, Laing Speirs:

> The first years of the twentieth century saw the Border championship emerging from the mists in a shape that is still recognisable today, but one which was totally lacking in the organisational strength, which was introduced by the League's secretaries and committees over the years. The results of the early games were listed in league form under the heading of the Border Competition, presumably to avoid confusion with the association football structure of these days which called itself the Border League. Club records of the first decade of the century are mostly silent on the progress of Border rugby matches, and often, even the speakers at the [clubs'] annual general meetings totally ignored their team's success in winning the league over the winter months.
>
> Suggestions that the Scottish Football Union [what was, in effect, the SRU], as it was then known, had frowned on the Border clubs organising competitive rugby have been exaggerated. But there was probably a reluctance, at least in the very earliest years, to upset anybody at headquarters with too dramatic a celebration of local success in a domestic competition which sometimes reached fairly lively conclusions.

Not everybody agrees with this interpretation of events and, from a distance, it appears too much of a coincidence that Borderers, en masse, effectively imposed a news blackout on their activities, following the foundation of the league. What on earth had they reason to be ashamed about? Yet, it can hardly have assisted the South's cause that, for a short period, their fledgling competition included Carlisle, who joined the original five participants in the 1904–05 campaign. At best, one imagines this would have sparked consternation among Scottish officials, considering that, irrespective of the close ties between the Cumberland club and their counterparts in Langholm, there was no rationale by which anybody could argue Carlisle was in any sense 'Scottish'. At worst, their bond with the Borders heightened fears that the leading organisations in the South of Scotland and North of England were considering a breakaway from the SRU and RFU.

This apprehension had little genuine substance, although the manner in which Carlisle suddenly exited the tournament hinted at some cloak-and-dagger intrigue behind the scenes. On the pitch, the Englishmen acquitted themselves well, with two victories out of three at the end of December 1905, whereupon they vanished! As Speirs explains:

> The most likely reason for Carlisle's departure, midway through the season, was that the Border clubs were already laying plans to have their championship fully recognised [by the SRU]. It seems likely that, as they prepared for their formal approach to Edinburgh, they realised that their chances of success would be greater if they confined the new structure to the five active senior Borders clubs. Certainly, the timing suggests this may have been the reason, but, whatever it was, Carlisle's disappearance was abrupt and uncharted.
>
> The first table of 1906 makes no mention at all of them, while there was no reference to the affair in the Carlisle minutes and, coupled with the suggestion that extensive travelling was presenting problems, the conclusion has to be reached that there were no great regrets about the parting of the ways. Whatever the truth, Carlisle faded from the Border League scene, leaving behind memories of a short spell in the spotlight.

Notwithstanding the suspicion of sports politics burbling beneath the surface, the birth of the Border League soon yielded positive ramifications, both for the clubs in the South and the wider good health of the Scottish game. The original five members were soon joined by Selkirk in 1908 and Kelso in 1912 – although Earlston's application was subsequently rejected in 1923 – and the competition quickly caught fire among the locals, who were understandably excited by the notion of winter derbies between community clubs who were separated by only a few miles, yet remained inherently proud of their own separate identities. From the outset the matches were passionate affairs, and anybody who has ever witnessed a full-blooded tussle between the likes of Hawick and Gala will appreciate the sheer visceral intensity of the combat between the 30 men on the pitch. This was often bone-juddering fare, not least because the hapless individual who missed a tackle or spilled a pass would be reminded of that fact by his townsfolk for the rest of the week – or the season – or, if the offence was especially glaring, the rest of his days! Players might be forgiven for lacking any special rugby talent – such as the redoubtable warrior who once piped up: 'We couldna play fitba', but Jings, we could hammer them' – but no excuses would suffice for those who seemed to be offering less than wholehearted effort or shirking a challenge when it mattered.

Referees, for their part, had to learn to be thick-skinned and ignore the taunts from the sidelines, because if any official tried to mess with the crowd, he soon discovered that he had chosen the wrong place to parade his pedantry. Supporters – and thousands of them were soon turning up for their regular dose of Border League thrills – included significant numbers of men and women, with the latter often providing stalwart support behind the scenes, as well as exhibiting their detailed rugby knowledge when it was required.

In the 1908–09 match between Selkirk and Jed-Forest, for instance, there was a telling interruption from one of the Philiphaugh club's redoubtable aficionados, Belle Murray, whose piercing cry of 'Coont the players, ref!' managed to filter through to the whistler, who, perhaps wisely in the circumstances, abruptly halted the game and discovered that Jed–Forest had 16 players in their ranks. The action was suspended for a few moments, but eventually, as Walter Thomson reported: 'The mystery was solved. It was found that Jed had arrived a man short. So their coachman, Bill Coltherd, offered to make up the team and, with a spare strip aboard, he took the field. Meantime, the absentee dashed into the pavilion just as the game began, and joined his team–mates in a scrimmage [sic] unnoticed by the referee or, for that matter, his own captain. And, but for the keen eye of Belle, Jed might have finished the game with one over the fifteen.'

On another occasion, the *Border Advertiser* related how a particularly feisty clash between Hawick and Gala had climaxed in a riot, with substantial numbers of the crowd invading the field to vent their anger at the referee. 'A scene of great disorder prevailed, with missiles being thrown at the official, and the county police had to intervene, as did some of the home players and officials.' Thereafter, a short ban was imposed on Hawick, which prevented them from playing within ten miles of their home ground for the rest of the month, and these types of incidents demonstrated how much these matches mattered to the crowd and those who were participating on behalf of their towns. In which light, it was hardly surprising that heroes from within the different organisations began to emerge; men whose names still evoke appreciative nods when they are mentioned around Netherdale or Mansfield Park, or the other clubhouses which hosted the fixtures.

Hawick, so often the trailblazers against the blazerati, won the first Border League title, a triumph which should have surprised nobody considering the stranglehold which they exerted on the competition, and the wider world of Scottish rugby, for much of the next 100 years. The now–legendary 'Green Machine', so beloved of Bill McLaren, had yet to crank into full gear, and the Teris [as the locals were known] were forced to cope with a variety of problems, whether in the decline of the hosiery industry in the 1890s, which led to many families leaving the town, or the unwanted (but constant) attention of rugby league scouts, on the prowl, from the North of England. But gradually, they turned the union pursuit into a religion, and produced men who were close to being super-men. There was Bill Kyle, who went on to represent Scotland, and who captained the original league champions, regularly inspiring his colleagues with his industrious energy and un-erring catching and dribbling; Sandy Burns, who was the epitome of an immovable object, and whose Herculean labours for his club rightly earned him folk-hero status; and a clutch of players who gained international calls, such as Walter Sutherland, Robert Lindsay-Watson, Billy Burnet and Carl Ogilvy, whose joint endeavours gradually, inexorably, ensured that Hawick had become the team that everybody else feared by the outbreak of the First World War.

Yet they had to work incredibly hard to wrest the initiative away from Jed-Forest, who won the league no fewer than five times in the first seven years of the competition. This was a testimony, both to the power of their forwards, and also the tireless endeavour of their committee officials, who toiled out of the spotlight, but to significant effect, as the 'Royal Blues' enjoyed a spell in the ascendancy which made them the best team in the South. They collected the first ever Border League cup – that prize had eventually been authorised by the Scottish governing body – in the 1906–07 season, and also prevailed in the unofficial championship of that campaign, as the prelude to their personnel being presented with gold badges for repeating their exploits in the following year.

As with all the best sides, Jed had gifted performers spread throughout their ranks. Even today, more than 100 years later, any of the worthies at Riverside Park will be able to regale visitors with tales of the derring-do of such characters as Michael Drummond, Adam Renilson, James Henderson and a veritable plethora of Williams with the surnames Hall, Jardine, Balfour, Watson, Purdie and Laidlaw. The latter has been one of the most famous names to emerge from Jedburgh, with generations of Laidlaws doing their birthplace proud. It must be said about these players that they dominated matters at the start of the 20th century as much as Melrose did at the end of it.

In the bigger picture, meanwhile, this was a period of regular success for Scotland on the international stage as the sport moved closer towards how it is recognised today. The Triple Crown, which required victories over the other home countries, was secured in 1901, 1905 and 1907, and the SRU, whose governors had often been criticised for their conservatism, were refreshingly forward-thinking in creating a purpose-built national stadium, with the opening of Inverleith in 1899. This was no mean feat and guaranteed that, for the first 50 years of its existence, the Edinburgh ground could accommodate a larger crowd than any other rugby venue in the northern hemisphere. The spectators flocked to these Test matches and, whether in the thousands of rugby followers who travelled to and from the Borders on the railway services, which would subsequently fall victim to the notorious Beeching axe, or in the manner that other countries copied the Border League format and launched competitions of their own, there was ample evidence of Scotland punching above its weight in the 15-a-side domain.

One could also marvel at the emergence of so many all-round individuals, who glittered like shooting stars before moving on to other pursuits or sacrificing their lives in the 1914–18 conflict. Some were reticent individuals who let their actions speak louder than any words could possibly have done and many in the Jed ranks excelled in that fashion.

Others, such as Kenneth Macleod, who was only 17 and still at Fettes when he was selected for his country against New Zealand in 1905, possessed a range of gifts which seemed hardly fair to ordinary mortals, as Allan Massie wrote in *The Scotsman.*

> He won 10 caps, all at centre-threequarter while at Cambridge University and retired, before he was 21, at the urging of his father, because two elder brothers had been seriously injured playing rugby. Macleod was famed, both for his running and his drop-kicking, and scored a memorable try in the 1906 victory over South Africa. He retired before reaching his full powers and, having already been Scottish long jump champion, went on to captain Lancashire at cricket, play football for Manchester City and, in middle age, win the Amateur Golf Championship of Natal [in South Africa].

Macleod was, by anybody's standards, a remarkable athlete. He was also undeniably a fellow from a privileged background, who could afford to heed his father's advice and seek sporting plaudits in other, less hazardous pursuits (although, in those days, there were probably more people killed playing cricket than on a rugby pitch). Most of the Borders participants, by comparison, hailed from a working-class background and yet there never seemed to be any problems when these men from starkly different vocations convened in the union code. I once asked Jim Telfer about this issue and his response was straightforward. 'If you love rugby, you love rugby. You don't care where a man has come from. If he's in your team, you all pull together. If he's in the opposition team, you go flat out to beat him and then shake his hand and have a beer with him later.'

Yet, despite the blunt common sense of Telfer's words,

there was often a queasy feeling of different worlds colliding in the early days of Scottish rugby. In 1920, the Border League committee asked the SRU to consider reinstating disabled professionals, while offering their opinion that these people 'could be of use to clubs or committees'. Two years after the Great War, when millions had died or suffered serious injury or permanent disfigurement, this appeared an eminently practical idea. But it was rejected out of hand by the governing body, who 'regretted that the Border League should have made such a proposal' in the first place. In the same year, Jock Wemyss, the Gala prop, who had turned out for his homeland against Wales and Ireland in 1914, asked for a new Scotland jersey and was promptly grilled as to what had happened to the old one. The fact he had fought with distinction in the war, had been injured, and lost an eye, were trivial affairs by comparison. These were the times when, along with the shunning of those from the Borders who went to rugby league in order to make an honest living in sport, union was left looking as if it inhabited a nonsensical ivory tower. Yet, if Wemyss was in any way annoyed by his treatment, he did not show it. Instead, he gained five more caps for Scotland and demonstrated that, whether with one eye or two, he could still do his job.

As for the Border League, it thrived because of the keen-as-mustard dedication of an army of volunteers in the committee rooms, the ferocious commitment of those who participated in the fixtures and the bristling and unrelenting rivalry between the seven clubs, on and off the pitch. Hawick and Jed-Forest were obviously to the fore in the early years, but what of the other teams in the competition? One might have imagined that Gala would be in the hunt for honours from the outset, but despite their victory in the 1905–06 campaign, any sustained success proved elusive at Netherdale, and some observers put that down to a mixture of their inconsistency and either their inability or reluctance to ram home their superiority when they held the upper hand. They produced a number of splendid performers in the early days – and have continued that pattern all through their history – but too often, circumstances or their own frailty let them down. There were no problems on that score with their victorious side of 1905–06, who defended as if their lives depended on it, and conceded only five points in the whole Border League season, and, bolstered by the sterling efforts of such players as their captain, G S Scott, and their wonderfully dextrous scrum-half, Willie McCrirrick, these Gala warriors were deserving of their prize. But too often, in other years, promising positions were squandered.

Langholm, for their part, were traditionally as tough as old boots, and unearthed a number of individuals who looked as if they had just engineered a break-out from a 'Scotland's Most Wanted' poster. But, despite their status as the original Borders club, and the manner in which they spread the union gospel all over Dumfriesshire, they were invariably more competitive than all-conquering in their Border League for-ays, which possibly helps explain why they have won the competition just once in their history – in 1958–59. That is not meant to denigrate the enterprise of the coruscating players they produced in the early years, including some uncompromising citizens in the mould of Tom Scott and Jim Elliot, both of whom were instrumental in their club vying with Hawick and Jed-Forest for the Border title. But, as historian Laing Speirs explained:

When Langholm's own standards began to decline, just before the First World War, their hopes of League success faded too. And, by the time of the 1920s, the economic prosperity of the town had declined and with it the quality of the local rugby. Players were often in short supply and desperate measures were needed to keep the team at full strength. At one time, these included drafting in some servicemen from the barracks in Carlisle to make up a team to meet Hawick. Sadly, nobody asked them their names and they go down in the Langholm records as 'three unknown soldiers'.

There was a similar anonymity to Melrose's labours at the outset of the Border League, but if truth be told, the picturesque little community was a village compared with the more substantial population centres of Hawick and Gala-shiels. It remains something of a minor miracle that the Greenyards faithful have orchestrated so much success throughout their history, and especially when the sport was moving headlong towards professionalism in the 1990s. In an earlier age, their maiden league triumph had arrived in the 1910–11 campaign, following a play-off with Hawick at Riverside Park, which the Melrosians won 10–0. The celebrations thereafter, which saw their captain and local grocer, Wattie Douglas, being carried along to the Market Square by his team's players and supporters in the company of some bracing anthems from a pair of pipers, confirmed a couple of things about these hardy fellows. Firstly, they, and the local newspapers of the time, knew exactly how to describe Bacchanalian evenings by the subtle deployment of euphemism – 'There was much cheering and toasting in the evening' – and, secondly, that Melrose was a place which had taken rugby to its heart, whether in Sevens or the 15-a-side version of the game, and would never surrender that passion. Their president, J E Fairbairn, was the man who had adroitly negotiated with the SRU for the new Border tournament to be granted proper recognition in 1906, and it was understandable that he and his confrères, allied to such stalwart performers as the aforementioned Douglas, his vice-captain, Jock Jardine, and Bob Davidson, revelled in their hour of glory. As it transpired, they needed to dine out on the memory for an awfully long time.

Selkirk and Kelso, of course, were latecomers to the party and therefore could hardly expect to march into the winners' enclosure immediately. Yet, such was the enthusiasm and efficacy with which both clubs embraced the Border League that they soon made their impact on the tournament and developed some of the best players ever to pull on a Scotland jersey in the process. Selkirk suffered a variety of problems in the early stages, and were forced to revert to junior status, which allowed their rival clubs in the South to generate greater early momentum, but one of the constant features of the Philiphaugh side was their capacity for engendering quality backs, and long before John Rutherford emerged to grace the game throughout the globe, Selkirk's sparkling passing and running had elicited the couthy approval of one Borders worthy, who exclaimed: 'If we had yon Selkirk backs and they Hawick forrits [forwards], we'd lick a' creation.' The remark had a touch of hyperbole about it, but the man's admiration was genuine and although the Souters had to be patient before finally winning their first Border League title in 1934–35, their achievement owed much to the energy and inspiration of Bob Mitchell, their indefatigable secretary, treasurer and president between 1907 and 1933: one of the myriad fellows in the Borders who devoted his life to rugby union and who was so devoted to Selkirk in particular that the club would have been a far less prosperous organisation without him.

Kelso, the last to arrive in the competition – or at least until Peebles were inducted in 1996 and Duns subsequently gained admission – were blessed with people as ambitious and single-minded as Mitchell and, although it was not until February 1912, when the townspeople turned out in significant numbers to debate the question of whether their club should join the

Border League – this was a pressing matter in the South – they marched forward, sidestepped reservations about finance, and embarked on a path which yielded glory as early as 1930–31.

In fact, they could have tasted success even quicker, considering the impressive fashion in which the Poynder Park team stormed out of the blocks. From the outset, they were cheered along by one of the most vociferous groups of fans in the region, and the North British Railways Company soon grew accustomed to laying on special trains to carry those supporters on their magical derby journeys. During that maiden campaign Kelso defeated the mighty Hawick, and, as the years rolled by, vied with the Teris on a number of occasions, and were assisted in their endeavours by luminaries of the quality of Jock Hume and Jimmy Graham. In January 1926, oblivious to a severe snowfall the night before the game, Kelso's warriors were involved in a bone-crunching contest with Hawick, watched by a crowd of between 3,500 and 4,000, and it was agonisingly close all the way to the death, only for the favourites to show their battling qualities to withstand some concerted pressure from their opponents and gain a nerve-shredding 3–0 win.

That sparked a play-off with the 'Green Machine' at the Greenyards, and again, Kelso fell tantalisingly short of their objective. But they were a persistent bunch, who simply refused to bow to adversity, and finally, four seasons later, they launched what proved a barnstorming charge to the main prize. In anybody's terms, this was a tenacious group of fiercely determined players, captained by the fearless 'Flood' Rogers and, with dervishes such as Jimmy Graham and Gordon Cottington among their number, they roared into their opponents' faces and rarely surrendered the initiative. They swept past Hawick, Melrose and Langholm, and recovered from a loss at Netherdale and the ravages of a chitteringly frozen winter to climb to the top of the league and set up a title decider against Gala. It was rough, it was tough and the language among the forwards was not for maiden aunts, but Kelso were not to be denied again and collected the spoils with an 8–3 win. For the victors there was unbridled joy, a night of carousing and the realisation that their names would be enshrined for posterity. As for Gala, they were angered at what they perceived to be the dirty tactics of their opponents and some unpleasantries were exchanged in correspondence, none of which mattered in the long run. This was the Border League and, almost from the first collision in the opening match, it was no place for softies – you had to be able to take it to dish it out and, by the 1930s, the clubs knew one another well enough to recognise that there was no point in whingeing about alleged injustices to higher authorities, be it in Edinburgh or anywhere else.

In the grand scheme, the competition may have had its detractors, but they could not argue with the innovation, organisation and dedication of the Border clubs, who had responded to the challenge of transforming a close-knit local circuit into a breeding ground for international talent and had done so, almost entirely by their own enterprise. Elsewhere in Scotland, significant areas of the country – such as West Lothian, Lanarkshire and the North-West – remained almost oblivious to rugby and the big-city schools continued to operate on the basis that they would nurture their own shoots of talent and leave soccer to the proles. All of which makes it undeniable – or so I would assert – that a glorious opportunity was missed by the failure of the rest of Scotland to wake up to what the Borders had achieved with a small population, but with a huge amount of foresight.

As for those who had paved the way at Langholm, Hawick and Gala, the fruits of their labours were evident by the middle of the 1920s. Crowds in excess of 5,000 were commonplace in the bigger towns, while even the likes of Melrose and Jed-Forest would often draw audiences which amounted to a staggering 20–30 per cent of their population. The local businesses noticed the increased trade which surrounded their communities' Sevens tournaments – and while Melrose had patented the concept, their rivals had been swift in picking up the ball and running with it – and the train services in the Borders were assured of extra revenue whenever there was a big derby tie on the Saturday.

It was as close to an ideal set-up as one could imagine and, considering the strength of the ties which bonded the organisations in the South, there was no reason to suspect that the structure might break down in the future. Yes, the participating organisations might have had their differences of opinion, and there were instances where the rivalry was stretched close to breaking point, but as Jim Telfer told me, the prevailing ethos of the competition revolved around hard, no-quarter-asked-or-given 80-minute battles, which remained mercifully free of any premeditated malice or the more cynical acts of foul play, such as eye-gouging and stamping, which occurred in other parts of the world.

In contrast, rugby officials elsewhere in Scotland were almost painfully slow in waking up to the possibilities of launching their own regional tournaments, possibly revolving around the East, the West and the North of the country, and organised on similar lines to the Border League. Instead, clubs outwith the South persisted with the unofficial championship, which was the only means by which the power of the various clubs in different areas could be measured, all the way through to the 1970s. And yet, this was never a satisfactory compromise when one learned that the various participants played a different number of matches, armed with separate fixture lists, which meant it was nigh impossible to judge which club was truly the cream of the crop in any one season.

The Borders, on the other hand, could proclaim their

annual champions on merit and that invariably carried greater kudos among their peers. Hawick, for instance, won the unofficial title in 1896, but the celebrations were as nothing compared to the ecstasy which greeted their victory in the inaugural Border tournament. Occasionally, there might have been an element of parochialism in all this, but usually, the lashings of bish and bosh, and rambunctious endeavour, allied to silky skill and shards of opportunism which were required to gain the upper hand over the rest, produced worthy winners, whatever the severity of the winters or the vagaries of the fixture list. And it was surely a telling yardstick of the competitive nature of the league that, within 35 years of it springing into existence, six of the seven participating clubs had tasted championship glory, with only Langholm missing out. That epitomised how difficult it was for any single organisation to dominate their rivals, and although Hawick eventually developed the momentum of an unstoppable juggernaut, consuming everything in their wake, even the Mansfield Park men has to wait until after the Second World War for that to happen.

Ultimately, therefore, the league was an unalloyed success. It was a tough breeding ground for youngsters, a seedbed of talent for future Scotland stars, and the Borders had an increasing part to play in some of the international success stories. Irrespective of any reservations at the outset, it has created characters, myriad tales of triumph and tristesse, and raised the profile of the sport to the stage where the words 'Borders' and 'rugby' went as naturally together as Rodgers and Hammerstein or 'argy' and 'bargy'. The rest of Scotland might have been only vaguely aware of the tournament in its formative years. But, in the final analysis, it was the rest of Scotland that missed out as rugby expanded its horizons.

Chapter Four

A SLAM, A SLUMP AND SOME BORDER HEROES

SCOTTISH RUGBY followers have always had to be pragmatic souls in the pursuit of success. Unlike the English or Welsh, who expect to collect major prizes and challenge for Grand Slams on a regular basis, the normal Murrayfield supporter has no illusions that, for every golden year, there will be other seasons where hope soon crumbles to dust. This was especially true in the 1950s and 1970s, decades which yielded such prolonged misery that they spawned the sort of gallows humour exhibited by the Saltire-waving fan who reacted to the Scots' 44–0 demolition by the rampaging South Africans in Edinburgh in 1951 with the observation that his compatriots had been lucky to get nil.

With that in mind, there were plenty of reasons to revel in the Scots' achievements during the 1920s, which turned into a halcyon period for the Caledonian game, with an overall international record of 25 wins and a couple of draws from 41 matches; a victory rate of over 60 per cent, which has rarely been equalled in the intervening decades. There was also the country's first Grand Slam in 1925, which prompted delirious scenes, but was not repeated thereafter until the twin triumphs of 1984 and 1990. Rugby, obviously, had changed dramatically during that time, and so had the influence of the Borderers on the national team. Because, despite the impact of the Border League and the emergence of a string of gifted performers from the South, only one of their number,

Hawick's Doug Davies, featured among those original Slam-winning heroes.

There were a variety of reasons for this small representation. Selkirk's gifted scrum-half, Willie Bryce, who shone for his country from 1922 to 1924, was forced to retire prematurely with injury, opening the door for his Glasgow Academicals compatriot, James Nelson, who subsequently made the No 9 berth his own. So, too, the Scots were reliant on a significant number of Exiles in their line-up, which included four Oxford University players, as well as others from Carlisle, Birkenhead Park and London Scottish, who are the only club in the history of the Scottish game to have produced a greater number of internationalists than Hawick. If one peruses the Border newspapers from the mid-1920s, there are occasional grumblings about this or that individual being unfairly over-looked by the selectors, but it is very difficult to argue with the latter's choices, given the magnificent manner in which they marched unbeaten through the campaign.

In so many ways, it turned into a scintillating winter for the Scottish game. Murrayfield was opened in 1925, and almost immediately played host to a memorable contest when England came calling in pursuit of the Calcutta Cup, even if their draw with Ireland had denied them any aspirations of gaining the Grand Slam. Scotland, meanwhile, had oozed power, panache and penetration in sweeping past the Welsh 24–14 in Swansea, prevailing over the Irish by 14–8 at Lansdowne Road and trouncing the French 25–4 at Inverleith. In which light, this was one of the infrequent occasions when the English were consigned to the role of would-be party poopers on their travels north.

Predictably, the tussle generated a massive amount of public interest, with rugby lovers and other sporting aficionados flocking to Edinburgh from every part of Scotland, whether from Aberdeen and Dundee, or Fife and the West of Scotland, with the starting XV featuring a quartet of Glasgow stars in the guise of the lustrous half-backs, Nelson and Herbert Waddell, the legendary Jimmy Ireland and the towering John Bannerman. Borderers, meanwhile, travelled up to the capital in significant numbers on the train, and it was probably just as well that Murrayfield had taken over from Inverleith. The latter held only 25,000, yet more than 60,000 fans swarmed towards the ground, sparking such clamour and confusion at the turnstiles that the kick-off had to be delayed while thousands of supporters made their way into the unfamiliar amphitheatre.

Eventually, they were rewarded with a classic confrontation, encompassing all the disparate qualities which tend to embody the best sides, regardless of the pursuit. The Scots boasted silk among their glistening three-quarters, in such nonpareils as Dan Drysdale, Ian Smith and the two Georges, Macpherson and Aitken. But there was also a bone-crunching steel about their front row, which featured Davies and Robert Howie, the Kirkcaldy prop, with Ireland in the middle of them, and a string of redoubtable customers comprising the rest of a formidable pack. Yet, unsurprisingly, the English were motivated, combative and fuelled by their desire to dash their rivals' ambitions, and the lead and balance of power changed time after time. The hosts were trailing 11–10 as the match entered the final quarter, but, despite the fluctuating fortunes, Waddell was an oasis of calm amid the hubbub, and eventually, coolness personified, landed a drop goal – which was worth four points at the time – and his team emerged as 14–11 victors.

It was a notable achievement, a thoroughly deserved honour, and few of the SRU's personnel would have been entitled to raise a toast that evening more than Davies, the lone Borderer in the ranks, who had endured an altogether unhappier experience in the previous year, when he had ventured to South Africa with the British Lions for what gradually, inexorably, developed into a miserable trek around the Cape. Those were the days when such tours dragged on incessantly, with the Lions participating in 21 matches, which were spread out from 12 July to 25 September. And although they won five of their first six fixtures, matters deteriorated thereafter with the visitors losing the Test series by 3–0, with their only consolation being a 3–3 draw at Port Elizabeth in the third of the four contests. On the party's return, two of their number, the Heriot's back Roy Muir Kinnear and Aspatria's Thomas Holliday, switched codes to rugby league, and there were approaches made to several others in the squad. Yet although Hawick would increasingly become a favourite destination for the professional sport's scouts, Davies shared the opinion of most of his compatriots that union was the superior version of rugby, and he reckoned he was better off as an amateur in the cut and thrust of the Border League, allied to the priceless opportunities to play in a gifted Scotland ensemble. As with so many of his contemporaries, he was an unassuming character off the pitch, and the thrills of a packed Mansfield Park or Murrayfield were sufficient reward for his endeavour. These fellows had no interest in such modern notions as celebrity or banging out a ghosted biography. On the contrary, as Jim Renwick told me, in matter-of-fact fashion: 'You thought you were lucky if you were chosen to play for Hawick and you gave it everything you had, because you knew that if you didn't perform to the best of your abilities, you weren't just letting yourself down, but your community as well. Fame didn't matter. What mattered was that you were playing for your town, your district, your country, and you knew you had to grab the chances when they came.'

That attitude was shared by the leading luminaries from the other Border clubs, who produced a clutch of inspirational players between the two world wars, individuals whose names still resonate in their towns, long after they departed this earth. Bryce, the pride of Philiphaugh, whose name might, in other circumstances, have entered the annals with the rest of the 1925 Grand Slam brigade, was a special performer, and yet had no grand pretensions. Indeed, judging by this account from the historian Walter Thomson, his gifts could easily have been overlooked at the very start of his career.

Willie Bryce arrived in Selkirk straight from school to learn the tweed trade in his uncle's mill. A slight youth, wearing glasses, almost the first question asked of him was: 'Do you play rugby?' He admitted to a slight acquaintance with the game and was given his chance in a local Factory Cup seven-a-side tournament. Bryce was an immediate success. His team, St Mary's Mill, simply romped through their ties and Bryce went straight into a navy blue jersey. The rest is part of Scotland's rugby history.

Gaining his first cap against Wales in 1922, Bryce developed into one of the finest scrum-halves of all time. He was an automatic choice for his country for three seasons until an injury on the field brought his career to a premature end, though not before he had gained the rare distinction of captaining Scotland. Bryce then turned to hockey and won a further string of international honours, while he was considered unlucky not to gain a cap for Scotland at cricket as well. His example as a player and a sportsman did as much as any single factor to establish rugby as the dominant game in Selkirk.

His name might hardly be known outside of the Borders, but the accounts of Bryce's displays in the Scottish cause brook no dissent: he was clearly exceptional, an individual blessed with vision and balance, poise and invention, who thrilled crowds as much as he scared the living daylights out of opponents. Precious few rugby players have the ability to win matches on their own – unlike in football, where one man's hat-trick can prove the catalyst for victory – but Bryce came close in 1923 in Cardiff, where his brilliance helped the Scots recover from a losing position and record their first success in the city since 1890. Their ranks included the likes of Eric Liddell, the future Olympic sprint champion and subject of the film *Chariots of Fire*, but it was the ubiquitous Bryce who sizzled in the Principality, growing in influence as the battle continued, sparking havoc among the Welsh, and creating a plethora of chances for his back line, who eventually transformed an 8–3 deficit into an 11–8 win, with the home team dead on their feet by the end.

If Bryce had merely been a richly gifted practitioner of his arts, that would have sufficed for most men. But – and it is a theme which kept recurring when I spoke to Borderers about their icons and talismanic figures – he poured his heart and soul into Selkirk RFC, later serving as club president, whilst his son, Bill, turned out as hooker in the early sixties. That continuity has always been one of the most noticeable aspects of rugby in the South; the sense of the torch being handed on from one generation to another, and of families keeping a steady hand on the tiller, either on the field or behind the scenes in the committee room. This is not unique to the Borders, of course, and the Scottish game has profited from famous father-and-son combinations, such as John and John-nie Beattie, and brothers-in-arms such as the Milnes, Calders, Browns and Hastingses. Yet, given the small population in communities such as Selkirk and Melrose, Kelso and Jed-burgh, the townspeople needed to be able to recognise the importance of eschewing complacency and continually look-ing ten or twenty years down the line, and, thankfully, they did so.

It meant that there were numerous cases of kith and kin embracing the oval ball. Some became famous in the wider world. Others were content to be local heroes, rousing themselves to prodigious exploits on their own patches. One such figure was Allan Smith, who helped Kelso to three Border League titles in the 1930s, and carried on supporting the 'Black and Whites' into his 90s. As Laing Speirs relates, he might not have been a world-class player, but this was a chap born to revel on a rugby pitch.

With a grandfather known as 'Strong Bob', the blacksmith who played for Kelso, and his father also a regular at the turn of the century, Allan came to the Kelso side with full understanding of what local pride was all about. He was a member of the side which won the League for the first time in 1930–31 and recalls the crowds of 3,000, which used to throng the field, ignoring the ropes and getting in the way of the action.

The personalities in the Kelso team included Tom 'Tinkle' Laidlaw, whose enthusiasm for training was lukewarm, to put it mildly. His preparations for any game generally included a pie and a bottle of beer. But he was a natural, according to Smith.

There may have been no professionalism in the 1930s and virtually nothing in the way of sponsorship, but there was one great incentive for young players to progress on the Kelso club scene. The treasurer at the time, Jock Laing, ruled that if you were in the first XV, you were given a high tea at away games, but if you were travelling with the seconds, the entertainment was scaled down to a plain tea.

Smith, an effective full-back with a natural aptitude for breaking tackles, was one of those individuals who felt blessed to have received the opportunity to parade his talent in front of the Borders people. Even nearly 60 years later, he could recollect precise details of various Border League encounters, while explaining that spectators were only charged two old pence admission for what usually turned into a stirring contest. No wonder they turned up in such multitudes – and there were instances of attendances in excess of 10,000 – when they could cheer (or jeer) such totemic characters as Kelso's Bob Smith and Alex Cameron, Hawick's Doug Davies and Jock Beattie, the Gala behemoth Jimmy Ferguson and the Selkirk powerhouse, Jack Waters. These were ferociously competitive customers, for whom the idea of taking a backward step was simply not an option.

They were also proud to play whenever they joined forces in a combined South team and, although the Scottish Inter-District championship did not come into existence until the 1950s, there were a number of illustrations of the exciting potential of a Border side, especially one which mixed Selkirk and Melrose's artistry and élan with the barnstorming Hawick, Langholm and Kelso forwards, and flung in a soupçon of the pace which Gala and Jed-Forest frequently exhibited on their Sevens adventures.

In the winter of 1931, for example, the South's elite locked horns with the touring South Africans at the Greenyards and earned a hugely creditable 0–0 draw in a match which they could have won, such were the quality and quintessential ingredients which the hosts exuded throughout the contest. This was no mediocre Springbok squad. On the contrary, Bennie Osler's typically hard-tackling and defensive-minded personnel prevailed against all the Home Nations. They recorded 8–3 victories over Wales and Ireland before beating England and Scotland 7–0 and 6–3 respectively, and eventually won 23 [and drew two others] of their mammoth schedule of 26 games between October 1931 and January 1932.

Yet the Borders kept them at bay, fuelled by the tireless exertions of such warriors as Doug Davies and Jock Beattie and the Selkirk duo of Tom Brown and Jack Waters, the latter of whom was another individual to serve his region and country with distinction. And this was not the only occasion when the South produced exhilarating, no-holds-barred performances against the giants of the southern hemisphere. Their most famous achievement came 53 years later when the Scots famously got the better of the great Australian ensemble featuring Andrew Slack and his compatriots – the only defeat which the Wallabies endured on their visit to Britain and Ireland – but the South also drew with the South Africans during the controversial 1968–69 tour and beat the Aussies in the midst of the latter's 1966–67 campaign. These tussles served up acts of individual brilliance from the home ranks, but, more importantly, testified to how well the cream of the Borders could rise to whatever challenges were placed in front of them. In which light, it is perhaps surprising that Scotland does not make more of these exploits, and particularly considering we never hear the end of Munster's 1978 victory over the All Blacks.

Indeed, the South were mighty close to a win against the New Zealand tourists at a packed Mansfield Park in October 1935, before eventually succumbing 11–8, in a match which was marked by the robustness of both sides' forward exchanges. This might not have been the best Kiwi contingent to have travelled to the northern hemisphere – as their defeats at the hands of Wales and England highlighted – but they were still good enough to beat Scotland 18–8 the following month, and the South could be proud of their endeavours. Here, as in so many other instances, they transcended any parochial concerns and amply demonstrated that the things which bonded them were more substantial than the local rivalry which came to the fore in the thick of Border League struggle. And it also helped that their selectors actually picked their best team on a regular basis.

Unfortunately, though, the same could not be said about Scotland in the years leading up to the Second World War, when they crashed like Wall Street, following the heady successes of the previous decade. On a positive note, they managed to secure another Triple Crown in 1933 and there was always the prospect of flashes of individual flair livening up the drabbest of international displays, but the Scots slipped into a losing habit and savoured victory only three times in 12 matches between 1934 and 1937. As Walter Thomson reported with a heavy heart, it did not help anybody that several of the Border clubs were enduring a rough patch, including Hawick, who regularly flirted with mediocrity – by their lofty own standards – during a miserable sequence of four wins in 14 matches, as Christmas was cancelled at Mansfield Park in 1937. With hindsight, these peaks and troughs should have been predicted given the slim resources at Scotland's disposal, but that did not ease the pain of the fans, who faithfully paid their admission money, irrespective of past travails, forever travelling more in hope than expectation: a state which made the occasional triumph all the more worth celebrating.

It was also difficult to establish any continuity or plan for the future when the Scottish selection panel changed every season and their choices were often, at best, debatable. But there again, apart from the Border League, how could they judge who was the best in the country at any given time when there was no national league competition? These questions taxed the minds of many in the South and some of the local newspapers in the South became quite vocal on the subject, arguing that Kelso should have gained greater international recognition in the midst of their splendid exploits in the 1930s.

Nonetheless, nobody disputed the fashion in which Hawick's Jock Beattie became one of the cornerstones of the Scottish pack throughout the 1930s on his way to amassing 23 international caps, which was a momentous haul in those days (and particularly given France's exclusion from the Five Nations Championship, over allegations of professionalism, for most of the Teri's career). Beattie was a fearsome opponent in his prime and it was remarked of him by the *Border Advertiser* that he would have run through a brick wall for Hawick and Scotland – 'but especially Hawick!' He made his debut against France in 1929, just a few months before they were temporarily booted out of the tournament, but he really came into his own in subsequent seasons and produced a string of juddering exhibitions of brawny forward play throughout his country's Triple Crown triumph. The winning margins were all tight: England were edged out 3–0 at Murrayfield as the prelude to the Scots travelling to Dublin and Swansea and prevailing 8–6 and 11–3 respectively. But, in terms of commitment, nobody could begrudge them their success.

Beattie would not have known it at the time, but his exploits were an inspiration to one of the children who followed these matches, namely Bill McLaren, who was growing up in Hawick and had already contracted the rugby bug with a vengeance. 'As an eight-year-old, I remember writing detailed accounts of fictional matches,' he later recalled. 'Scotland once beat the Rest of the World 85–11 and I think that I had Jock Beattie [that's B-E-A-T-T-I-E] scoring three tries.' McLaren's grasp of detail and the minutiae of these contests was phenomenal and, despite his beloved Hawick struggling in the Border League for a number of seasons, the youngster took solace in journeying to all parts of Britain with his father, soaking up the atmosphere of international sport. He was there at Twickenham in 1936 for what proved to be

Beattie's swansong in a Scotland jersey, but it was another of his Mansfield Park comrades who suffered a worse afternoon. 'Rob Barrie had to go off with a broken collarbone after just ten minutes and you could see that he was in agony. He was tackling the Sale wing, Hal Sever, who was a massive hulk of a man, and there were no substitutions in those days, so it looked as if it would be another painful visit to London for the Scots,' said McLaren. 'But they dug in and battled with everything they had and it made you proud to be there and watch their efforts, even with all the odds against them. They ended up losing 9–8, but they got a huge cheer from the crowd when they walked off at the finish and they deserved it.'

If that was a nerve-shredding encounter, there were sunnier dispositions on the next occasion when the Scots pitched up in London, two years later, with a team that had already defied expectations by defeating Wales 8–6 with a late penalty in Edinburgh, prior to dispatching the Irish by a comfortable margin of 23–14. That allowed them a crack at another Triple Crown, and two Borderers, Tom Dorward of Gala and John Hastie of Melrose, were among the ranks as they prepared for a contest which became famous for several reasons, not least because it was the first to be televised, but principally as a consequence of the fabulous display which was unleashed on the English by the mercurial Wilson Shaw, with whom this tussle will be forever inextricably linked.

Allan Massie recently painted a vivid picture of the game in *The Scotsman*.

It was a remarkable and memorable match. The English forwards did all that had been expected or feared, and opinions vary as to whether they won three or four times more ball than Scotland. But the Scottish back row of Duff, Young and Crawford spoiled and scavenged tirelessly, while

Shaw ran as if he had been shot from a gun and the centres cut through [England's defence] at will. The match was won 21–16. More tellingly, Scotland scored five tries, Shaw himself getting two of them, and England only managed one. Shaw was hailed as the greatest rugby player of his generation and he was carried shoulder-high in triumph from the field. The Triple Crown had been won by a team that was originally despised and despaired of. But then, after the victory over Wales, *The Scotsman* had declared that 'Scottish rugby XVs come into existence to confound their critics or, often, to disillusion the hopeful'.

The next year, things were back to normal. With characteristic perversity, the selectors ignored the evidence of 1938 and shunted Shaw back to the wing. With him at No 10, the Scots had scored ten tries and won all three matches. In 1939, they lost all three.

This dramatic shift between soaring towards the stratosphere in one instant and suffering Icarus' fate in the next, regularly beset the Scots, but if Shaw was the shining star, the contributions of the two unsung Borderers should not go unnoticed, especially in these pages. Dorward only gained five caps for his country, at scrum-half, and subsequently perished in the war in 1941, but gratefully seized his opportunity to be part of one of the most astonishing afternoons in Scotland's rugby history and it could be argued that Shaw would not have had the chance to tear England apart if his half-back partner had been delivering him hospital passes. His brother, Arthur, also stood proudly behind the thistle, making 15 appearances between 1950 and 1957, and once again, as happened with a remarkable frequency, the family connection was maintained despite the ravages of conflict, and the Borders – and Scotland – gained hugely from the phenomenon.

John Hastie, for his part, never played for Scotland again

after collecting what was his third cap at Twickenham, which makes one wonder how many performers in the modern era would have been discarded in these circumstances. Yet if the Melrose hooker felt aggrieved at his treatment, he was not inclined to go bleating to the press about it. As he and so many of his peers told the likes of Walter Thomson, they had never entered rugby in pursuit of Test recognition or getting their names in the Fourth Estate; they had done so for the pure, undiluted joy of picking up a rugby ball and working in unison with their allies in the Borders. And whether they earned one cap or 51, nobody could ever take it away from them once they had offered their all with the rest of their team-mates.

It was a simple philosophy, an approach forged on industry and camaraderie in the heat of sporting battle, allied to these staunch fellows' collective ability to be inspired rather than terrified by representing their towns, their district and their country. As the 1930s reached their conclusion, there were far more important hostilities to worry about than mere games of rugby – and, just as in the first global conflict of 1914–18, where so many Borderers perished, there was a heavy toll on their numbers in the fight to save the free world. Ultimately, the powerful strands of family, faith and fighting for what was right mercifully prevailed, although every community suffered grievous casualties and many of their number returned with dreadful memories indelibly etched on their consciousness. They included a young Bill McLaren, who served in the Royal Artillery as a teenager from 1942 onwards. He recounted his memories in his autobiography, *The Voice of Rugby*, recalling one particular scene which was straight out of Dante's *Inferno*.

Early one morning, in 1944, just after the sun had come up in Northern Italy [McLaren was involved in the bloody struggle for Monte Cassino], I was leading a group of men on a reconnaissance. I was looking for a gun position, which was one of my duties as a forward observance officer. As we came into a small town, we quickly became aware of a peculiar smell. It was a very strong, sweet, sickly sort of smell and it seemed to fill the air. It was winter, so we could discount the scent of overripe flowers wafting on the breeze. Any old soldier will already have a good idea of the source of this cloying stench. We moved carefully towards the town centre. Nobody seemed to be about. All we could see was destruction: buildings bombed and shattered, broken down and wrecked vehicles lying in the street. In the middle of the town, we turned a corner and saw a graveyard. What confronted me there was a sight that remained with me for ever.

There must have been, piled up on the ground within this one cemetery, around 1,500 dead Germans and Italians. The bodies lay there, frozen in their death throes, grotesquely contorted, one of top of the other and four or five deep. Both the smell and this nightmare vision were indescribable. Many of the corpses had had limbs blown off: there were men, women and children without feet or arms, children with legs missing. It was the most horrific thing I had ever seen in my life, indeed would ever see. I was 21.

Apparently, the Germans had put down a huge barrage and had hit the village, accidentally it was said. Once it was taken, they had dug in and, some time later, had confronted the advancing British Army. There had been an absolute bloodbath. Local men, women and children, as was all too vividly evident, had been caught up in the battle and paid a terrible price. The Germans, too, had been wiped out and their corpses lay, strewn in heaps in the graveyard, along with those of the townsfolk.

I had seen dead bodies before, since arriving in Italy, but nothing on this scale. Somehow, this pitiless slaughter seemed to encapsulate the greater conflict into which we had been dragged. It was a vision of hell on earth and we were right in the middle of it, watching our chums, our enemies and innocent civilians alike, losing their lives right in front of us. For weeks afterwards, I could not get that shocking image out of my mind, nor the stench of decaying bodies out of my nostrils. The boy I had been was gone. I suspect that he disappeared for ever on that awful morning.

Understandably, in these circumstances, when a semblance of normality was restored to life in Scotland and the rest of the planet in 1945 and beyond, it was with as much a huge sense of relief as anything else that rugby gradually became a high priority again for the South. Some people might believe that too much emphasis is placed on sport, and matters have definitely changed during the last ten or twenty years from the time when those who had witnessed atrocities, such as that encountered by McLaren, adopted a proper perspective towards games. There were no 'tragedies' or 'disasters' from McLaren at the mike. If somebody missed a tackle or sclaffed a penalty, it was unfortunate, nothing more.

Nonetheless, it was necessary for everybody to try and pick up the pieces of their lives and thank their lucky stars they were in a position to be able to countenance any kind of future. Soon enough, amid the rebuilding of towns and cities, and development of such innovations as the National Health Service, sport was on the agenda once more. At which point, we began to witness rugby's progress towards modernisation, while affairs in the Borders were increasingly dominated by an all-conquering Hawick infantry.

Chapter Five

THE GREEN MACHINE

VERY FEW SPORTING success stories happen by accident. They might be the consequence of one special group of players coming together at the same time, whose exploits cast a long shadow over those who follow in their wake, or they may spring from the vision of a solitary far-sighted benefactor. But, speaking as somebody who has covered all manner of pursuits in the last 25 years, experience tells me that Celtic and Manchester United would not have risen to greatness in the 1960s and 1990s without the efforts of a whole range of behind-the-scenes architects of their clubs' heroics, whether in the scouting system which served Jock Stein so well, or the en-deavours of mentors in the mould of Teddy Scott and Eric Harrison, who unearthed diamonds for Alex Ferguson.

On a smaller scale, Kingussie have prospered throughout the decades in shinty, because of the development work, which carries on year in, year out in their hamlet, just as Freuchie won cricket's National Village Cup in 1985 because their captain, president and general factotum, Dave Christie, devoted count-less hours of unpaid energy to ensuring that every single person in the Fife community had the opportunity to pick up a bat and ball and discover for themselves the treasures involved in the summer game. As he told me, in terms which explained why this doughty individual has a street named after him in his birthplace: 'I've never believed that Scots are born thinking that football is the only sport which matters. If they end up playing football, because they were never offered the chance to try their hand at anything else, I think that's a pretty sad state of affairs. But, from what I have seen over many years – the last 50 years in fact – Scots love sport and will take an interest in cricket, rugby, tennis, golf and any other pursuit if you catch them young and make them realise the enjoyment they can get from hitting a ball, or serving an ace, or scoring a try. But it's up to us, the adults, to capture their imaginations.'

In Scottish rugby, the means by which Hawick rose from being a good club to a feared institution owed precious little to mere fortune, but was more a natural by-product of the network of fiercely-committed players, coaches, committee officials and teachers, whose labours transformed the Mansfield Park organisation from the prime club in the Borders into the best in Scotland by a country mile in the 1960s and 1970s. Indeed, whenever and wherever there have been innovations in the Caledonian game, Hawick have usually swept all before them, whether winning the first ever Border League or repeating that feat when Scotland finally established an official national championship. Even in the 1990s, when the Scottish Cup sprung into being, who else should bring thousands of their townsfolk up to Murrayfield, replete with specially-composed songs and other tokens of pride in their roots than Hawick, who duly triumphed in the inaugural competition?

Perhaps predictably, the efficacy of their fabled 'Green Machine' has elicited a degree of envy and criticism from some of their opponents, although the Mansfield men simply have to point to their wondrous roll of honour – including 43 Border League victories and 12 'official' Scottish titles, in addition to boasting all of 58 Scottish internationalists – to drive home the message that their awe-inspiring passion for rugby has yielded a rich seam of talent, both for themselves and the wider Scottish community. Of course, it helped that Hawick was the largest town in the South, but they only had a tiny fraction of the population of Glasgow or Edinburgh (the 2001 census listed the figure as 14,801), yet progressed to the stage in the early 1970s where they were virtually able to field a first XV with international experience. That process did not come to fruition without lashings of perspiration on the pitch, but more importantly, a tremendous amount of missionary work at the grass roots, from selfless characters who did not suffer fools gladly, but whose fervour and inherent love for the game guaranteed there was never any danger of their precious club developing into a clique or, in modern parlance, a vanity project.

We have already highlighted how they were born, initially as a means of keeping the town's cricketers fit during the lengthy Scottish winters. But, by the time we advance to the late 1940s and early 1950s, there were other reasons why Hawick flourished. In the first place, recognising that they had to tap into every conceivable well of talent, they created a junior system which sparked a mustard-keen rivalry among their emerging talent and ensured that nobody's place was ever secure, particularly if they were foolish enough to treat selection as a right and not a privilege. Thus we had the establishment of Hawick Trades and Hawick Wanderers in 1946 and 1954 respectively, who augmented the links which had previously been formed with Hawick PSA (founded in 1919), Hawick Linden (1921) and Hawick Harlequins (1930). With such a disparate strand of rugby on offer, it was hardly surprising that the community became as famous for the sight of hundreds of youngsters playing on Saturday mornings as it did for the town's annual Common Riding festival and the quality of the produce from their mills.

Then, there was the influence of a triumvirate, whose combined efforts, on and off the field, were pivotal to their organisation's prodigious achievements during the next three or four decades. The first of these Three Wise Men was Hugh McLeod, the redoubtable prop, who represented Scotland on 40 occasions between 1954 and 1962 and travelled with the

British and Irish Lions to South Africa in 1955. This fellow, who earned the sobriquet of the 'Hawick Hardman', soaked up the lessons from his stint with the Lions and gradually, as much through the sheer force of his magnetic personality as the quality of his performances, instilled in his compatriots an attitude that rugby union players might be amateurs, but that did not have to prevent them from being professional in their training and preparation for matches. McLeod could make the toughest of opponents wilt under his glare and once, according to his great friend Bill McLaren, delivered the following speech to his forwards: 'Come here, my wee disciples. Now, ah want to tell ee that ah've been asked to lead this pack tomorrow. Ah'm no very keen on the job, and if any of you lot want to be pack leader, just let me know and I'll put in a word. Meanwhile, the next one who opens his trap will get my boot bloody hard at his arse.'

The second of the trio was Robin Charters, the resplendent Hawick centre who made three appearances for his country in 1955, and later became the SRU president at a stage when rugby was moving inevitably towards the pay-for-play era. In between, he was a master motivator and astute thinker on the game, whose passion for the union code was only equalled by his conviction that traditional Borders values remained vital, no matter what else might change. He said the following in 2000:

For years, Hawick won the Border League and if we didn't, then we were considered to be a poor side. It was all a question of numbers. Hawick had more players and it had all to do with local prosperity. Despite the economic problems [as the 20th century moved on], rugby was a great attraction. Townsfolk always supported their club – it was a place to go – and there was a wonderful social life. There was a lot of patter with the opposition and it was great fun.

But somehow, all that has gone in the professional game. We

know that the game had to change and we had to change with it. But I take the view that we call it sport still, but it's not sport. Our definition of sport was something else – you played hard and you played to win, but you enjoyed yourself doing it and, whatever the result of the match, you enjoyed mixing after the game with the opposition. The fact is that somebody has to come second. But nowadays if you lose, then nobody wants to know you.

The third member of the triumvirate was Derrick Grant, another in the long line of Borderers whom it would be preferable to have as a friend rather than an enemy. He served his community and his country with singular distinction, whether winning 14 caps as an indefatigable flanker between 1965 and 1968, or graduating into the role of Hawick's hugely-successful coach in the 1970s and 1980s. Grant, as one might have anticipated, could be a tough customer when it was necessary, but none of the illustrious former stars who were interviewed for this book had a single negative word to say about their erstwhile mentor. Instead, they testified to the meticulous nature of his pre-match preparations and rigorous analysis of his opponents, his openness to new ideas such as organising team meetings on the Fridays before games, and improving the athleticism of his squad by putting them through 2,000-yard gallops when they pitched up at Mansfield Park on Tuesday evenings. And the overriding impression which emerged was that he shared many of the qualities of Jock Stein; namely, that while he detested players who squandered their talent, and had no patience with those who settled for second best, he could mix the carrot and stick to such mes-merising effect that his players would willingly have walked over hot coals in their bare feet if he had asked them to do so.

The cumulative impact of these characters can hardly be overstated in steering Hawick towards a position where they shared Queen Victoria's approach to the possibility of defeat. In the seasons immediately after the Second World War, the club could not crank up sufficient momentum to leave their rivals trailing in their wake, and Gala, Melrose and Selkirk all enjoyed a share of the honours prior to Langholm celebrating their solitary Border League triumph in 1959. Yet, just as the times they were a-changing in music with Bob Dylan and the Beatles to the fore, so, too, Hawick began churning out a remarkable number of gifted personnel, fuelled by the twin peaks of their burgeoning junior set-up and the work of McLeod, Charters, Grant and Bill McLaren, the latter of whom nurtured scores of rugby-daft youngsters from the region's primary schools.

The consequence was an abundance of riches and a diverse range of personalities with glimmers of magic in the back line from such gifted performers as George Stevenson, Wattie Scott and Norman Davidson, allied to the formidable graft of forwards in the mould of Hugh McLeod, Adam Robson and Jack Hegarty, even as a clutch of stars from the younger generation started making an impression in the town's junior ranks.

Ian Barnes, who later went on to represent Scotland in the 1970s, was one of the youngsters who was exhilarated by the atmosphere around Hawick during that period, even as the club capitalised on the foundations laid down by the likes of McLeod.

It all began when Hugh came back from the Lions trip, bursting with ideas he had picked up on his trip to the southern hemisphere, and suddenly, you had this group of people coming together, who created a synergy around Mansfield Park, and it was a brilliant time to be growing up in the town if you wanted to play rugby. The thing is that there was plenty of money in Hawick at that stage – the mills were going full pelt – and my generation was very lucky, because we had this situation where there were great players, such as Hugh and Robin Charters to look up to, and a natural progression between these fellows and the likes of Derrick Grant, while Bill [McLaren] was working in teaching and doing a terrific job of getting more and more children interested in the sport. It meant that rugby was as popular down in Hawick as football was in parts of Glasgow and I can remember going out and playing touch rugby when the weather was too bad or it was too dark, and a lot of people's lives revolved around the game.

With all the other sides in Hawick, such as the Linden team and the Trades team, you had what was almost the perfect structure, and the rivalry between the various clubs in the town was incredible. I was involved in some of these games and, believe me, they were some of the most savage encounters in which I ever took part, because everybody was absolutely determined to force their way into the Hawick first XV. There were other times where we travelled down to England and played against opponents like Whitehaven and Workington Town and it was f★★★ing brutal, no-holds-barred stuff. But, because of these experiences, you soon learned that you had to stand your ground, and it meant you were ready to make the step up if you saw your name on the Hawick notice board.

Looking back, it was a really vibrant town in the 1950s and 1960s and I suppose that there was also a bit of good fortune in the fact that people of the calibre of Jim Renwick, Colin Deans, Norman Pender and Alan Tomes all came through in the same group. But, on the other hand, Derrick left pretty much nothing to chance, and he was definitely ahead of his time in so many different ways. To be honest, I remember going to a Scotland session after being called up into the national team [in 1972] and it was quite embarrassing when you compared how basic it was to what Derrick was doing with us down in the Borders. I don't want to sound too nostalgic, but there genuinely was a huge amount of community spirit about the town and rugby was the glue which held everything together. I grew up living next door to Bill

[McLaren] and he was the first person in the street to own a television and when we weren't playing or training, we were round there watching *Champion the Wonder Horse*. And everybody was spurring everybody else on. But, of course, people had jobs in those days, and the youngsters didn't have to go elsewhere to search for work. So that made it easier for the people who were running rugby in Hawick to hang on to the best of the emerging talent.

The results allowed no room for argument. In the period between 1945 and 1972, the club's supremacy over the rest of the competition, not merely in the South, but the whole of Scotland, eventually grew all-pervading. They wrapped up 15 Border League titles, secured the unofficial championship eight times, and even earned fame as Sevens specialists, although they gradually encountered a rising challenge from Gala in that sphere. But, unsurprisingly considering these exploits, no Scotland team was complete without at least one or two Teris in the line-up and McLeod (40 caps), George Stevenson (24), Adam Robson (22) and Grant (14) accumulated 100 caps between them, while another 15 members of the Green Machine pulled on their country's jersey and the rugby league scouts swarmed around Mansfield Park like wasps at a July picnic. Even if we accept that Hawick had a numerical advantage over their Border neighbours, this was still the stuff of which dreams were made and it was a testimony to the boundless energy, vaulting ambition and volunteer corps who were content to be part of a process which brought them no personal glory, but made them feel part of something special.

Opinions vary as to which of the various Hawick ensembles was the pick of the bunch.

The older fraternity sang the praises of Jack Hegarty's team of the 1959–60 campaign, with Derrick Grant's brother, Oliver, an integral member of their fearsome pack, while

Drew Broatch and Glen Turnbull formed an incisive, imaginative half-back pairing. This latter pair were subsequently lured to England by the professional league code, but it was a measure of the strength in depth which the club boasted that replacements slotted into their places almost seamlessly. Even once Grant retired from playing, his coaching expertise ensured that the trophy cabinet was never empty at Mansfield Park, and one could sympathise with their opponents, who must have felt akin to poor old Sisyphus shoving his bloody rock up the hill for all eternity. The Border League turned into something resembling the modern Scottish Premier League in football, where all the participants bar the Old Firm are scrapping for third place, and if it was not Jim Renwick and Alastair Cranston teaming up in the centre, it was Ian Barnes and Norman Pender forming a juddering partnership and knocking seven bells out of opposing packs. Nothing lasts forever, of course, but it must have felt very close to heaven for the Hawick confrères when they transferred their collective skills from their club to Scotland without any visible drop in quality. Renwick, who is one of most unassuming people it would be possible to meet, and yet glittered on so many of his 52 caps for Scotland, had this to say:

We had our moments at Murrayfield with a 10–9 win in 1973 against a Welsh side with nine Lions and we also beat them in 1975 and 1981. I can still remember the year of the snow down there in 1978, though, where we had seven Hawick men on the field by the end. We didn't win, but I remember that as a special day which probably won't happen again. We started with six [Renwick, Cranston, Deans, Pender, Tomes and Brian Hegarty] and then 'Greco' [Graham Hogg] came on, up against Gerald Davies, on the wing. Never easy!

Bill McLaren used to say to me that he enjoyed commentating in the seventies the most, when Gerald, JJ and JPR

Williams, Phil Bennett and Barry John were the men. Folk wouldn't have guessed it, but he told me he got carried away during these games and you could well understand why. It was not as predictable as rugby is now: boys just played off the cuff and were prepared to be adventurous. Yes, there were a lot of mistakes, but you were out there trying to use whatever skill you had to outfox your opposite number, and we had plenty of good players who reacted to that and thrived on it.

It obviously helped these individuals' collective confidence that Hawick had settled into such an all-conquering groove, winning the Border League eight seasons in a row and an astonishing 21 times in 26 seasons from 1959–60 to 1984–85. There was continuity, the ability to shove opponents backwards in the mud and glaur or scythe through them with some sparkling back play on the days when the sun shone and the pitches were more conducive to running rugby. Mansfield Park became a fortress, an arena from which visiting Glasgow and Edinburgh collectives rarely escaped without injury, either to their person or their reputations – or both! – but they could at least reflect on how they were involved in one of the truly phenomenal periods for any Scottish team in any sport.

Renwick, for his part, was both a centre of evidence and a chap who could slip into the background of any picture, rather like Zelig. When we spoke for this book, he was instinctively inclined to heap praise on others in the Hawick ranks, whether in the early guidance he received from the Three Wise Men, or the totemic influence of such doughty stalwarts as Jack Hegarty, Norman Pender and Norman Suddon, or one of his own icons, George Stevenson. Yet nothing should disguise the myriad qualities which this little marvel possessed at his peak, nor how he broke through the ranks at Mansfield Park to ignite the dullest game and spark excitement from any position on his field.

For me, Derrick Grant was the real driving force. He had a vision, he had ambition and he had such an incredible sense of purpose that he drove the ship forward. This was in the early days of coaching, but he was a pioneer who pushed us to become better players than we might otherwise have been and I don't believe that his contribution to Scottish rugby and his vast knowledge and experience have been properly recognised.

In the 1950s and 1960s, Hawick was just crazy about the game. You left school and you got a job, and you poured your heart and soul into working during the day and playing rugby at night and at weekends. My dad and my brother both played for the club as well and it just seemed the most natural thing in the world to get up early in the morning, put in a decent shift, get home, pick up your kit, and head down to the rugby ground. We never even thought about whether we were tired. Tired!! We were young men and this was a fantastic life and there was so much going on that it was really exciting.

In the early days, I looked up to George Stevenson, because he was so unpredictable – he could be making an arse of it one minute and then suddenly produce a piece of magic, which took your breath away in the next. There were lots of heroes, Hugh McLeod, Colin Deans, Alan Tomes . . . where on earth do you stop? And, of course, there was the constant presence of Bill McLaren in the background, keeping an eye on you, and always passing on a quick word of encouragement whenever he could. He was a one-off as well.

I remember him teaching us and you weren't allowed to go overboard about scoring a try with Bill, because you had to show respect to your opponents. I think he would have looked at somebody like the English guy [Chris Ashton, whose extravagant celebrations were a feature of the 2011 Six Nations Championship] and told him to cut it out. Bill loved the game and he had the words and the enthusiasm to make others love it as well, without feeling the need to bang on about winning all the time. His message was that enjoying what we were doing was the main thing. And it rubbed off on most of us.

Don't get me wrong, we were brought up in a pretty hard school, and the supporters in Hawick made sure we never let our standards slip or, when we did, they were quick to let us know about it. There was pressure, it was there when you walked up to the notice board in the town centre to discover whether or not you were in the team for Saturday's match – because nobody bothered to telephone you one way or the other – and if your name wasn't on the list, you were shattered. Of course you were. But you weren't playing for money or fame, so it wasn't the be-all and end-all. You still wished your team-mates well, and wanted them to succeed, but it made you doubly determined to do everything you could do to guarantee that your name would be there the next time around.

I think that system taught you about the euphoria which rugby could bring. It also got people used to the idea that losing was no disgrace as long as you had given it everything you had. During my career, whenever and wherever Hawick played, we were the king pins, everybody wanted to knock us off our perch, and that can be tough to deal with if you haven't been properly prepared. But, because we had all risen through the structure together, the knowledge that everybody wanted to beat us simply made us better and better players. Derrick knew that, he had worked out what was required for us to keep making progress and retain our hunger, and if he ever caught you slacking, well . . . you just didn't! There were so many players trying their damnedest to get into the team that you had to regard every game as being very, very important, not least because Derrick never lost sight of the fact that we were out there fighting on

Saturdays, not for ourselves, but for the town which had given us the opportunity to play in the first place. Some people thought he was hard. He had to be. Introverts don't make good coaches!

With these ingredients, allied to the spirit of collectivism which infused Hawick teams throughout their decades of success, it was no wonder that the Green Machine left fans and journalists alike incessantly searching for new superlatives. There were epic tussles, classic confrontations, both in the Border League and the Scottish championship and, occasionally, the two competitions converged, such as when Hawick made the short journey to Netherdale to confront their deadly rivals, Gala, in the winter of 1982. By this stage, the hosts had not merely caught up with their local adversaries, but surpassed them, en route to winning two consecutive Scottish titles and, in advance of the match, there was a sense that Hawick had perhaps relinquished their aura and former majesty.

With hindsight, the quality of both sets of combatants was lip-smacking; the national selectors could have chosen a first-rate XV from these team sheets. Gala were bolstered by such sterling performers as the usually metronomic full-back, Peter Dods, the future Grand Slam-winning captain, Jim Aitken, and such tenacious and talented warriors as Tom Smith, Derek White and Gordon Dickson among their impressive pack.

Yet the visitors also oozed class and clout in most departments, with their side featuring the likes of Renwick, Cranston, Deans, Tomes, Derek Turnbull and Alastair Campbell when the action commenced in front of a massive − and voluble − audience, who screamed their support for the respective endeavours of the Maroons and Greens.

This was the kind of afternoon in sport when minuscule fractions often make a massive difference, and when tabloid journalists had their pens ready – in the days before laptops and the Internet – to commend or condemn players as 'battlers' or 'bottlers'. Sadly, from Gala's perspective, the normally rock-solid Dods suffered a nightmare day with the boot, missing half a dozen kicks, which might have made all the difference at the end, while Colin Gass, who had only recently switched allegiance from Gala to Hawick, was almost as profligate for his new club, in squandering four penalty opportunities. Given this litany of blemishes, the tussle remained nail-bitingly tight all the way through to its dramatic denouement: and despite the visitors leading 9–3 at the interval with a brace of penalties from Gass and Renwick and a drop goal from the former, to a solitary penalty for Dods, his side gained renewed hope when Jim Maitland scored a wonderful individual try, latching on to his own kick ahead and duly touching down. Normally, Dods would have slotted the conversion in his sleep, but this was not a run-of-the-mill encounter, and his attempt drifted wide, to the groans of the home fans.

Nonetheless, their mood improved considerably when Maitland sent Gala 10–9 ahead with the clock ticking down on Hawick's hopes of regaining the ascendancy in the Borders. Then, suddenly, in the fourth minute of injury time, who should pop up to apply the *coup de grâce* with the boot than Renwick, when his opponents were penalised for killing the ball. He had been in these tight spots so often before that the derision of the Gala aficionados went clean over his head, and he kept his cool to snatch an improbable victory. 'I looked over to Colin, or to anyone else who fancied the kick, to take it,' recalled Renwick. 'In the end, I just took it myself. I thought: "Just keep your head down and hit it." ' It had been a narrow squeak for the Green Machine – who had earlier gained a reprieve when the referee, Brian Anderson, ruled out a Smith try for offside – but the sizzling atmosphere inside the ground, the realisation that this truly mattered to both clubs and their adherents, and the dramatic, fluctuating fortunes at the death, reflected Renwick's own view that nothing on the club circuit surpassed a pulsating derby between the Borders elite, whether it was taking place in February 1902 or 1982. As he told me: 'We sometimes won matches because we never knew when we were beaten and kept fighting until the final whistle, not because we were the better side on the day.' And that is the mark of champions in every pursuit, and goes a long way towards explaining why Hawick had the capacity to grind out victories where any rational analysis of the statistics in the contest would have decreed they should lose.

In a sense, even when their feeder system stuttered, the buzz around the community and desire of those who lived in it to play rugby at the highest level transcended any early reservations about some of the great components of the Green Machine. It might seem incredible nowadays, but Colin Deans, probably the best hooker who has ever worn the Scotland jersey, struggled to convince his mentors that he was anything other than a journeyman forward at the start of his career. 'I didn't play for the High School, because my PE teacher, Ernie Murray, told me I would never make a player. And I never wanted to be a hooker as such,' said the stalwart individual, who subsequently accumulated 52 Scotland caps in that position and shone for the Lions. 'My father [Peter Deans, who wore the No 2 shirt with distinction for many years at Mansfield Park] told me always to be the first to every line-out. It's advice which I still pass on to youngsters.'

Even Derrick Grant remained to be convinced and initially selected the young Deans in the second row, where he battled away with trademark industry and dedication, until he eventually persuaded the Hawick sages to see sense and field him where he could dictate the tempo of matches and exhibit his powers to best effect. More than anyone else, it was Bill McLaren who spotted the potential of the nine-year-old, when he took part in the following exchange, which later supplied the title to Deans' autobiography.

McLaren: 'Hey you, Tubby, what's your name?'
Pupil: 'Colin Deans, sir.'
McLaren: 'Is your father Peter?'
CD: 'Yes sir.'
McLaren: 'You're a hooker, then.'

Many years passed before the rest of Hawick grasped the wisdom of that judgement, but it was a testimony to Deans' dedication that he was less interested in where he turned out for his community, than being allowed to gain entry to the Green Machine at a time when they were the most formidable organisation in Scotland. He had grown up watching Hawick Wanderers, where his dad was the president, and it encapsulated the attitude of the youngsters in the town that no amount of setbacks or teething problems dashed their aspirations to excel at rugby. Instead, they used them as a motivating force and, in Deans' case, were assisted in their endeavours by the tutelage of the ubiquitous McLaren.

Bill was a god to us. He wasn't as well known at the time as the 'Voice of Rugby', because he only covered the four international matches a year, plus tour games. There was no *Rugby Special* at the time, but he was actively involved in all the schools, and the amount of work which he put in was invaluable, both to the town and the club. I remember once, during an international, Bill said: 'There's Colin Deans, an old school pupil of mine. If you look closely, you can still see the belt marks!' Well, somebody wrote to *The Scotsman*, complaining about that, and Bill phoned me to apologise. But you can't underestimate how much he did for us. He used to take us country dancing. And teach us about cricket as well as rugby. He was a very big influence on so many people and if you saw him down here, you could understand why he was loved in Hawick.

Deans was a towering presence, somebody who could transform a game and inspire his colleagues with acts of sporting heroism, which gradually earned him near-mythic status. In the South, he slotted into the Hawick ranks, as a Jim Clark or Jackie Stewart might have done in any quality racing car, and this was a time when silverware was the rule rather than the exception at Mansfield Park, and when Deans could walk down his town's main street and everybody knew his name, even those few people with only a passing interest in rugby. (And they did exist in the Borders.) In these circumstances, it would have been easy and perhaps even understandable if the young star had developed a trace of arrogance or a whiff of look-at-me narcissism, but Deans had never forgotten being left on the sidelines in the early days, and he actually questioned his own abilities when he gained the call from the Scotland selectors, ahead of his debut in 1978.

I suppose I always had this inferiority complex and I never thought I was as good as the newspapers said. Scottish players tend to have this perception – I think it might be the nation in general, not just rugby players – that we're not as good [as other countries]. Anyway, it said on the invitation that I had to indicate if I was unavailable or unfit for selection [against France in the opening game of the Five Nations Championship], and I remember wondering if this was a get-out clause for if you didn't think that you were worthy to represent your country. So, I sat down and asked myself: 'Right, am I really fit to play for Scotland?' Then I thought: 'Aye, let's give it a go!'

These words might surprise many people, but these indomitable Borderers were so used to keeping their feet on the ground that they rarely became prima donnas. In any case, despite the ferocity of the Hawick juggernaut sweeping away everything in its path on the domestic circuit, the policy of building the Scotland side around a nucleus of Mansfield Park behemoths only had limited success. The likes of Pender, Hogg and Hegarty saw their international careers extinguished in 1978, following a dismal sequence of 13 international matches without a win for the Scots, and even characters of the calibre of Deans and Renwick grew as familiar with disappointment in their country's cause as they basked in success in the Borders. The decision, which many in the South had opposed, to launch a Scottish club championship in the 1970s eventually bore fruit, but there were slim pickings for the first few years and Deans was one of the few of that golden Hawick generation to endure into the 1980s and progress towards an eventual Lions call-up.

Even then, on what proved an ill-fated trip to New Zealand, the hooker was frustrated, both by the inclusion of Ireland's Ciaran Fitzgerald – a man who could barely throw the ball straight by the end of the series – and the lack of faith shown in his qualities by those who picked the team. This was not the fault of the coach, Jim Telfer, a proud Borderer who knew all about Deans and the gifts he could bring to the party, but a consequence of the selection process, where Fitzgerald and Lions manager, Willie John McBride, made some peculiar decisions, which not only impacted on Deans, but the peerless John Rutherford, who was only picked for one Test and that out of position at centre.

In short, the Green Machine could rule the roost when they were playing in their homeland, but they held less sway on the international stage. Yet, even if somebody such as Renwick only savoured victory away from Murrayfield twice in his 52-cap span, they provided rugby aficionados with a scrapbook of unforgettable images and vignettes.

As for Hawick, there may be some people who berate the Teris for dwelling in the 'Land that Time Forgot' or their 'Aye-been' tendencies, but the fact is that their achievements will never be surpassed in Scottish rugby. They created a development system which was the envy of the rest of Scotland, and even today, there are plenty of youngsters performing with distinction from the town, who have sufficient talent and ambition to pursue Test honours and follow in the footsteps of their predecessors. Yet, as Jim Renwick pointed out, the major difference lies in how they will chase these goals.

Scotland's clubs could have taken their chance when the game turned professional [in 1995], but they didn't and the SRU went down the district route, so there is no point in crying over spilt milk. I still live down here and I don't think there is any less passion for rugby among the Border clubs than there was in the past, but you have the situation nowadays where a lot of our young folk have to move to the cities to find work and, once they start playing rugby in Glasgow or Edinburgh, they don't come back as often as they used to and it is just a fact of life that we have economic problems in the South.

Some people find it hard to get to grips with the modern game, and even more difficult to accept that Hawick is now just a stepping stone for the best players, before they leave the town in search of a professional contract, either with the SRU or in England. But I am not too pessimistic about the future, because I know there are still lots of hard-working folk doing their best around Mansfield Park and these things tend to be cyclical. I was at the Common Riding [in June of 2011] and I met up with a lot of the old crowd, and, of course, we chewed the fat about the past, and talked about how things are at the moment. And, what came across to me was that people still really, really love their rugby in Hawick and I have no fears on that score. It is how we help the clubs which is important, because they *are* Scottish rugby and nobody should ever forget that. And recently I have sensed they are springing back into good health and are showing the sport is still alive and well at the grass roots. So who knows what will happen from here?

Renwick is one of his country's finest rugby performers. He is also as much in love with Hawick as he was in the early days when he and Colin Telfer were vying for the stand-off berth at Mansfield Park, and he talks vividly of refulgent afternoons, such as kicking that long-range penalty to sink Gala in the last act of an enthralling, title-deciding contest at Netherdale in 1982. That kick secured another championship for his team and although they lost out to their maroon-clad rivals in the following season, the Teris rebounded with typical effervescence to maintain a stranglehold on the national title for the next four years, as the struggle continued between the rival organisations in their region.

That is how it has always been in the Borders and when one examines the fashion in which rugby captured the imagination of so many diverse individuals, we have to be grateful for the tireless exertions of those in the Hawick Hall of Fame, such as McLeod, McLaren, Grant, Charters and the raft of wonderful players who were inspired to take up the game from the 1950s onwards. Ultimately, the marauding feats of these characters might cast an imposing shadow over the present Hawick generation, but men such as Renwick and Deans are not stuck in a time warp; they appreciate that they were privileged to enjoy so much success, but that the focus must now switch to the men and women who are doing their utmost to maintain the tradition and keep the Green Machine on the road.

Chapter Six

A Toast to Selkirk, Langholm and Gala

THOSE WHO PLEDGE allegiance to Scottish football clubs other than Glasgow's Old Firm giants will probably appreciate the lurking frustrations which were occasionally experienced by Hawick's opponents in the midst of Border League battle. Season after season, regardless of the lashings of enterprise expended on the pitch, there was, more often than not, a familiar look about the champions, and they were usually wearing green. If the men and women who toiled away behind the scenes at such rugby citadels as Selkirk, Langholm and Gala had been so inclined, the easy thing would have been to admit they were scrapping for second best every winter, before hitching their carts to the Hawick bandwagon, and basking in the reflected glory of the Teris' triumphal procession.

But thankfully, that defeatist idea never occurred to the army of volunteers who continually ploughed their time and effort into improving the standard of rugby at Philiphaugh, Milntown and Netherdale. On the contrary – and soccer aficionados will appreciate this too – the long fallow periods only made the occasional successes all the sweeter, because they had been achieved against the odds, and often in circumstances where other Borderers were waiting for them to fall flat on their faces with an almighty thud. Selkirk, for instance, hardly set the heather on fire in the years after the Second World War and there was little reason to suppose that they would suddenly unearth a squad which was capable of sweeping everything before them. But they did and their exploits in the 1952–53 campaign, where they surged to the double by winning both the Border League and the unofficial Scottish championship, were as exceptional as they were surprising. Indeed, though it happened nearly 60 years ago, the Souters still talk about it with dewy eyes, much as Aberdonians marvel about getting the better of Real Madrid in the European Cup Winners' Cup final in 1983, or Partick Thistle aficionados reminisce how they famously trounced Jock Stein's Celtic in the League Cup final of 1971.

At the time, their achievement elicited astonishment and time has not dulled the feeling of wonder at how Selkirk, however briefly, glittered in the spotlight. Yet, if some of their fans thought they were in dreamland, there was nothing airy-fairy about the stalwart brethren who turned romantic reveries into hard reality. Consider, for instance, the fact that the side was captained by George Downie, a man steeped in Selkirk lore, and who also happened to be one of the toughest and most unstinting props in the Borders of that vintage. This fellow had fought for his country in the RAF, in which light he was hardly going to be fazed by rousing his rugby troops to new levels of intensity and lion-hearted resolve.

One man does not make a team, of course, but Downie had willing confrères in the front row in the guise of redoubtable hooker Jock King and Jim 'Basher' Inglis at loose-head, with the latter's nickname providing an ample confirmation of his disinclination to take any nonsense from his rivals. And this trio were a fearsome sight for anybody in their homeland, even the likes of Hawick legends of the calibre of Hugh McLeod, so much so that King and Inglis both gained Scotland honours between 1952 and 1955 while there were plenty of observers in the Borders who were mystified as to why the prowling, growling Downie was denied his opportunity at international level. But there again, this was the period when the Scots were enduring such a desperate spell on the Test stage, with 17 matches lost in a three-year stretch, that the words: 'Abandon Hope All Ye Who Enter Here', might as well have been engraved on the gates of Murrayfield.

However, if there was misery on the wider stage, Selkirk's supporters were entitled to focus on the feats of their own heroes, who boasted formidable scrummaging power, but also dangerous backs, including Archie Little, a No 15 with the confidence to launch counter-offensives from his own territory, and whom Bill McLaren would probably have described as 'running like a scalded stag' when he was in the mood to test the pace and defensive skills of opposing teams. There were others, such as the Cowan brothers, Stanley and Jack, whose qualities not only became common knowledge throughout the Borders, but also – regrettably for the Philiphaugh faithful – filtered down to the world of rugby league, whose scouts soon came calling, but not before Selkirk had bewitched and bewildered the rest of Scotland with their own brand of high-intensity rugby.

Perhaps part of the reason for their success stemmed from the limited expectations which surrounded the team at the start of the 1952–53 season. It was not that they had fallen off the radar exactly, but they hardly commenced with an all-conquering flourish, losing two of their opening five fixtures and the second of these was a comprehensive 37–5 demolition at the hands of Edinburgh club, Royal High School FPs. So far, so familiar for the long-suffering Selkirk fraternity, and yet gradually, Downie and his colleagues began to put the squeeze on their opponents, recording a meritorious 8–0 win against Hawick, even as the winter arrived with a vengeance and frost forced the cancellation of a string of matches throughout the country. That might have stalled the momentum of lesser individuals, but it seemed to invigorate Selkirk, who signalled their potential with consecutive wins over Glasgow High School, Dunfermline, Jed-Forest and Edinburgh Accies, which forced even the most sceptical followers in the town to acknowledge that Selkirk were a force to be reckoned with. Indeed, even though Hawick gained revenge in the corresponding game by securing a narrow 6–0 victory, Downie's personnel had shrugged off their earlier inconsistency and embarked on a sequence of five straight wins and that run was only brought to an end when they slipped to a 3–0 defeat at Gala.

By now, the excitement in the town was palpable and the likes of the *Border Advertiser* began to engage in heady praise of the Selkirk lieges. The captain's endeavours brought him glowing reviews from Walter Thomson, while other, anonymous scribes delved into their dictionaries for synonyms for 'industrious' and 'immovable'. March turned to April, and when Selkirk orchestrated back-to-back triumphs over Melrose and Watsonians by 11–0 and 11–6, their strengths were no longer in question. What remained unclear was whether a club, which had experienced few reasons to be cheerful for more years than they cared to remember, could handle the pressure and complete the job.

This was heady stuff, particularly for a support base that had gradually grown inured to disappointment. And, as the proud Souter Allan Massie wrote in his book *100 Years of Selkirk Rugby*, Downie and his men had turned into a big box-office attraction.

There were still obstacles to be cleared and Gala were still in the running for the 'double' themselves. So when they came to Philiphaugh for an evening game, excitement was intense and the ground saw a crowd of over 4000 (and gate receipts of £132 – a record then – almost £2000 in today's values). If ever a game proved that you don't need high scoring and lots of tries to produce gripping rugby, this was it. Selkirk took an early lead when Tom Brown, playing in the centre, dropped a goal, but thereafter, Gala were on top. Wave after wave of attacks threatened the Selkirk line, but the defence held firm, and time and again, Archie Little appeared, as Walter Thomson recalled, 'from nowhere to pluck the ball from the air and drive Gala back a few precious yards.' The Souters displayed the spirit of Flodden where, as Sir Walter Scott wrote:

> 'The stubborn spear-men still made good,
> Their dark, impenetrable wood,
> Each stepping where his comrade stood,
> The instant that he fell . . .'

But this time, the outcome was triumph, not disaster. The line held, Gala were repulsed, and when the final whistle sounded, Selkirk had won.

There remained Jed-Forest to be beaten before the titles were securely in the Souters' grip and, over the years, Selkirk have always found Jed among their hardest opponents. This match was no exception, a game that stretched the already taut nerves of those at Philiphaugh. Again, Selkirk took the lead, this time from a long-range penalty goal, which was kicked by Archie Little. Again, they could not add to that score. Again, they were thrown back on doughty defence. Again, the tension held to the final minute when Jed-Forest attempted a mighty drop goal, which flew high towards the Selkirk posts, but happily just wide. The game was over and, at last, after almost fifty years, Selkirk were [unofficial] Scottish and Border [League] champions.

It was a marvellous achievement and the community rightly basked in the warm glow of what had been an incredibly hard-fought campaign. Downie's players had been forced to withstand concerted pressure during these last brace of fixtures and had responded with the kind of sporting heroism which only happens once in a blue moon. They were a disparate bunch, ranging from the unprepossessing bish and bosh of

'Basher' and his front-row confrères, to the fleetness of foot of Little, the dexterity of Brown, and the athleticism and aggression of the Cowan siblings. As for the captain, Downie, this was his apotheosis and one has to wonder how his qualities could have been overlooked by Scotland, or at least until one recollects the vagaries which existed within the selection panel of that era. This was 1953 and there were other exploits which commanded bigger headlines in the rest of the British press, such as the FA Cup final between Bolton Wanderers and Blackpool, which the latter won 4–3, courtesy of a posterity-sealing performance from Stanley Matthews and a Stan Mortensen hat-trick; the 26-time champion jockey Gordon Richards' only victory in the Epsom Derby on the massive horse, Pinza; and, of course, it was the year of the Coronation. But, as somebody who has been in Melrose, in Hawick, in Kelso, when rugby titles have been won, and especially in against-the-odds struggles, it is not too much of an exaggeration to declare that Selkirk's exploits were the main source of jubilation in a never-to-be-forgotten spring.

These kinds of triumphs were to be relished – and the celebrations were raucous. Yet, in many instances where sporting underdogs prevail and relish their time in the spot-light, their success turns out to be the prelude to a reality check, and so it proved with Selkirk. Some of their more pessimistic followers had even expressed reservations about the overall quality of the 52–53 brigade in their hour of victory, and, bit by bit, the victorious squad was dismantled by a combination of factors. Downie, a banker by profession, had to relocate to Dunfermline and subsequently represented the North of Scotland. Stanley Cowan was tempted by the offer of financial security and switched to the league code, whilst his brother, Jack, moved to London and joined the Metro-politan Police. Several of the younger players were called up for national service; a few of the older personnel, perhaps recognising that they were unlikely to replicate the fantastic achievements of lifting the double, elected to retire, or at least bow out of first XV action. But it was no disgrace to revert subsequently to the status of middle-of-the-table honest artisans, who occasionally performed above expectations. And, ultimately, the fact was cast in stone that nobody could ever take the glories of that sweet winter away from them.

There were similar heroics later in the 1958–59 campaign when Langholm finally made the breakthrough, which gen-erations of players had striven for, by lifting the Border League for the first time since their foundation, all of 88 years earlier. Their teams had always been renowned for their battling qualities and the club itself had made a virtue of their modest resources – particularly in comparison with the likes of Hawick – so there was a sense of shared pride in the Borders at the fashion in which the Milntown personnel dominated that season, not merely gaining ascendancy over their rivals in the South, but posting records which earned them coverage the length and breadth of Britain.

Much of their success derived – as elsewhere in the Borders – from the influence of a number of families, including the Armstrongs, Copelands and McGlassons, whose exertions en-sured that the club was capable of surviving through turbulent times. By the late 1950s, Langholm had assembled a potent squad, which featured such flinty characters as Christy Elliot, Jimmy Maxwell and Tony Grieve, and they started recording some impressive results, especially once Ernie Michie, a former British and Irish Lion and the human equivalent of Mount Rushmore, travelled down to the Borders to work in the forestry industry and lent his myriad talents to the Langholm cause. In many respects, Michie was the missing link for whom the club had been patiently waiting and was one of the pivotal performers when they began to dazzle in the autumn of 1958.

As with Selkirk, everything just clicked into gear and the rest of the country bore the brunt. The Souters were the first to experience the ferocity of the Langholm hurricane, blown away by a 40-point margin. Then, one by one, Melrose, Hawick, Gala and Jed-Forest came off second best against Michie and his confrères, whose forwards created the platform for a string of emphatic victories. Christy Elliot was consistently outstanding, both in his kicking duties and in discombobulating rival back lines, Jimmy Maxwell glittered with or without the ball, John Armstrong oozed class and solidity in the full-back berth, and the cumulative impact of these performers meant that when the national press listed the league tables at the climax of the season, Langholm stood out as the only one (of 420) who had avoided defeat throughout the entire season. They demonstrated their quality on the wider stage when they overcame a powerful London Scottish contingent in the Borders, with Michie once again to the fore, urging on his troops, seemingly covering every blade of grass, and generally exhibiting the sort of powers which belong in the pages of comic books, while his club sped towards the title.

Yet, if he was a source of inspiration, so was the captain, Jimmy Maxwell, who constantly hunted down rivals and tackled as if his very life depended on it. Once or twice as the winter progressed there were difficult afternoons, where they might have relinquished their unbeaten record, and there were four draws in the run, which testified to the number of occasions when they were involved in hard-fought wars of attrition. But, undaunted by the knowledge they were – to paraphrase Jim Kirk – boldly going where none of their fathers or grandfathers had gone before, the Milntown militia marched on. Others in the South kept awaiting a slip-up, or a hint of vulnerability, but it never materialised. On the contrary, Langholm's members grew in stature as the spring arrived, as if appreciating they were now within touching distance of feats which would live for posterity.

In the end, it boiled down to a fraught visit to the Greenyards to tackle Melrose on an April evening in 1959, with the visitors being cheered on by a massive travelling support, who probably realised that seasons such as this might be a once-in-a-lifetime thrill. They were made to fret for sustained passages of the match, which was scarcely a classic, and the outcome remained in doubt until the denouement, with both clubs stuttering and sparkling at various stages of the encounter. In their defence, Langholm had never remotely been in this situation before, of chasing both the Border title and the unofficial Scottish championship crown, and, unusually, their pack struggled against their Melrose counterparts. The visitors did manage to take the lead after 15 minutes with a long-range penalty from Elliot, but Alec Hastie responded with a superb individual try, and that was how it stayed until a few moments before the break, when Elliot landed another kick to push his side 6–3 in front. Yet there was little between the combatants and that pattern continued when the action resumed, with the hosts' Andrew Hewat replying with another fine try, following Elliot's third successful kick at goal. That proved the catalyst for an almighty Melrose surge and their opponents were forced to dig deep into their reserves of commitment and could have been cruelly denied at the death when the dangerous Hastie attempted an opportunistic drop goal, which went only narrowly wide of its target.

You could have sliced the tension with a knife as Melrose kept attacking. But finally, with the visiting fans anxiously counting down the clock, the game finished. Langholm had prevailed 9–6, and their players, officials and supporters rejoiced. The party carried on into the next morning and the day after that. This was their dual triumph, their chance to revel in the midst of being showered with honours which normally went to Hawick and the bigger communities in the Borders. When they eventually escaped the attention of well-wishers and returned to their own community, the details of the famous victory had already filtered back to Langholm, and there were 1,500 of their townsfolk on the streets, all waiting to acclaim their rugby heroes.

The team's labours had yielded fitting rewards, both within their district and throughout the rest of their homeland, and nobody with any sense of sporting theatre could possibly have begrudged Langholm this belated recognition. After all, they had been the first club to come together in the Borders and it must have been as frustrating to be the trailblazers and find themselves being eclipsed by the rest, as it is for the pacemaker in a long-distance athletics race, who leads for most of the journey, only to be swept aside on the last lap. Understandably, therefore, the proud men who participated on that hallelujah trail have clung to the memories of that wonderful year and one of those in the throng, winger John Smith, told me about his experiences with Langholm's finest.

It is now 52 years since we were champions of Scotland and the Borders, yet to the players who were involved in that historical season, it seems like only yesterday. That season will never be forgotten in the Muckle Toon because, as if winning the unofficial title and the Border League was not enough, the Milntown side also beat the mighty London Scottish with all their internationalists, and we were the only undefeated team in Britain for the season. We also won our own Sevens to add to the Selkirk Sevens Cup and had a record of: played 26, won 22, drawn 4. Points for 309, points against 81.

I was not a regular in the team, being one of the younger members, but reserves were needed at times when the leading players were either in action for the South or injured, and the whole squad, which only totalled 25, played their part in making history for the club. Everything just seemed to click into place that season when Ernie Michie, who originally played for Aberdeen Grammar School [and was capped 15 times at lock from 1954–57], came down to the town. He had only recently returned from a tour with the Lions in South Africa, and he brought us terrific knowledge of forward play.

Michie joined up with the captain Jim Maxwell, who was unlucky to only get the one cap in 1957 in a snowstorm. Christy Elliot was another stalwart in the backs and got his first of 12 caps in 1958. The youngest in the squad was his brother, Tom, and like myself, he was reserve for the wing. He later switched to back-row forward and was capped five times for his country between 1968 and 1970. I missed several midweek games at the end of the season because of injury, and would possibly not have been in the side anyway for the championship decider at Melrose which Langholm won 9–6, with a massive crowd attending the night match. But I was on the team bus that evening, along with my mate John Armstrong, who was the team's regular full-back, but was also out injured.

The memories of that night will remain forever, from the moment that Hector Monro, the Border League president, who later became an MP [and future sports minister], and was a former Langholm player, presented the cup to our skipper, Jim Maxwell. After celebrating for a while in Melrose, the bus eventually arrived back in Langholm and it was an amazing sight which we witnessed. The two local bands met the bus on the outskirts of the town and played us down a thronged High Street, which must have brought every resident out, and there were loud cheers as the players embarked towards the Town Hall. It was one of those occasions where you understood exactly how much rugby meant to the people in the town and, to be honest, it sent shivers up all our spines.

Later that year, the Town Council held a civic reception for the players at the Ashley Bank Hotel and there was a celebration for the club in the Eskdale Hotel. There was also the joy of the players getting together, one last time in that historic season, for a photo session. Sadly, some have passed away over the years, but it was great the championship squad were special guests at the Langholm rugby dinner in 2009, with Tom Elliot and John Beattie making it back from overseas. In the same year, the Rotary Club also invited the players to a special function where the BBC's Andrew Cotter was the guest speaker. His grandfather, Jimmy, who played for Scotland, was the minister at Langholm Parish Church for a number of years and was greatly involved with the club.

There are obviously many memories from such a successful season, such as beating all the Border League teams. Yet what sticks in my memory, as much as anything, was playing in a 3–3 draw, with one try each, against a strong Edinburgh Accies side at Raeburn Place, with Scotland half-backs Tom McClung and Stan Coughtrie playing for the opposition and making sure we had to be on our toes. McClung continually thumped huge up-and-unders at our full-back, John Armstrong, and I kept racing behind him from the wing to cover any mishaps, but he never flinched and you could have sworn that the ball would come down with snow on it. It was that kind of attitude which helped us to stick together, through thick and thin, and it was a terrific club to play for.

It was not surprising that Langholm were unable to maintain their success in the following years. Some of their leading lights retired, while they were no longer an unknown quantity for rivals and we were entering the period when Hawick began establishing a stranglehold, not merely in the Borders, but over the whole country. Yet, as the local newspapers reported, there were other noteworthy achievements in the future, including a commendable victory against the Green Machine at Mansfield Park in 1972 – when Christy Elliot, in his 22nd season at the club, scored the game's only try – and precious few opponents have ever relished the journey to Milntown in the dead of winter.

These tales of the unexpected prevented Borders rugby from becoming stale, and even at the height of Hawick's powers, there were afternoons, and even seasons, when they bumped into an immovable object. Such a fate befell them in 1966–67, when they had to surrender the limelight to their near, and not so dear, colleagues at Gala, who had sparkled only fitfully in the Border League, but stamped their authority all over a campaign in which they combined prolific try-scoring feats with some parsimonious defence, which defied almost anything which opponents could fling at them.

This was a fiercely formidable Netherdale collective; a multifarious band of brothers, who were superbly organised and adroitly captained by the pivotal figure of John Gray, who excelled in the second row alongside a sedulous pack, which habitually gained sufficient possession to release their mesmerising back line, which featured such luminaries as Duncan Paterson, Jock Turner and Peter Townsend, who nowadays might be better known as the father of Gregor, but was a quicksilver performer in his own right. Considering the pace and panache which they had at their disposal, Gala's trophy-winning success on the Sevens circuit was only to be anticipated.

But this ensemble was more than just a serious force in the abbreviated version of the game, as they demonstrated by amassing 115 points in their first three matches of the 1966–67 fixture schedule. Their ability to unlock rivals with individual acts of derring-do was underpinned by the Scrooge-like tightness of their cover, which saw them conceding only a paltry nine points in their opening four Border League matches. Indeed, from early in the campaign, it was clear that Gray and his charges were *the* team to beat. And, as the skipper told me: 'We had the attitude that if we played to our potential, we could leave other sides to worry about us. There had been previous years where Hawick had virtually won matches before they even took the field, because their opponents didn't really believe that they could beat them. So we talked about what we could do to change things and one of the most obvious things was to concentrate fully on our own game and not worry about the other clubs. It worked to pretty good effect, because we came racing out of the blocks and, once you have built up momentum, that is half the battle.'

Gray's personnel essentially seized the initiative and clung on thereafter, on their way to dishing out a series of emphatic beatings to the likes of Melrose and Jed-Forest and subsequently gained a major psychological advantage when they defeated Hawick, as they wrested control of the league away from the other contenders. Not even a mounting injury list could dent their advance – although there were understandable concerns about the long-term absence of Paterson, one of the most elusive No 9s of his generation – but, whatever problems arose, Gala responded to the challenge and they ventured to Poynder Park on the penultimate day of the season, aware that victory over Kelso would earn them their first Border League crown since they tied for the title with Melrose in 1949–50.

Predictably, tension surrounded this contest, not least because Gala's pre-Christmas dominance had gradually ebbed away, to the stage where their earlier prowess was replaced by a fragility which has often surfaced around Netherdale teams. John Dawson explained this tale of two halves succinctly in his book *The Ambassadors*.

Up to the end of December, Gala played and looked like a championship side and the Maroons were all set for the Scottish and Border League titles. In the two tables, up to this stage of the season, Gala had played 16, won 13, lost two and drawn once. But the second half of the season brought mixed blessings, and they only had themselves to blame [no sympathy for injuries here!] for letting the double slip from their grasp. The Braw Lads just could not overcome the challenge of the city clubs. After New Year, 10 matches were played, four were lost, with two drawn, and only four were won.

Gala played attractive rugby and they proved to be crowd-pleasers, especially in Border League games. In the first 16 matches, a total of 63 tries were recorded, whereby, in the second half of the campaign, only 13 tries were scored in 10 matches. Five of these tries came from one game. In four of the others, Gala failed to score any tries.

The contrast was remarkable, but there again, it should not be forgotten that Gray's side were missing the influential Jock Turner for nine of these contests while Paterson was out of commission for seven – and five of them in a row – and they only had access to a full-strength XV on a handful of occasions, and proved their worth in these tussles. Yet, in these circumstances, one could comprehend why many Gala supporters were anxious in the build-up to the potential title-decider with Kelso. Their heroes had flattered to deceive too often in the past for the diehards to take anything for granted and they appreciated that Kelso would provide stern resistance. But, as it transpired, there was to be no anticlimax. Instead, as Peter Donald wrote in the *Scottish Daily Mail* on 6 March 1967, it was their rivals who were left questioning their decision-making at the death.

Kelso held a post-mortem at the weekend on a mistake that helped Gala to win the Border League title at Poynder Park. The mistake was made before Saturday's match when the home team won the toss and elected to play AGAINST the wind in the first half. Kelso officials were amazed at the decision. Gala, needles to say, were delighted and proceeded to take full advantage by harnessing the strong wind and building up a 9–0 first-half lead. They held on to that until five minutes from the end, when Drew Wood went over for Kelso's try, which was converted by Jock Common.

Gala thus clinched the title – their first outright win in 45 years – with nine wins and a draw from 11 games. Their twelfth fixture, a postponed game with Selkirk, will not now be played, as no other side is within reach of Gala's 19 points. Nervous tension, the near gale-force wind and injuries combined to deprive this Poynder Park occasion of much of its entertainment value. The Gala players have been on tenterhooks for the past month – and their form has undoubtedly suffered. This has probably also contributed to Scotland centre Jock Turner's indifferent displays of late. His form, at fly-half for his club, has been mixed, and Saturday's display would not encourage the national selectors.

At the same time, one must not lose sight of the fact that Turner won the game for Gala with two penalty goals and a drop goal, and his play was interspersed with some characteristically neat covering and touch kicking. It can have been of little help to Turner's form that he has had to play alternately with two scrum-halves, Jim Dobson and Lyall Houghton, during Duncan Paterson's enforced absence. Houghton suffered slightly on Saturday through the lack of cover afforded him by his forwards, who seemed to think their job ended once they had effectively bottled up the Kelso halves. Kelso, however, missed the inspiring influence of former cap Charlie Stewart, who was out with a leg injury, and their cause was not helped by a first-half injury to young Brian Kelly, who deputised for Stewart. He played for most of the match with a heavily-bandaged right knee. This took some of the sting out of the Kelso forwards, who could never get on top of the Gala pack. Scott Wilkinson and John Gray won their team a lot of ball from the line-out and even when Kelso did get possession here or from the set scrum, their young backs seemed limited to one idea – the inside break of Alan Tait.

There is not much here about what happened in the match itself and yet, as Gray told me, it was a genuinely helter-skelter affair, with plenty of barn-stopping tackles, chances for both clubs to profit on the weather-induced mistakes of their rivals, and a collective frustration at the finish that neither side had done themselves justice. The *Border Advertiser* was not the only newspaper to run analytical articles, discussing whether Gala had been 'lucky to win the league'. This, surprisingly enough, focused as much on the victors' perceived collapse in the second half of the season as it did on the excellence which they had shown while winning their first seven fixtures. It was a negative slant on what had been a creditable achievement by Gray's injury-depleted squad and perhaps demonstrated that negative sports reporting in Scotland did not start with the collapse of Ally's Tartan Army in Argentina in 1978.

At any rate, nobody around Netherdale was inclined to waste too much time worrying about these supposed deficiencies. Irrespective of the gripes from their opponents, the trophy was in their cabinet and they had orchestrated more wins than anybody else during the course of the competition. So what was there to complain about? On the contrary, it was time for the Sevens to usher in the dawn of spring, whereupon Gala, bolstered by the presence of their electrifying backs, followed up their success in the 15-a-side game with triumph in the abbreviated format. In short, this was a golden campaign for the Maroons, and three of their number – Jock Turner, Les Rodger and Scott Wilkinson – went to South

Africa during the summer with the Scottish Border Club and enjoyed their visit to the Cape. Gray, one of the linchpins of his club's success, was one of the reserve pool of players for the tour, and was unfortunate not to be included in the party. But at least he had the satisfaction, not only of leading his warriors to their first title for two generations, but also of later helping to bring into the world a son called Richie, who would subsequently maintain the family tradition by captaining the Gala side which snaffled another league crown in fabled fashion 31 years later.

That pattern of 'like father, like son' was one of the most heartening aspects of the Borderers' attitude to rugby and it crops up time and again in the chronicles as an affirmation of the manner in which the torch was passed on from one generation to another. Less defensible, though, was the flippancy with which the South continued to maintain sporting relations with South Africa, whose apartheid philosophy had become common knowledge the longer that the 1960s advanced. This notoriously sparked the cancellation of England's cricket tour to the Republic in the winter of 1968, when the inclusion of Basil D'Oliveira was opposed by the South African prime minister, B J Vorster, setting in motion a chain of events which led to the country being banned from future Olympic Games. It was facile to argue, as some people did, that 'sport and politics don't mix' – of course they do and always have done – and yet the union code in particular continued to lend succour to the Springboks, after almost every other sport had cast Vorster and his ruling party's discriminatory policies into the wilderness.

This showed Scottish rugby in an unflattering light and it was not the sole issue that provoked controversy within the sport and wider society. This might be a celebration of the Borders, but it will not suffice to pretend that these things never happened.

Chapter Seven

THORNS AMIDST THE THISTLES

I T MUST BE ONE of the great questions for those who test their sporting knowledge on a regular basis in bars and taverns across Scotland. To wit: 'Who was the only Scottish player to win the World Cup in rugby?' I have posed this teaser to some of the brightest and most beetle-browed members of the pub quiz fraternity, and they usually scratch their heads for several minutes, and query whether it is a trick question, before admitting they are stumped. But there is no shame in that. After all, one will not find a statue of Dave Valentine in Hawick town centre, nor a stand named in his honour at Mansfield Park. To all intents and purposes, the Teri might never have been born, and yet, back in 1954, he skippered the Great Britain rugby league team to glory in the inaugural World Cup, more than 30 years before the union code got round to organising such an event.

However, such was the antipathy which existed between the rival codes for most of the 20th century that Valentine's anonymity – outwith those who cherish League – is hardly surprising. There were always likely to be tensions between those who believed that union should live and die by the tenets of amateurism and those who saw nothing amiss in working-class sportsmen being permitted to earn an honest wage for their endeavours in what was a transient sporting career. The Borders was one of the regions where hostility simmered for decades, sparking a situation where those who departed to the rugby league fold found themselves shunned if they later returned to their roots.

Even in the late 1980s, when Kelso's Alan Tait decided to sign terms with Widnes, and I journeyed down to the latter club to interview him for *Scotland on Sunday*, there was little indication of the rift being healed, despite widespread rumours of 'shamateurism', and most notably among the southern hemisphere countries, being rife in union by that juncture. Tait, quietly, in matter-of-fact fashion, told me: "I knew that my decision to go to league would be controversial, but you have to do what you think is best. I have absolutely nothing against my former team-mates who are committed to union and I would hope that they wished me well at Widnes. But I suppose I am realistic enough to understand that there will be plenty of people in the Borders who accuse me of selling out or letting down the folk in Kelso, especially those who helped bring me through the ranks at Poynder Park. Basically, there's nothing I can do about that now. I just have to do my best to make a success of my new life and I am having a fantastic time at this club."

In the event, Tait was one of the few exceptions to the general rule, not merely excelling in rugby league, but being welcomed back into the Scotland union fold in the second half of the 1990s and performing an instrumental role in his country's remarkable success during the last ever Five Nations Championship in 1999. But, for the most part, the manner in which the Borders treated their league converts was an unedifying story, and even if one accepts that union aficionados were entitled to be suspicious of the scouts, who were regularly witnessed at Border League fixtures – there was bitter resentment in Hawick throughout the 1950s when as many as 15 players were approached and offered terms – the treatment of those who ventured to England was often shameful. These men had broken no laws, nor crossed any picket lines, and yet they were immediately banned for life from returning to the union code, and were frequently blanked by their former friends and rugby colleagues when they attempted to heal the wounds in later life.

Valentine, for instance, had a terrific story to tell, but pariahs rarely command an audience. Yet, as Scotland Rugby League historian Gavin Willacy explained to me, there was something genuinely uplifting about his role in a global triumph.

There may be no primary schools named after him in his birthplace, but when Dave Valentine captained his side to glory in Paris in 1954, he was leading Great Britain and not Scotland and had won the first ever rugby league World Cup. What is more extraordinary is that Valentine was not the only Scot in the team and not the only Borderer. Days before the tournament started, David Rose was summoned from his Jedburgh home to replace Welsh superstar, Billy Boston, in the British squad, and the Jed-Forest product went on to score one of GB's two tries in the final.

Valentine remains the most iconic Scot ever to have been involved in rugby league. Winning the World Cup obviously helped, but the man, who was born in Hawick on September 12, 1925, has legendary status in Huddersfield as well. After winning two Scotland caps, he was tempted south by one of his compatriots – the Huddersfield chairman, Bill Cunning-ham – in 1947 and, following a season playing loose forward in the club's star-studded side, was picked to play for Great Britain against Australia. Tall, dark, and ruggedly handsome, Valentine was an ideal leader, enjoying the midfield battles as much as skilfully bringing his backs into the action and he was an impressive presence, both for GB and with the talented Huddersfield squad, who were champions in 1949, runners-up in 1950 and Challenge Cup winners three years later.

He replaced a fellow Hawick man, Drew Turnbull, on the wing in the Lions tour Down Under in 1954 and stepped in as captain when Willie Horne joined a string of players who were unavailable for the World Cup, which followed in France. A ludicrously under-prepared and under-strength squad was given no chance, but victories over Australia and New Zealand and a draw with France saw the Britons face the French again in a final play-off in Paris. They triumphed 16–12 and Valentine duly made history.

A year later, his international career ended in style: after 18 GB test caps and 16 appearances for Other Nationalities, he captained the latter for the first time during their win over England! A triple break of the ankle in 1957 meant that his career went into steep decline and he retired from the game in 1961. Yet his heroic status at Huddersfield was to be increased with a short spell as coach in which he led the 'Fartowners' to Wembley and the league championship in 1962, which remains their last title.

Valentine died in 1976, aged just 49. But his story was retold and his memory has been celebrated in the 21st century: the Super League Academy Grand Final man of the match wins the Dave Valentine Memorial Trophy, Scotland's Player of the Year wins the Dave Valentine Award, and Scotland Rugby League's official tartan features Hawick green in honour of the man, whose grandson, Rob, has played rugby league for Scotland Students. Quite simply, you can't underestimate the impact which he made on his sport.

Hawick certainly suffered from the impact of losing personnel to the rival code on a regular basis. Their internationalist, Alex Laidlaw, became the first capped player to join the 'rebels', after being snapped up by Bradford in 1898 and proceeded to score for them in the 1906 Challenge Cup final. His move pre-cipitated a wave of defections, which weakened the potential might of the Green Machine, with their three-quarter, Andrew Hogg, forming a devastating Scottish pairing with Bob Wilson at Manchester club Broughton Rangers, as the prelude to

Hogg swallowing his pride and eventually turning out for England against New Zealand and Wales in 1908. Even by this stage, the code-switching had become sufficiently complex to tax the boffins of Bletchley Park and, although it still constituted a gamble for any internationalist to leave Scotland, Anthony Little was the next man to do so when he agreed terms with Wigan, penning his contract by candlelight in Hawick to ensure that nobody spied his mysterious visitors.

In those days, Scottish players tended to be signed in pairs, and especially those from close-knit Border communities, where club colleagues were likely to be friends and fellow workmates. This meant that they could travel to England together and reside in the same lodgings, in addition to offering each other moral support. Billy Jardine followed his older brother, Adam, from Jed-Forest to Oldham, becoming a stalwart of the Roughyeds team, only to perish, like so many others, in the First World War. And although Hawick had most reason to rue the trend, Gala lost James Aitchison to Wigan and Harry Paterson to Halifax, who also acquired the services of Selkirk winger John Ewart and Melrose forward James Brown for £90. After the war, Halifax continued their policy of plundering from the Border League, signing the Gala trio Andrew Murdison, George Swan and Jock Beattie, along with second-rower Jimmy Douglas, from Riverside Park. While the first two of this quartet gained honours with the Other Nationalities ensemble, Douglas participated in the 1932 Challenge Cup with Leeds before becoming the secretary of Salford, for whom he signed the Northern Irishman Tom McKinney from Jed-Forest, who lost a third of their squad in the space of one season. This was when the 13-a-side game was enjoying a golden period of prosperity.

Perhaps predictably, these actions provoked anger in the South of Scotland and there were several instances of rugby league scouts being threatened and chased out of clubhouses by furious locals, not that it prevented these doughty individuals from carrying on their recruitment drives. In many respects, union only had itself to blame: it was one thing for the SRU and the private-school sector to maintain a deep-rooted antagonism towards any suggestion of players being remunerated for their efforts, but they went to ridiculous lengths to protect the so-called 'sanctity' of the 15-a-side pursuit, and when Scotland stars from working-class backgrounds were expected to pay for new jerseys and shorts when the one set they received every season were torn or damaged beyond repair, it created a situation where poorly-paid individuals, many from agricultural or labouring backgrounds, were being asked to shell out money to represent their country.

No wonder that so many of them decided to switch codes. And 1933 saw two of the most dramatic swoops on rugby union's ranks when the 21-times-capped Hawick veteran, Willie Welsh, elected to move to England and ply his trade for London Highfield, who had recently relocated from Wigan. They trained in Lancashire and played for a season at the White City Stadium, with the redoubtable Welsh featuring in a win over France and scoring a record-breaking four tries in their final game before the club moved to Liverpool. In the same year, Alex Fiddes, who had yet to be capped by Scotland, turned professional with Huddersfield and proved to be a sufficiently talented stand-off that he was given his debut against Australia and developed into a star at Fartown, captaining them in the 1935 Challenge Cup final, winning the 1945 War Cup, and earning a Great Britain call-up for the cancelled 1940 Ashes tour to Australia.

There were further foraging raids in the 1950s and 1960s, with the biggest signing being that by Leeds of the Scotland and Selkirk winger Ronnie Cowan, who had toured South Africa with the British and Irish Lions, when he chose to follow his brother's example and move to the 13-a-side game. A few months later, the Yorkshire club also handed a contract to Drew Broatch, a highly-rated centre from Hawick who was the nephew of Alex Fiddes, but he never matched Cowan's achievements and, around this time, the exodus of Scots to the league code started to dry up, as Gavin Willacy explains.

With most players facing social isolation from their original clubs upon their return from rugby league – some were even ostracised by whole communities in the Border towns for their alleged disloyalty – the supply line to league dried up well before union turned professional. Unless they were joining a top club, with a guaranteed multi-year contract, it was simply not worth risking their livelihoods to make the move to England.

For 40 years now, English rugby league clubs have not actively recruited in Scotland. There will probably always be an exceptional few who journey from the Borders to try their luck with Cumbria's semi-pro clubs, but it is no longer financially attractive to most people. Even Scotland Rugby League (founded in 1994) has little presence in the Borders, with almost all its activity in Glasgow and Ayrshire, Edinburgh and Fife.

But there is no doubting the part that men from the Borders played in the league game. Of the 77 Scots who crossed codes before 1995, almost all of them came from the Borders. Of the 15 who were Scottish rugby union internationalists, 14 were from Border clubs. Not only was the Borders home to the vast majority of Scotland's best players, but its club rivalries created a competitive scene, as close to that which was found in Yorkshire and Lancashire, as anywhere else on earth. And the fact they were geographically closer [to England] than the rest of Scotland also meant that most rugby league scouts only got as far as the Borders when they were searching for new talent.

The last of the great Scots to make the transition in the one direction — bearing in mind that Alan Tait glittered in both versions of the game — was George Fairbairn, the gifted Kelso full-back, who agreed terms to join the once-mighty, but then-struggling Wigan in 1974. Within six months, he had been selected for international duty and, whether in his rock-hard tackling, his tremendously reliable kicking or his attacking qualities, he illuminated the league circuit, eventually gaining 15 caps for England and 17 for Great Britain, his last against the invincible Australians in 1982. He won the 'Man of Steel' award in 1980 for steering Wigan back to the top flight as a player-coach, and subsequently signed for Hull Kingston Rovers for a world record fee of £75,000 in 1981. At Craven Park, the voracious Fairbairn, a fellow with a Bunteresque appetite for trophies, snaffled a brace of championships and performed in a Challenge Cup final, prior to entering management. He enjoyed spells at Rovers, Huddersfield and, latterly, with the Scottish officials at two rugby league World Cups. Once again, his name is not widely known outwith his domain. Once again, the thought occurs it ought to be.

> It was a huge risk when I moved down to Wigan, because I was only 19, I had just finished my apprenticeship, and was starting to gain recognition for Kelso and the South team, and I knew that once I joined league, that was me finished with union. But Scotland had Andy Irvine in their team, and he was a great full-back, and Arthur Brown was another excellent No 15, so it wasn't as if I was ever guaranteed gaining a place in the Scottish national team and I have no regrets about what I did. I think the tide was turning by that point, because my mates backed my decision, I still have plenty of friends in the Borders, and everything was positive when I moved down to Wigan. It was a big learning curve, because, whatever some people might think, there are massive differences between the two codes, and

I had to put in an awful amount of work when I first arrived in league. The two versions of rugby did come closer together for a while in the 1990s, but they're moving apart again; union has gone back to rucking and mauling and that makes it a completely different experience from what happens in league. But I've never had any problems enjoying 13- and 15-a-side; they're both smashing games.

Scotland seems to have built up a bit of a following for league, but, to be honest, the game will always struggle unless they can establish a Super League team, because that is where the focus, the major attendances and the media coverage are. But I've been pretty lucky: I grew up with some great players in Kelso, and I have rubbed shoulders with the best in the rugby league world. You can't really ask for much more than that.

Fairbairn now runs a pub called 'The Mill' in Hull, and obviously is not bitter about how the door was slammed shut on his union aspirations when he journeyed to England as a teenager. But there were definitely problems with the whole union/league divide, allied to the feeling that, where a compromise should have been possible, intransigence held the upper hand, with both codes suffering from stereotypical perceptions. Thus, the land of league was portrayed by its detractors as a place of Eddie Waring, endless rain and grotty Working Men's Clubs, which produced comedians in the mould of Bernard Manning and blasted brass band music. The union realm, meanwhile, was perceived as an elitist sphere for toffee-nosed patricians with Barbour jackets, chaps who tucked into their kedgeree as they perused their *Daily Telegraph* every morning and lived by the philosophy of Cecil Rhodes. Neither of these images was remotely applicable to the Borders, nor their players and officials, but sometimes it was easier to adhere to ingrained prejudices than go searching for a fair picture. And this was one of those instances.

The saddest aspect of the schism was the squandered opportunity to establish a rugby format which could have appealed to both sets of supporters, and might even have challenged football in popularity. Tony Collins, of the Rugby Football League, put this view: 'The interesting thing about the Scottish players is that most who switched to league were from the Borders, so socially, they were very similar to rugby league players in the north of England. If the union authorities hadn't banned for life anyone who played league, there would have been much more back-and-forth movement between the regions and a much stronger link forged between them. Rugby, as a whole, would have been very different and probably much stronger in relation to soccer.'

There were other areas where elements of 'Aye-Been' intractability led to disharmony in the Borders and the wider Scottish community. One of these revolved around the issue of South Africa, whose government's notorious introduction of an apartheid system brought them into increasing conflict with international sport as the 1960s carried on. Even at this distance, it should have been obvious that such discrimination was contrary to the whole essence of international sport and society in general, but rugby was notoriously slow in challenging the South Africans and continued to organise reciprocal tours, to and from the Republic, long after other pursuits such as cricket, football and the Olympic Games had implemented action to cast the Vorster government into isolation. Thus it was that a Borders select travelled to the Cape in 1967 and the Springboks were invited to Britain in 1969 and 1970 for what eventually descended into a shambles, which became better known for the riots and demonstrations than anything which happened on the pitch.

Jim Telfer, befitting his reputation as an individual who was blessed with intelligence and conscience, recognised the grand folly of the old maxim that 'sport and politics don't mix'. His critics might retort that the Melrose man had no qualms about journeying to South Africa in 1967, but at least he was prepared to witness for himself and learn about the discrimination which existed in their society. 'I remember being struck by how it [apartheid] was an accepted part of life – black people would walk with their heads down as if embarrassed and not make eye contact with you. If you met a black man walking along the street, he would often cross the street to stay away from you,' said Telfer. 'Clearly, that wasn't what we saw in the media, with coverage of riots and the ANC campaigns, but, on the ground, I saw this deference by black people to whites, which was unsettling. With apartheid now gone and rugby having played a part in bringing the "Rainbow Nation" together, with the World Cup success there in 1995, there is obviously more equality and hope shared across the country now. But I have to say that some things haven't changed a great deal. I was back in 1999 and 2003 with Scotland and still black people appear to do, and are expected to do, the menial jobs – the waiters, handymen, cleaners were still mostly black. I didn't see any white people doing these jobs.'

There was no sign of a black presence in the touring party which arrived in Britain in 1969 on what was always going to be a controversy-strewn campaign and the Anti-Apartheid Movement, fuelled by such resolute campaigners as David Steel (or Baron Steel of Aikwood, as he is now titled), and the activist Peter Hain, mobilised their resources to sufficiently impressive effect that even the most apolitical rugby follower in the country grew accustomed to encountering protests and being showered with leaflets. In December of the previous year, the Scots had beaten their Springbok opponents 6–3 at Murrayfield and would have triumphed by a greater margin but for the repeated deficiencies of Ian Smith, who only managed to convert one of six kicks, but the victory was overshadowed by the scale of the demonstrations against the trip and, it should be added, the outrage of many fans, who believed that nothing should be allowed to interfere with their game, as summed up by Sandy Thorburn, in his history of Scottish rugby.

'Straight away, mention must be made of the almost intolerable strain placed on the tourists throughout the entire tour by the actions of those who professed to oppose the apartheid policy of the South African government,' wrote Thorburn. 'For this match, some 75,000 spectators were contained in the stand, or in one section of the terracing directly opposite, where a highly efficient group of policemen, assisted by stewards, saw to it that the game was never interrupted by those militants, who did come inside.' One can almost smell the distaste in the writer's nostrils, and this was not the finest hour of many in British rugby, not least when the South Africans met the South of Scotland in Galashiels in the middle of January 1970. (The contest finished 3–3).

To his credit, Steel was one of the few people prepared to stick by his principles, but this neither yielded any short-term comfort, nor was he allowed to forget his alleged apostasy by many of those who had previously voted for the Liberals in the region.

'Living in Africa for four years and having black servants and being educated separately from other races all spurred me to make my mark,' he later declared. 'My most difficult time came when the Springboks played one of their matches at Netherdale. Rugby is a religion in the Borders, but we held a public protest meeting and stood outside the ground, handing out leaflets. This was deeply unpopular, but clearly I had no choice. At the general election a few months later [in June], my Tory opponent issued a brilliant last-minute leaflet, showing a rugby ball going over the bar between the posts. The slogan was "Convert to Conservatism". Many people did, and I only held my seat after three recounts.'

But this is not being wise with the benefit of hindsight. By the stage that Dawie de Villiers and his confrères touched down in Blighty, the D'Oliveira affair had already become a cause célèbre in international cricket and even if many of the spectators at Murrayfield, Netherdale and Linksfield Stadium in Aberdeen might have claimed to be ignorant of politics, there were others who should have been able to sift through the propaganda and arrive at the conclusion that rugby was one of the few things which South Africa could export to the wider world and therefore, demonstrating against the tour in these circumstance was a practical way of delivering a resonant message to their rulers.

But sometimes, even radicals stick their heads in the sand. For most of their history, the Borders people had been proudly independent and their contribution to rugby epitomised their ability to think on their feet, forge ahead with fresh ideas and make them flourish from their own exertions. The formation of the Border League, the invention of Sevens, the development of a coaching structure in Hawick which was the envy of communities ten times their size . . . these were just three of the positive factors which deserved the support of all those who loved the oval ball game. Thus, when the SRU and the leading clubs in other parts of Scotland eventually appreciated that they were trailing in the slipstream of their counterparts in the South, and decided to create a new Scottish championship structure commencing in 1973–74, one might have envisaged that the Borders would embrace such a concept, considering how it would bring an end to the unsatisfactory and anachronistic unofficial set-up, which had trundled way beyond its sell-by date, even as Scotland began to slip down the international pecking order.

Instead, there were widespread concerns and an initial refusal among some Borders officials to commit their organisations to the novel proposal. This reluctance partly stemmed from fears that any new competition would compromise the integrity and/or the credibility of the Border League, while diminishing the significance of the Sevens circuit. As it transpired, this apprehension was not wholly unfounded, and there was logic in the South's decision to entrust Dr George Balfour (of Jed-Forest) with the task of articulating the opinions of the seven Border League clubs, whose misgivings led to them contemplating whether they should opt out of the pan-Scottish format altogether. Yet, while they eventually steered away from that course, and joined the new structure – with Hawick predictably romping to the maiden title – the Borders were uneasy about the future and historian Laing Speirs pointed out the reasons why this was the case.

Even after the arrival of competitive rugby at a national level [in the winter of 1973–74] the Border clubs remained anxious about several issues. The clash of representative fixtures with championship matches exercised them, as did the particularly sensitive communication from headquarters [aka Murrayfield], which suggested that Border League fixtures on Saturdays should be cancelled to allow National League fixtures to be played. This point was raised initially by Hawick, who were concerned at a suggestion that their Border League fixture with Gala should be cancelled to allow a National League fixture with West of Scotland to go ahead. The importance of the Border clubs sticking together in the face of such proposals became – as was the way of the League – the banner under which the Border case was presented in Edinburgh.

Nearly 70 years had passed since the Union had formally blessed the Border League, but, for a short period, it looked as though the relationship was under serious strain. But with compromises, promises and co-operation, plus some deft work by fixture secretaries, the threat to the long-standing harmony was averted. The fact that the Border clubs, and particularly Hawick, made such an impact on the first National Leagues did no harm either. But, by the late 1980s, the Border League's concern with the proliferation of games and the impact they were making on the competition was undiminished.

Having coped with the problems created by the national competition, the Border League had to face even more serious complications caused when the Cup, Bowl and Shield knock-out games arrived on the scene. The meeting, in 1990, was initially unanimous in condemning any competition which interfered with April Saturdays and agreed to support it, only if it was completed by the end of March. The Sevens, while not formally a matter for the Border League, [then] began to intrude on the League agenda and the Border clubs, driven by their desire to protect their local structure, engaged in lengthy debate and even longer correspondence with the SRU, in an effort to protect the traditional dates. Within a few weeks, the SRU had made it clear that the [Scottish Cup] quarter-final and semi-final games were to be played in midweek and compromise was in the air. But, faced with the response of other Scottish districts, who were in favour of using April Saturdays, the strong line taken by the Borders was gradually eroded.

The natural response to this litany of woes would surely be to inquire: who on earth would want to be an official in Caledonian rugby? Damned if they do, damned if they don't, there was never any prospect of all the different parties being satisfied with any fixture schedule and, regrettably, many of these issues are still being discussed and arousing heated emotions in 2011. But what was evident, once the dust had settled on the debate surrounding the new Scottish championship, was the continuing dominance of the Border representatives, while standards undoubtedly rose elsewhere, once the leading clubs in the Central Belt and the North had grown accustomed to performing on a national stage. From that perspective, the shift in emphasis was to be applauded. But, of course, that was not how the situation looked to many in the Borders, who felt that, bit by bit, the myriad elements which kept the sport in rude health were being dismantled.

As a neutral, it seems only fair to observe that these objections had some merit. Whatever one's views on Sevens – and there are many in the major Scottish cities who regard the abbreviated format as a big snooze – they had become an integral part of the Border sporting calendar and the bottom line was that they generated priceless income for the likes of Melrose, Gala and Selkirk. So too, those who administered and participated in the Border League were entitled to fight for their territory and although it is now clear that the national championship has taken precedence over the South's own competition, the latter was a brave, bold step into the unknown and one which should not be brushed aside as an irrelevance. After all, just as was the case in the 1970s, there are weekends where thousands of fans watch local Border derbies, whereas attendances at the public-school clubs are in the hundreds, with the average age of those watching above 50.

In short, there were fights which the Borders picked which were worth scrapping about, and other issues where their silence or complicity was deafening. None of this was unique to the South – and rugby, in recent times, has become a byword in Scotland for stramashes and spats which invariably prove a puzzle to the wider world – but if the drain of talent to rugby league left a bitter taste in some people's mouths, as did the manner in which the Border League and Sevens gradually relinquished a semblance of their former lustre, there were positive consequences for the man who emerged from the Borders and set about transforming the fortunes of the sport in his homeland.

Chapter Eight

MR TELFER COMES TO TOWN

I T WAS EARLY IN THE 1990s, with Scottish rugby on the crest of a wave, and I was sitting in the reception area at Murrayfield Stadium, waiting for an interview with the inimitable James Telfer, Esquire. Suddenly, as the clock ticked towards the appointed hour, a well-known internationalist caught sight of me and inquired on whom I was waiting. When I told him, he winced, turned a peculiar puce colour, and declared, prior to making a sharp exit: 'Well, I hope you've got a sturdy book to shove down your trousers!'

It might be unfair to describe that as a common reaction from those who played under Telfer, but there is little doubt that the Borderer possesses the ability to induce trepidation and fear among his charges and has resorted to expletive-laden tirades whenever he has divined it will provide the necessary verbal boot up the backside. One such memorable outburst arrived in the build-up to the British and Irish Lions tackling the Springboks on their 1997 tour of the Republic when – or so one of the Irish players told me – his rage was so all-consuming that several of his team were genuinely concerned that he might conk out with a heart attack towards the end of his Malcolm Tucker-like diatribe.

That is Telfer in a nutshell: forever passionate, stubbornly non-conformist in his socialist tenets, amid a sport which is still, rightly or wrongly, perceived as being the preserve of private schools and the affluent middle classes, and robustly committed to ensuring that nobody on his watch ever entertains a sliver of complacency. Little has changed in his dedication to education since he came into the world in 1940 and worked as a shepherd's boy on the Cheviot Hills. From the beginning, Telfer was an outsider, a man whose parents, Willie and Peggy, were barely interested in rugby, but who quickly recognised that their son was too bright to be consigned to some menial job and eventually packed him off to become a teacher. In these circumstances, it appears even more amazing that he subsequently became one of the most important figures in the history of the Scottish game, and celebrated his 44th and 50th birthdays on the same days that his country won their only Grand Slams of the modern era. And yet, he was moulded by the Borders, grew addicted to mentoring and schooling youngsters, and, whether in his suit and tie in Hawick, or with his tracksuit on in Melrose, there are literally thousands of children who have grown up with a passion for knowledge which they learned from Jim Telfer.

Many people have attempted to fathom what makes him tick. Allan Massie provided a good thumbnail sketch with the assessment: 'Telfer is a man of innate authority. There's a wealth of quiet reserve and self-knowledge, touched by that form of self-mockery, which appears as understatement, in the way he will describe himself as a dominant personality.' Bill McLaren, speaking in 2003, responded thus: 'Jim has never forgotten where he came from, he is one of the most honest men you could ever hope to meet, and he is also somebody with an endless thirst for learning and hard work.' That much was obvious even during my brief visit to his office inside Murrayfield, where he was carrying out endless video scrutiny, examining the weaknesses of opponents, drawing up a raft of new tactical formations, and generally confirming that he is, and always has been, an advocate of the mantra that genius is an infinite capacity for taking pains.

At the outset, his interest in rugby originated from him

growing up in an area where it was the number one pastime. Indeed, it is not particularly difficult to envisage that if Telfer had been born in Glasgow, he might have developed into an Alex Ferguson figure in football coaching. Yet there was something else in his make-up, which he later admitted had motivated and spurred him on to pursue fresh challenges, and that was his own sense of inferiority. It sounds absurd, given his glittering CV, but he constantly felt the need to prove himself and that was one of the reasons behind his inspirational performances in a Scotland jersey and further explained why he hated slackers on the rugby circuit.

My upbringing was one where there were no privileges: you had to work for everything you got. I was not born into a family with money, so I had to earn everything. I took that into my rugby and my teaching, probably in the way I would choose to develop someone, no matter what his background was: he was judged by me, only on his ability and his attitude. I would always do my best to encourage the trier; the boy, who maybe wasn't the most talented, but the one who showed lots of commitment and worked as hard as he possibly could to improve himself. I came from a non-rugby family, and I had to start from scratch, so I have never had that much time for people who think that they are better than they really are, either in rugby, or in education, or in life. The players who always had excuses for not training could disappear as far as I was concerned.

When I was making my way, I developed a huge fear of failure that was always with me. It drove me on as a player and it drove me on as a coach. I had, and still have, an inferiority complex. Coming from the background that I did, I suppose that it was inevitable. Being raised in an environment where the landlord and the duke were the kingpins made me feel small, despite me railing against the system. It also made me a bit of a rebel, to be honest with you. I saw that you were being judged on what you owned, rather than what you are, and I didn't like it. No, I didn't like it one little bit.

What Telfer *did* relish was wholehearted endeavour, physical self-sacrifice in a sporting cause, an appetite for hard graft, and the recognition that the team mattered more than any single individual. There is a photograph of the young Telfer, standing along with his Melrose comrades, at the climax of their double-winning success in the 1962–63 campaign. The majority of the players in the picture are smiling, as they were entitled to do, following a harsh and protracted winter during which they had clung on to Hawick's coat-tails in the early stages, as the prelude to stalling the Green Machine 5–0 in a classic encounter at the Greenyards, which was watched by more than 4,000 supporters. Yet Telfer's expression is unflinching, with even a trace of defiance, as if delivering the message: 'See that trophy sitting in front of us. *We* won it. *We* deserved to win it. And we'll win it again next year if it's anything to do with me.'

That attitude became a familiar one during the next four decades, whether Telfer was excelling in the No 8 berth for his club or country, or exhorting and encouraging a string of teams, both in Scotland and with assorted Lions ensembles in New Zealand and South Africa, to aspire to ever loftier standards. This perfectionism made him one of the best of his generation; and he performed with distinction for Scotland, after making his debut in the Five Nations Championship against France in 1964 at Murrayfield, where the hosts won 10–0, as the prelude to earning his next cap in the no-scoring draw with the All Blacks at the same venue. To this day, the Scots have never beaten New Zealand, but when Telfer started talking to the men from the Land of the Long White Cloud on their visit to the northern hemisphere, he developed a comradeship with them which shaped his whole rugby philosophy, both on and off the pitch, for better and for worse.

He ventured to New Zealand with the Lions in 1966 and
with Scotland a year later, and his initial passion turned into a
full-blown love affair. I once asked Telfer why he laid such
great store by their methods and his reply was typically to the
point. 'You don't get into their team because of who you are,
or where you went to school, or because you have been given
an easy passage up the ladder. You get to wear the All Black
jersey because you have earned the right to wear it and their
whole rugby structure, from primary school right up to the
provinces, is based on giving every single youngster in their
country an equal opportunity,' said Telfer, who hardly needed
to mention the stark contrast between this situation and the
prevailing climate in Scotland in the early 1990s. 'In Scotland,
we don't really seem to like team sports that much. We
produce individuals who are good at golf and athletics, boxing
and swimming. But when it comes to team sport, far too much
effort is devoted to football, and we're not even any good at it.'

These trenchant opinions meant that Telfer could never
have considered an alternative career in the diplomatic corps.
Not that keeping his head down and trotting out party lines
ever held any appeal for him. Instead, he thrived on his own
obdurate terms, initially as an attacking player with plenty of
pace and acceleration, then, as the wear and tear from injuries
stacked up, through his ability to focus on mastering and
refining new skills. As a player, he was one of life's natural
leaders, forever cajoling and coaxing those around him, and
even when his speed started to fade, little by little, he amply
compensated with powerful running, canny positional sense,
an abrasive determination to burst through a brick wall if it
was required, and the knack for transforming contests by the
sheer force of his personality and the savvy to be in the right
place at the right time. These ingredients added up to one
seriously formidable player and although he only gained 25
Scotland caps, he would almost certainly have secured more

but for a number of injuries, which restricted his Scotland career to the years between 1964 and 1970. Telfer's indefatigable sense of commitment reached the stage where he instinctively dived into the fray where other, less courageous, souls would have ducked for cover and he showed no fear against some of the most imposing opponents in the game, such as the famous occasion when he pounced to score the match-winning try against France in Colombes in 1969. This, of course, was screened repeatedly for the next 26 years until the Scots, inspired by Gregor Townsend and Gavin Hastings, triumphed in Paris in 1995 on their final visit to the Parc des Princes, with Telfer in attendance and, as he put it, bloody glad that he would not have to sit through any more viewings of his effort in black and white.

Raw-boned and steely-eyed, with nary a hint of fat in his body, Telfer was as fit as a fiddle and was as uncompromisingly tough on himself, if he detected his standards slipping even a fraction, as he ever was on anybody else in his teams. Perhaps we should not strive to build him up into some sort of Borders Superman, but there again, similarities existed between the comic-book hero from Smallville and his Scottish counterpart from a diminutive region. By day, in his workplace, Telfer was always the bookish chemistry teacher, lean of build and studiously disinclined to flaunt his fame, preferring to keep a low profile and concentrating wholly on teaching his pupils without any distractions or sideshows. It was only when he entered the realm of rugby that his personality changed and his rivals glanced around for any spare bits of kryptonite.

In terms of his contribution to Melrose, Telfer captained the Greenyards club for six seasons and, despite the marauding qualities of his Hawick and Gala rivals of the period, his contributions were as immense as they were consistent, and proved the catalyst for his team's hard-fought Border League success in the 1970–71 season. Yet, in some respects, with

Telfer by then in his thirties and no longer in international contention, his thoughts were already turning to how he could influence and assist his country on the wider stage. His visits to New Zealand had convinced him that there was no point in Scotland stumbling along from one miserable sequence of results to another – and, after a promising start with a brace of victories over England in the space of a week in 1971, the decade was a wretched one for the SRU's teams – and therefore, he turned his attention and scrutiny to learning from the Kiwi template and transporting it to the Scottish game. This, of course, was far from easy, not least because Murrayfield's officials were slow to recognise the value of appointing a full-time coach, allied to the fact that, whereas rugby was the number one sport in New Zealand and thus commanded all the attention from school upwards to the regional structure and All Black enclave, football was the kingpin in Scotland, a state of affairs which only increased as the national team began qualifying for the first stages of World Cup tournaments.

In short, Telfer faced an obstacle course, which was strewn with hazards, and it was not until 1980 that he was finally presented with the opportunity to try and improve matters in his homeland when he took over from Nairn MacEwan, who had produced some entertaining teams, but generally without the forward strength and technical expertise to convert promising positions into regular victories. Telfer knew, even before he accepted the national coaching role, that he would have to implement a dramatic change in the fitness, the mindset and the physicality of future internationalists and none of this was ever going to be accomplished in a month, or even a year. Yet, if there was one feature of Telfer's personality which had earned the respect and admiration of even those who quibbled with his methods, it was the fellow's thirst for knowledge and learning, to the extent where he was capable of soaking up information like blotting paper and, once it had been stored in his brain, it was never forgotten. As Sherlock Holmes remarked of his brother, Mycroft: 'His specialism is omniscience.' This meant that when Telfer sat down to pick his squads and addressed the various issues of which players were best suited to every position and how he could bolster competition for places, nothing was ever left to chance, as Colin Deans, one of the men who thrived under his guidance, told me.

Jim was the sort of guy who got to know you first, who took the time to find out what made you tick, before he fathomed how he could inspire you from there and he was brilliant at man-management and persuading players to push themselves to the limit. I remember going on a 1980 development tour to France and we were beaten in our first game, with the forwards not doing themselves justice, and Jim went through us like a dose of salts and the next ten days were probably the hardest of my rugby life.

Later on the trip, we came up against a French Barbarians side, which comprised the players who had won the 1975 Grand Slam for France, and Jim knew that it was going to be a really tough contest. So he started winding up one of our lads, George Mackie – who was a nice big lad from Inverness, who didn't have a malicious bone in his body – and by the time Jim was finished, George was flinging punches at him in the changing room. It was totally out of character for him, because he was one of life's gentle giants, but Jim had obviously decided he needed battlers against the French and by the time George walked out on to the field, he was fighting mad and really up for the challenge.

As for Jim, he just rolled with the punches and seemed happy at the reaction he had provoked, which tells you a lot about the qualities which he brought to the job. He knew how to push people, and I suppose there was something reminiscent of Alex Ferguson about the way he was always searching for new standards and bringing the guys closer together. In any sporting side, you have different characters, different personalities, and one of the hardest tasks is getting everybody to pull in the same direction, especially in rugby, where you can have one or two world-class players in your ranks, but that isn't much use if you're not performing as a team. But Jim knew what buttons to press, he would push you, punish you, and you could liken his methods to SAS training: in that only the very best would succeed when they were put to the test. Personally, I've got a hell of a lot to thank him for, because he taught me that you never know how far you can go until you have been tested and he definitely drove Scottish rugby in the right direction, because he knew that we couldn't continue with just hoping things would turn up. If that meant sending us to hell and back, training in the morning, in the afternoon, in the evening, he soon found out which of the guys were ready for international rugby and which weren't going to make it. And it is called 'Test' rugby for a reason.

Nonetheless, it should not be forgotten that MacEwan had carried out some sterling work of his own in the Scotland cause, despite the largely disappointing results for his XVs in the seventies. As a consequence, Telfer was able to concentrate on improving his forwards, with backs of the calibre of Andy Irvine, Jim Renwick, Keith Robertson, Roy Laidlaw and the peerless John Rutherford perfectly capable of capitalising on any decent stream of possession from their pack. Yet it was not simply the case that Telfer continually shouted and screamed blue murder at his charges: any loudmouth could have done that and relied on invective at the expense of innovation. Instead, he gradually revolutionised the manner in which the sport was organised in Scotland, both by enhancing the fitness and durability of his troops and bringing his admiration for the New Zealand game to bear on his personnel at Murrayfield, as well as relying far less on Exiles than past generations. He was also fortunate that the national leagues, which came into existence in 1973–74, were responsible for raising the standard of club rugby in his homeland, even if they began to overshadow the Border League, just as the South's leading organisations had feared would happen. (This explained their opposition to the scheme.) In which light, and although there were no quick fixes, the Scots, slowly but surely, started to produce displays which proved they had exorcised the travails of the previous decade.

Alan Tomes, the formidable 48-cap-winning lock forward for his country and a staple of the Green Machine in the 1970s and 1980s, offered some telling points when we discussed the contrast between Jim Telfer and his Hawick confrère, Derrick Grant.

Jim and Derrick were totally different characters. I worked under Derrick at Mansfield Park and I thought he was a great 15-a-side coach, whereas Jim was more fixated with forward play and getting his pack working as he wanted. Don't get me wrong, we all benefited from Jim's efforts, but he was absolutely ruthless, he challenged you as a player and as a person, and if you didn't measure up, the bottom line was that you wouldn't stay in the picture.

He needed to be like that to get the best out of his players, but it's only natural that I have such a high regard for Derrick, because I worked with him week in, week out at Hawick, and when you are that close to somebody, you form a bond with them and you have to bear in mind how absolutely devoted Derrick was to keeping his club great. By the late 1970s, the rest of us had cars and we would drive down to the ground in the middle of winter, but Derrick came on his bike, whatever the weather was like, and I don't think that he has been given the recognition he deserves, and the same applies to Nairn

MacEwan for that matter. After all, Jim already had the backs
to do damage when he got the job; so he just had to get the
forwards sorted out. Yes, he succeeded in that aim, and he was
a terrific coach, but let's not forget that Scottish rugby didn't
start and finish with him. There were others who did a
smashing job as well and when you look at the number of
Hawick players who won international recognition for Scotland during that period, it seems clear to me that Derrick
made a huge contribution to the process.

This appears a prescient assessment and Tomes was one of the
proudest and most industrious of the myriad characters who
served both Grant and Telfer to the best of his abilities. But, all
the same, the latter's arrival as national coach sparked a resur-
gence which led all the way to the 1984 Grand Slam success and,
as soon as he stepped down the following season, the Scots had
plummeted back to earth in collecting the wooden spoon. This
cannot be coincidence. Better, surely, to regard the Melrose
mentor as the fulcrum of a new inner conviction within his
compatriots, which ensured they no longer feared anybody.

That much was evident as the 1980s rolled on. In 1981, the
Welsh and the Irish were defeated at Murrayfield, with the
invariably daunting away trips to Paris and London yielding
narrow 16–9 and 23–17 losses. That was the prelude to Telfer
stiffening the sinews of his charges with a hastily-arranged visit
to the southern hemisphere and another clash with that All
Black magic. 'It wasn't on the schedule originally, because
South Africa had been due to go to New Zealand for 12 weeks,
but the authorities cut it to six, following all the [anti-apartheid]
protests,' recalled Deans, who was one of the cornerstones of
Telfer's grand design. 'So it was a late booking and Jim and the
SRU were both delighted. These kinds of tours really helped
Scotland develop and brought us closer together and I have no
doubt they sowed the seeds of our future success.'

On a positive note, the experience demonstrated to the visitors that they had no reason to harbour inferiority complexes when sparring with the All Blacks and they provided their opponents with a stern challenge in the first Test in Dunedin before succumbing 11–4. Unfortunately, this outcome had the negative effect of convincing Telfer that what his men required was a diet of ever more gruelling training sessions and they were driven relentlessly in the build-up to the second Test in Auckland, which ended in a 40–15 defeat. This was not the first occasion, and it would not be the last, when Telfer's teams were pushed through the wringer, to the stage where the forwards were virtually dead on their feet from the rigours of their training-ground exertions, by the time the match, for which they had been preparing, kicked off. Ultimately, it proved that even the best coaches made mistakes, or asked for too much, but the refreshing aspect of the whole experience was the strength in depth of the home-grown Scots who were emerging.

They included players of the lustre of the Watsonians centre, David Johnston, a fellow blessed with genuine pace in the midfield; the mercurial Roger Baird, a livewire winger who created opportunities for others, even though he is probably destined to go down in posterity as the man who never scored a try for Scotland; and Keith Robertson, the nuggety Melrose winger, who was part of an increasing number of Borderers who were forcing their way into the international mix. This had nothing to do with favouritism – as Deans told me: 'Jim always picked his guys on merit and it was irrelevant to him whether they came from Glasgow, Edinburgh, the Highlands or Hawick' – but simply reflected the fact that the South was, once again, punching above its weight in Scottish rugby.

The success of and razor-sharp rivalry between Hawick and Gala had grown in intensity once more, with the Maroons shedding their 'nearly men' mantle and they not only secured back-to-back Scottish championship titles in 1980 and 1981,

but also recorded their first brace of victories over the Green
Machine in the same season for nearly 30 years. Telfer scru-
tinised these matches with more than his usual interest, because
they featured a veritable plethora of past, present and future
internationalists and whether admiring the leadership qualities
of the Gala skipper, Jim Aitken – who had already proved his
worth with Scotland since making his Test debut in 1977 – or
poring over the talents of such rising stars as Derek White,
Alastair Campbell, Peter Dods and Derek Turnbull, Telfer
knew that there was sufficient potential for the Scots to
transcend their long-time inconsistency and show the rest of
the world they could win on the big stage.

Better still, there was a fresh air of confidence among the
players who had recently started strutting their stuff for Scotland,
including Keith Robertson, who had earned his first cap against
the All Blacks in 1978 and, despite finishing on the wrong end of
an 18–9 defeat, viewed these encounters as the reason why he
was involved in rugby, the more so because he had prospered
under Telfer's tutelage and recognised a kindred spirit.

In the early days at Melrose, we didn't have a big pack, so we
had to take risks. People at the club tended not to get after me
too much for doing that, because they trusted my instincts.
Creamy [the nickname for Jim Telfer] eventually did mind
when we started gaining a bit of control up front, but he
understood that we had to take the fight to the opposition.
And, to be honest, I was happiest when I was doing that. It
comes from a feel, knowing what's round about you and how
to use the ball. A lot depends on the situations you find yourself
in. Sometimes risks come off, more often than not, they don't.

But even though it might sound strange, I found it quite
easy playing international rugby. There was very little immediate pressure as a winger, compared with turning out at
centre [for Melrose] week in, week out. Also, I came into a

side which was struggling, and we only gained the occasional chance to work with the ball, so we had to try things when we did get it. And when Jim took over as coach, he already knew what I could do. He rammed the message into us that we had to show greater control, because there was no point flinging the ball around like headless chickens and scoring an occasional great try if we were gifting chances to the opposition and conceding three or four at our end. It sounds simple now, but he had a way of conveying these things which made sure you never forgot them. And, bit by bit, the results came along to back him up.

This was true, but any signs of progress were invariably followed by a reality check. The Scots, for instance, achieved a creditable 24–15 victory over the Australians in Edinburgh towards the end of 1981, and approached the following year's Five Nations event with a justified amount of confidence, only to commence their campaign with a dull-as-ditchwater 9–9 draw with the English on a frozen afternoon in Auld Reekie. Telfer's pursed lips on the periphery testified to his frustration, although there was little difference between his reaction to his side's lacklustre performance during their 21–12 loss in Dublin and their 16–7 win against France at Murrayfield. In both matches, chances were squandered, and legends such as Renwick and Irvine, the latter in his final international season, were culpable during the defeat to Ireland, who claimed their first Triple Crown since 1949. At this point, it was, at best, a B-minus for their championship display.

Yet, at least from Telfer's perspective, there were signs of improvement. Not so many that he was prepared to express public optimism about the trip to Cardiff – a city where the Scots had not tasted triumph for 20 years – but sufficient to instil a quiet expectation in his troops. For starters, the Welsh had slipped a notch or two from the majestic force they had been in the 1970s. And secondly, Telfer reckoned that his pack could get into their opponents' faces and run them off their feet if they played to their potential.

As it transpired, they fared better than anybody could have anticipated, first weathering an early onslaught, and then cranking up the momentum with such a wondrous exhibition of pace and continuity that they might have been asked to do the haka at the climax. Jim Calder rounded off one electrifying incision from Baird and Iain Paxton. Then David Johnston produced another glimpse of magic with a sublime outside break which left the Welsh cover tackling fresh air. Generally, with Rutherford at his scintillating best, it was a masterful exhibition and while some people in the Valleys proclaim that you never actually beat the Welsh, you just score more points than them, there was no arguing with this display or with the eventual winning margin of 34–18, which was a trouncing in anybody's terms.

This was Telfer at his best, acting as the catalyst for improbable heroics, allowing his team the chance to express themselves, and the normally reticent Renwick was one of the men who viewed this contest as a stepping stone on the subsequent glory trail.

The tactics were to wait and be patient for the chance to counter-attack, the chance to go from wherever, and when it came to just go for it. We had a few guys who had been on the British Lions tour [of South Africa] in 1980, we had all been to New Zealand as a squad, and Jim Telfer had come in and started to work with the forwards. We had beaten both Romania and Australia before the Five Nations. We had beaten France before going to Cardiff and Terry Holmes and Jeff Squires cried off for Wales, so they brought in a boy for his first cap at scrum-half, and old Clive Burgess came back into their back row. All these different things helped lift our confidence that day. We knew we could beat them at home and a lot of us were pretty desperate to do it away by then. We kept it pretty simple, but we were ready for the counter-attacking chances which came our way and we had boys who were able to finish them off when it mattered. So, looking back, it was off the cuff. But it was also planned. That sounds daft, doesn't it!

As if that was not reason enough for cheer, the Scots next embarked on a sojourn Down Under, in the summer of '82, and duly gained a memorable triumph over the Australians. It is the only time they have beaten any of the southern hemisphere 'big three' away from home in their history, even if they had to perform out of their skins to emerge with a 12–7 win at Ballymore in Brisbane. It seemed as if Telfer, the master strategist, assisted by his growing coterie of Borders foot soldiers, was guiding his country towards previously unscaled peaks. Yet, as always when dealing with Scotland, it pays to be pragmatic and the elation from that first Test success had barely abated before the tourists were being overrun 33–9 in the rematch in Sydney. Once again, Telfer had drilled his forwards into the dirt, and once again, they had nothing left to offer when the Wallabies rushed in their direction, scenting blood and revenge. This was in danger of becoming a familiar story, but what ensued in the 1983 Five Nations deviated from the script altogether.

In fact, 1983 turned into Telfer's *annus horribilis*. At the outset, in what was the third season of his four-year tenure, he must have imagined that his team would have a decent opportunity of challenging for the championship, as the prelude to him leading the British and Irish Lions to New Zealand in the summer. But any coach, even one as skilled and multifaceted as Telfer, can only control so many factors and juggle so many balls before the whole edifice comes crashing down on top of him. He was slated for taking a year out to prepare for the Lions crusade – while Derrick Grant and Colin Telfer stepped in as temporary replacements – then found himself repeatedly outvoted by the Irish duo of the captain, Ciaran Fitzgerald, and the tour manager, Willie John McBride. As the barbs and criticisms stacked up, the Kiwis rubbed their opponents' noses in the dirt, en route to a 'Blackwash' and some scathing comments from the non-Scottish press about Telfer's alleged tactical deficiencies. As a proud Borderer, albeit one who had grown up with a self-confessed inferiority complex, this was a bitter pill to swallow and Jim was typically honest in discussing the mental scars which afflicted him in his autobiography, *Looking Back for Once*.

No amount of reasoning could lift my personal feelings of failure. My overriding thought when that tour finished was that I had believed I was ready to be a Lions coach, but that the tour had shown me I wasn't. I failed to find a game that would beat the All Blacks, who were always better than us, technically and tactically. People asked me at the end of the tour whether I feared facing the Scottish media on our return. I said: 'No, I am more worried about hearing the comments as I walk along the street in Selkirk.'

I could not fault the players, because they had come through a system that wasn't good enough to beat the All Blacks. I failed and maybe I wasn't the right person to coach them. Saturday, 16 July 1983 – the date of the fourth Test – remains one of the saddest days in my life. A 38–6 defeat, a 4–0 series loss, there was no coming back from that. The dreams I had held three or four months earlier were in tatters. I was very disillusioned with coaching and with rugby and I was also totally against the whole Lions concept by this stage: it was so difficult to get the team together and prepare properly before going into the biggest Test matches these players would ever experience. Willie John [McBride] spoke to the press at the end of the tour and said he hoped the Lions would pick me to coach the next tour, as this experience had been invaluable. But I remember my own response to the media. In reply to one question about my future involvement, I asked them: 'Is there life after death?' It summed up how I was feeling.

Yet, in at least one respect, this adversity yielded a positive outcome in bringing the Scottish contingent closer together. And, despite the 1983 Five Nations developing into a tale of woe for the most part, with the Scots losing their opening three matches – notably in the absence of their injured playmaker, Rutherford – to Wales and France by 19–15 margins and Ireland by an even tighter 15–13 scoreline, they responded with a reaffirmation of their trademark thrawn pride to beat England 22–12 at Twickenham for what remains the last occasion on which the Scots achieved victory over the Auld Enemy in London. Ultimately, if it was a poor championship, it hinted at so much more and Telfer derived slivers of consolation from the optimism of his Borders confrères, Roy Laidlaw and John Rutherford, who were always disposed to look for the positives in any situation. Indeed, they defiantly told Telfer: 'We may have lost this tour, but we will return to Scotland and win the Grand Slam next season, because we have learned about the weaknesses of the other [British] teams in the last few months.'

Rutherford was back for that against-the-odds outcome and it was a measure of the man's abilities that I could not find a single person – from the Borders or anywhere else – with a negative word to say about the Selkirk stand-off. Instead, superlatives abounded, with 'Rudd' being variously described as 'a genius', 'a prince', 'a true great', 'a legend' and 'one of the best there ever was in rugby'. And these were words from the mouths of hard-bitten Borderers such as Colin Deans, Alan Tomes and Keith Robertson.

What was undeniable was that Scotland were a diminished force without the presence of Rutherford and the same applied in the case of Telfer, who returned from the southern hemisphere, understandably crestfallen from his Lions experiences, but determined to make sure that he would finish his term as national coach on a high note. From this analysis, it might seem that he endured mixed fortunes during his time in charge, but Rutherford had another way of defining his mentor's impact on his country's fortunes. 'I thought that, at Murrayfield, the team became almost unbeatable and Creamy's record was magnificent,' said the great No 10, in referring to the fact that the coach did not lose a single match at home in his tenure between 1980 and 1984, with the only minor glitches occurring in the drawn games against England and New Zealand.

Ultimately, perhaps that last contest offered the best summation of the symbiosis which existed between these sons of Melrose and Selkirk. It would have been easy for Telfer to have been sick of the sight of the All Blacks, such was the ruthlessness with which they had shattered his dreams. Yet, only a few months later, with even the most patriotic supporters possibly fearing the worst, the Scots, brimming with gusto and chutzpah and the bonnie panache of Rutherford, excelled in the task of pushing New Zealand all the way to the brink of defeat at Murrayfield, before the match finished tied at 25 points apiece. It was another case of so near and yet so far, but the Scots had talent to burn, and plenty of options at their disposal, and a true sense of their own worth. This was surely the abiding memory which they could take into 1984. And here was the evidence that the Borders could not only play a bit part in Scotland triumphs; they could emerge as protagonists in unforgettable pieces of sporting drama.

Chapter Nine

THE CORONATION OF A BORDERS PRINCE

HE BORDERS INFLUENCE on Scotland's first ever Grand Slam in 1925 was marginal at best. Only one player – Doug Davies – turned out in the team which made history and almost half of their number played their rugby in England. Yet, it was a measure of the dramatic shift in the balance of power, which occurred after the Second World War, that the Scots became increasingly dependent on their representatives from the South. By the time that Jim Telfer took over as coach in the 1980s, and implemented his radical policies, there was no longer any point in denying that the old days and old ways of cosy, cloistered public-school traditionalism were an outmoded luxury in an age when several countries, and most notably the All Blacks, were almost openly flaunting their professionalism when the latter word was still anathema among the home unions. The question was: what was to be done about squaring the circle between those who stuck to their belief in amateurism and those who argued the union code was adhering to an anachronistic ethos?

Sometimes, though, the sport provided less fractious and more positive matters on which everybody could sing from the same hymn sheet. One of these rare instances happened when Telfer's personnel began their inexorable march towards the Grand Slam in 1984. One could query the philosophies and tactics of the different sides in this struggle for European supremacy, and endlessly debate the abilities of many of the tournament's leading participants. But, in the final analysis, what was *not* up for discussion was the fact that John Rutherford was operating on a different stratosphere from everybody else. Even his opponents could scarce forbear to cheer at the insouciance and sublime free expressionism with which this Selkirk prodigy illuminated his pursuit.

Rutherford had never been anything other than a special talent, one of the few Scottish performers who could have waltzed into the New Zealand or South African ranks and blazed a majestic trail. He was first capped in 1979 and, straight from the outset, the partnership which he had forged, during their joint assignments as comrades on South duty, with the Jed-Forest scrum-half, Roy Laidlaw, ensured that both men intuitively knew what the other was planning. This meant they were able to devise attacking ploys with the strategic nous of chess grandmasters, while the relationship between them was almost telepathic. In the early days of his career, Rutherford absorbed valuable lessons from Ronnie Cowan, a former darling of the Souters, who had blotted his copybook – indelibly, in the eyes of the diehards – by switching codes to rugby league, sparking a slightly farcical situation where Cowan was treated like a leper in Selkirk, even while he was passing on tips to the young Rutherford from his family's greengrocer's shop. It was another reminder of the slightly absurd hostility which existed between the two codes, and the drain of talent from the Borders continued right into the late 1980s when the gifted Alan Tait of Kelso announced he was moving to join Widnes, prior to returning to the Scotland fold when union finally embraced profession-alism in the mid-1990s.

Heaven only knows how much moolah Rutherford might have commanded if he had chosen a similar route, but there was never any chance of this happening because he had been transfixed by the 15-a-side code from an early age, as he told me.

It must have been about 45 years ago, when we were involved in this school tournament and I was a member of the Philiphaugh team, and we were having the time of our lives. We battled hard to get to the final, and eventually won the competition, and who should come over and congratulate us than Bill McLaren, who was already a bit of a legend in the Borders, and we were absolutely thrilled that he was taking the time to wish us well. It made everybody's day, and there was a huge amount of interest in rugby at that stage. You could walk up the High Street of any of the towns in the region and you would see people carrying rugby balls and practising with them and either heading to a park or going to the local club for training. It never occurred to any of us not to play rugby and with people like Bill around, it just added that extra piece of inspiration.

Rutherford advanced almost seamlessly from the youth ranks into the Selkirk side, which provided him with the opportunity to start learning his craft at senior level. It actually assisted his development that he grew accustomed to performing behind a pack which offered him a limited supply of possession, in which circumstances, he quickly refined his decision-making and displayed a maturity when he was still in his late teens. There are precious few individuals who are blessed with sophistication, swiftness and sangfroid, but the young stand-off began making an increasing impact on the Border League and Scottish championship circuit and word spread about this immensely gifted player.

To his credit, Rutherford was never dazzled by fame or inclined to be cocky. If anybody perceived arrogance about the manner with which he routinely destroyed opponents, they were wide of the mark, because it would be difficult to meet a more humble person away from the grand rugby stages. When we talked during the preparation for this book, he repeatedly spelled out his conviction that he had been 'lucky' to have emerged in the era he did, and had been 'fortunate' that so many other talented performers rose to the challenge under the 'magnificent leadership' of Jim Telfer. In one sense, it was wonderfully refreshing to encounter somebody with such a manifest lack of prima donna-ism; on the other, one was left wondering how much Rutherford might have profited from the sport had he been born 15 or 20 years later, rather than in 1955.

It helped, of course, that he and Laidlaw built up such a remarkable bond once they combined, first for the South and then when Scotland came calling. Yet while both members of the duo possessed significant abilities and duly operated with the natural fluency of the best double acts, it was Rutherford who sparked most fear because he could kick wonderfully well – whether it was the garryowen, the grubber variety, or deft cross-field chips, whenever he was working with small, pacy back divisions – or weave his way beyond strings of would-be tacklers with a mesmerising nonchalance which was so bejewelled with class that it seemed inadequate to describe it merely as a change of pace. In all sports, the men and women who make the biggest aesthetic imprint tend to be those who always have time to spare or extra room in which to glisten, and Rutherford was no exception. And whether excelling with Scotland in their demolition of Wales in Cardiff in 1982, or being chosen for the ill-fated British Lions tour of New Zealand, where he was scandalously overlooked for the Tests, the Selkirk player never gave the impression he was doing anything other than loving his opportunity to shine.

How they treasured him at Philiphaugh! And the scale of the reverence was summed up by one of that club's most famous supporters, Allan Massie, who watched and marvelled at the fashion in which Rutherford brought his majestic presence to the Test arena.

Above. The good shepherd: Jim Telfer has been one of the greatest figures to emerge from the Borders and has stamped his imprint on rugby, as a player, coach and administrator.

Left. The Hawick mechanic: Hugh McLeod was one of the driving forces in the success of Hawick's fabled 'Green Machine' and proved equally formidable throughout his Scotland career. *Scran*

Right. An underrated figure: Derrick Grant was, for some people, a rugby version of Jock Stein, and he certainly steered his Green juggernaut to unprecedented success in the 1960s and 1970s.

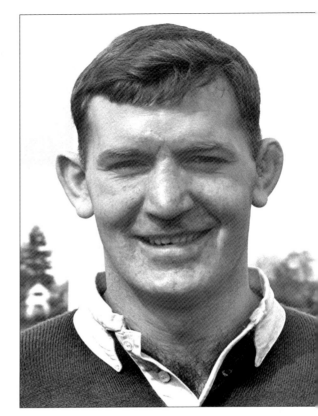

Below. Look at the crowd!: The South were always formidable opponents for touring sides between the 1960s and 1980s and their warriors did themselves proud against South Africa at Netherdale in 1969. The game finished 3-3. *Scran*

Above. Another year, another title: Hawick's players celebrate at Mansfield Park, following the clinching of yet another championship title. *Scran*

Left. Masters at work: the Borders were spoiled for talent when the likes of John Rutherford and Jim Renwick linked up to bewitch, bother and bewilder opponents. *Southern Reporter*

Centre of excellence: Renwick, who was one of the true greats in the history of Borders rugby, unlocks the English defence at Murrayfield in 1980. *Newsquest*

Scrum on down: Roy Laidlaw was one of the best in a veritable conveyor belt of scrum-half talent to emerge from the South, forging a memorable partnership with John Rutherford. *Getty Images*

Left. Substance and style: Rutherford had it all: pace, precision, panache and the precious capacity to weigh up his options in the blink of an eye. *Getty Images*

Sunny Jim: He could be a hard task master, but Jim Telfer relished success as much as anybody and was understandably delighted when his players clinched the Triple Crown against Ireland in Dublin in 1984 before going on to win the Grand Slam against France at Murrayfield. *Getty Images*

Campo follies: The great David Campese was unable to prevent the South from recording a famous 9-6 victory over the Australians in 1984. However, the winger and his colleagues gained revenge by thrashing Scotland a week later on their way to securing a Grand Slam.

Diving for cover: The mercurial Roy Laidlaw orchestrates another attack for the South against Edinburgh in 1986. *Scran*

Above. Stanger than fiction: Scotland were the underdogs when they met England in 1990, but Tony Stanger's famous try, early in the second half, brought them Grand Slam glory at Murrayfield. *Press Association*

Left. A Melrose maestro: Craig Chalmers, so assured, self-confident and mature for a man of 22, was a prime performer during the Scots' march to the 1990 Grand Slam.

Shark bite: He hardly requires a caption, such was the distinctive sight of John Jeffrey, the Scotland and Lions flanker, in full flight – here in the thick of the action at the 1991 World Cup. *Getty Images*

Championship material: Alan Tait's middle name is Victor and the redoubtable centre was one of his country's leading luminaries during their 1999 Five Nations Championship title win. *Fotosport*

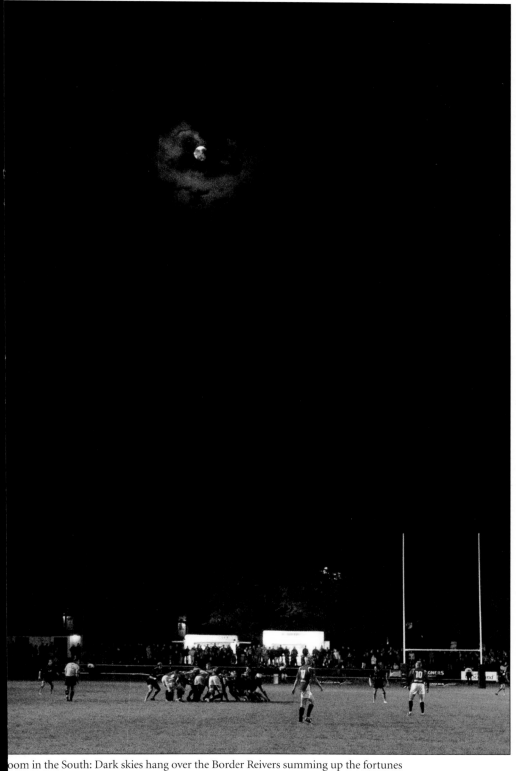

oom in the South: Dark skies hang over the Border Reivers summing up the fortunes
the professional team, who were eventually scrapped by the SRU in 2008. *Fotosport*

April in Paris: There have been few sweeter afternoons than the 36-22 demolition of France in 1999. The Scots ran in five first-half tries and the ubiquitous Gregor Townsend was in the thick of the drama. *Fotosport*

The South rise again: After a gap of nearly 15 years, the South, coached by Craig Chalmers, took on and beat Northumberland in front of more than 2000 fans at Netherdale in December 2009. *Digitalpic*

21st century star: Chris Paterson has appeared in four World Cups for his homeland and became the first otsman to win 100 international caps, when he played against Wales in Cardiff in 2010. *Fotosport*

Melrose heaven: The proud Greenyards club have punched well above their weight in the last 20 years and gained another prize by beating Heriot's in the Scottish Cup final at Murrayfield. *Fotosport*

History makers: Melrose bequeathed the game of Sevens to the world and proved their ability in the abbreviated pursuit when they triumphed at their own Sevens in the spring of 2011. *AB Images Scotland*

one but never forgotten: Bill McLaren might have died in 2010, but the 'Voice of Rugby' has left us
th a library's worth of priceless commentaries and enduring phrases.

On the way up: The beetle-browed Craig Chalmers has successfully made the transition from player to coach and steered Melrose to their first Scottish title for 14 years in 2011. *Fotosport*

Tall (by the standards of Welsh fly-halves), fast, beautifully built and a finely balanced runner, John was, in the early days, completely uninhibited. But he still had to learn how to control a game, because he then lacked the attribute which all great fly-halves have possessed: the ability to put the ball where his forwards want it and to perplex and tantalise opposing full-backs. Realising this, he worked very hard on his kicking, until he became as good and effective a tactical kicker as Scotland and Selkirk have ever had. He was a master of every kick and nobody who saw it has ever forgotten his demolition of the England full-back, Dusty Hare, in the 1984 Calcutta Cup match.

Nevertheless, he remained by instinct and inclination essentially an attacking player and daring runner and, in all, he played 42 times for Scotland. It is easy to measure the scale of that achievement; before him, the most-capped Scottish stand-off was Gordon Waddell, with a mere 18 appearances. Since then, first Craig Chalmers and then Gregor Townsend have left John's record behind them, but there are, of course, so many more international matches nowadays. You can play eight or ten games a year, and more when it is a World Cup one. The plain fact is that, from his first cap in 1979 to his last in 1987, John was never dropped. He was out of the team only when he was injured and Scotland lost all but one of the matches that he missed.

This latter statistic demonstrates the myriad qualities which Rutherford brought to his country's cause. And they were rarely better highlighted than during his involvement with Scotland in the 1984 Five Nations Championship. Quite simply, if the previous year's campaign had been a massive disappointment until the face-saving exercise at Twickenham, this was one of the winters where the cold and the snow seemed immaterial, at least for those who were transfixed by the oval ball. The Scots had absorbed lessons from their trials in New Zealand with the Lions, and they had noticed that their British rivals were deficient in some areas. They were coached by Telfer, a man who was ruthlessly determined to exorcise the demons of that trip, and he was in the final year of his tenure, so this was the ideal moment to set the record straight. And he had assembled a clutch of ferociously competitive and talented forwards, in the mould of David Leslie, John Beattie, Iain Paxton, Derek White and Jim Aitken, the latter of whom was a juddering bulwark in the front row for his country. Then there was Rutherford, restored to rude health, and, at 28, approaching his peak. It was a potent combination on paper and, mercifully, they were equally efficacious when they commenced their title bid. It culminated in one of the great chapters and towering campaigns in Scottish sporting history and much of it was a direct consequence of Border class and power.

As Rutherford told me, this was a year where all the components came together.

When you join up with the Lions and you're Scottish, you tend to be a bit overwhelmed at the start of the trip and you don't have the same confidence as the English and Welsh guys, but then, when you begin training with them, you discover that they aren't actually any better than you. It took a wee while for that to sink in, but there were eight of us on the tour – and the likes of David Leslie didn't even make the party – so we recognised pretty quickly that we didn't have any reason to have an inferiority complex and I remember Roy [Laidlaw] saying to me, on the flight home, that he fancied Scotland's chances in the 1984 championship. We didn't make a big song and dance about it, but, no matter if we were underdogs, we knew – as a squad – that we were capable of beating anybody in the Five Nations and we had France and England at Murrayfield, which is usually the schedule which gives us the best chance of challenging for honours.

That said, though, we wouldn't have won the Grand Slam without Jim Telfer being in charge and I have never strayed from that belief. When you played for Scotland and Jim was the coach, you always thought that you could win, because he worked on everything to the nth degree, he put a huge amount of effort into devising his tactics, and studied the opposition for signs of weakness, and even checked on the weather forecast, in advance of matches. Maybe we take these things for granted nowadays, but Jim was utterly meticulous and methodical and I think it does him a disservice to say that he achieved what he did purely because he was a great motivator. Yes, he *was* that, but he always drew up his plans astutely, got his message across to his players, and he could teach you about technical aspects of rugby and keep you interested and that was because communication was another of his strengths. Derrick Grant was a big influence on anybody who grew up in the Borders, and what he achieved should never be forgotten, but Jim had an aura about him, he was fearless in everything he did, and when he told you in his team talks that you could go out and beat England or France or whoever, you absolutely believed him 100 per cent. Not many coaches have that sort of drive and desire, but it was one of the cornerstones of our success during the whole of the 1984 championship campaign.

The Five Nations crusade commenced with a trip to Wales, who were still smarting from their comprehensive defeat of 1982, but it was one thing to be aggrieved, another thing entirely to translate that into a reversal of fortune. The Scots, buoyed by Telfer, knuckled down to their task with vim and vigour, ignoring the attempts of their opponents to needle them into losing their discipline. The visitors were altogether too potent for their hosts, who crashed to a 15–9 loss which was more emphatic than the result might suggest. The Scots controlled the forward exchanges, with such warriors as Iain Paxton and Jim Aitken scoring tries, although this was undeniably a case of the whole Scotland juggernaut contributing to a merited win. This was the third time in the space of five games that the Scots had dowsed the Dragons, which, considering that the Welsh had only lost three of these contests in the preceding 57 years, reflected the manner in which Telfer and his compatriots were battering down the doors of the status quo. But the SRU's charges recognised that greater challenges lay in store. Next up were England, who could scintillate one day and plumb the depths the next, with their selectors almost constantly unsure of what their best XV was on any particular weekend.

Telfer was aware of the danger of his personnel being complacent. So were his Borders contingent, who numbered 12 out of 20 of the brethren who rolled up their sleeves and proceeded on the path to glory. Rutherford, for his part, a stellar figure in an ensemble which was dominated by belligerent back-row members beating the living daylights out of rivals, clung to his opinion that the Lions odyssey had illustrated that Scotland had nothing to fear from their northern hemisphere adversaries and gradually, bit by bit, he was vindicated in that judgement. This was the 100th meeting of the Auld Enemies, and England would clearly have to rely on their muscular pack, which featured the likes of Maurice Colclough, Steve Bainbridge and Peter Simpson. But it was also a period where their sides could change dramatically between Tests and Telfer appreciated that they were always capable of pulling rabbits out of hats. Rutherford, though, was more upbeat. 'When you are up against a country which has ten or twenty times more players that you, there is never any room to be complacent. But we just thought we were better than them that season. It was actually nothing to do with the baggage which sometimes surrounded this match, but more the fact that we knew all about their players and the Lions tour had demonstrated to us that we were every bit as good as what they had to offer. You never take anything for granted, but we felt pretty optimistic.'

That assessment was amply vindicated by what transpired at Murrayfield. Rutherford, replete with classy touches, kicked with fiendish design; his partner in crime, Laidlaw, bossed, bullied and bothered his frazzled opponents and Telfer's initiative in changing his tactics, given the soggy conditions, simply exposed the one-dimensional nature of England's limited strategy. The Scotland coach opined:

We decided to use Roy and John to kick on to their full-back, Dusty Hare, and we recognised that our scrummaging would be the key in the wet. We played with the normal south-westerly wind in the first half at Murrayfield, and the first try was the result of a ball over the top of the line-out. Paxton hacked it on and David Johnston dribbled on and scored. The tactic of putting pressure on Hare obviously worked, because he missed six penalty goals out of eight.

Our second try is one that sticks out clearly in my mind, because it was an occasion when everything just came together perfectly. England took a 22 drop-out, and the Scots caught it, drove and rucked, then Roy chipped over the ruck and Dusty Hare was caught in possession. Jim Calder ripped the ball from him and the Scottish forwards, with David Leslie and Alan Tomes in the van, rucked perfectly, laid it back, and Roy passed to John, who took it off his toes, drew [Clive] Woodward, and gave a short pass on the burst to Euan Kennedy, who went in at the posts. We won 18–6, but unfortunately, both Euan and Bill Cuthbertson were injured, to be replaced by Jim Pollock, [who, sadly, is one of the forgotten men of that triumphal season] and John Beattie [who isn't!].

Telfer was entitled to feel satisfied with the relative ease of this victory, particularly given the opposition. More tellingly, perhaps, Rutherford guessed that nothing had yet been achieved. And yet, the symbiosis between him and Laidlaw was usually worth the price of the admission money alone. I spoke to both these masters and commanders and they will hopefully forgive me for reproducing their comments in this fashion.

RUTHERFORD: There was pressure, of course there was pressure, because we had beaten two of the major countries in the championship, and suddenly the talk among the fans was all about us winning Triple Crowns and Grand Slams. But, as a player, you honestly never think any further ahead than the next match. Roy and I had built up this relationship and we understood each other and knew what we needed to do in any number of situations. We had the experience at half-back and, at that stage in rugby's history, it was pretty simple. We got most of the ball, and we had to decide what to do with it. If we got it wrong, our team would normally lose, so you had to make the most of the possession. If we got it right, well, we always had a decent chance.

LAIDLAW: John and I had grown up in the Borders, we both had similar backgrounds − both of us had a parent from the West [of Scotland] and one from the Borders, and we were one of three sons − and we understood the other's game from playing together for under-21 sides, from South matches and moving up to Scotland duty, so, by the time we got to 1984, there wasn't much that we hadn't experienced together. Neither of us was ever dropped and we just got on, almost as if we were brothers, and going after the Grand Slam was the sort of challenge which just got the juices flowing in both of us.

RUTHERFORD: What you have to appreciate is the quality of the players that Scotland had at that time. Jim [Telfer] had worked incredibly hard, as had Derrick Grant and Colin Telfer, to take us forward and, more importantly, Jim and the SRU got us into the habit of going on tough tours to the southern hemisphere and, although there might not have been too many results to get excited about on these visits, they sorted out the men from the boys and we knew we had a realistic chance of going all the way in 1984.

LAIDLAW: That was Jim Telfer's master plan, and don't let anybody say otherwise. The majority of the Scotland squad had been together since 1981 and we kept going close and producing the occasional good performance, but we knew we were capable of much better than just one or two wins every term. John was missing from most [three out of four] of the 1983 championship and Jim wasn't there either, and yet we came really close in every match. You could sense that the frustration was swelling up in the squad and when we travelled to New Zealand with the Lions, it just made us even more determined. After all, I went away on that tour for three months with no wages and two young children at home and my family had to rally round to make sure I was able to concentrate on rugby. So you aren't going through the motions in these circumstances.

Understandably, the Scots had built up a significant head of steam and their media profile heightened in the build-up to the meeting with Ireland in Dublin for the Triple Crown. Jim Aitken, the team's grizzled skipper, was a pillar of common sense amid the hubbub and, together with Telfer, they shared the attitude that forecasting is for the foolish. Yet, if the mood in public was one of caution, there was an almost SAS-style approach to this contest in the Emerald Isle. For starters, the SRU's squad switched hotel venues from their normal Dublin locale and stayed well away from the city, in the countryside: this fostered team spirit, increased the sense of mystery over which tactics Telfer might employ, and, according to Rutherford, allowed the players to concentrate on their task, without being waylaid by supporters, no matter how positive the latter might be.

Next up, Telfer pulled a masterstroke. On the day before the match, he showed his squad a video, not of *Rocky* or *Chariots of Fire* or anything else with a positive message, but rather an X-rated rugby exhibition, which involved the South being trounced 30–9 by the All Blacks during the previous autumn. This featured ten of the Scots who were in the line-up which would meet Ireland the following day, and the sight of their efforts being thwarted had the desired effect. Rutherford said later: 'We knew that New Zealand were a tougher proposition than the Irish, but that was an extremely effective wake-up call by the coach. Looking back, it was typical Jim: he always wanted us to learn from our mistakes and the only way we could really do that was to confront them head-on.'

Screening that match was an insightful piece of reverse psychology. It might have backfired with the wrong type of player, but Telfer knew the mettle of his troops and reasoned that they would be inspired by comprehending the areas in which they had to improve. It worked! On a windy afternoon in Dublin, the Scots swept out of the blocks and the Rutherford–Laidlaw axis worked like the sweetest of dreams. The nimble little scrum-half scored a brace of terrific tries in the same corner of Lansdowne Road and duly made that part of the ground his own little piece of turf for posterity. In the midst of a swarming, all-pervasive attacking declaration of intent from the Scots, the referee, Fred Howard, awarded the visitors a penalty try and, almost miraculously considering the Scots' normal anxieties on the road, they went in 22–0 in front at the interval.

The Irish could barely believe what had hit them and, perhaps understandably, the contest petered out thereafter, although Laidlaw had to retire with a head knock which meant that Gordon Hunter, the Selkirk scrum-half, took his place in the second period. But this merely accentuated the influence of the Borders of the Scottish team, because Rutherford was obviously au fait with his Philiphaugh colleague and the pair worked a treat together in the second period, while Scotland wrapped up a comprehensive 32–9 triumph which steered them towards touching distance of a hallowed Grand Slam.

Let's just recap for an instant. Here was a Scotland XV, coached by a Borderer with more than half of the number in their squad similarly from the South. Pedants might point out that Jim Aitken was not born in Gala – even though he played for the Netherdale club – and Iain Paxton was originally from Fife, despite turning out for Selkirk, while David Leslie, a towering performer in these cauldrons of battle, hailed from Dundee. Yet, such considerations should not be allowed to detract from the massive influence which the Borders had on this lustrous team, and, as Rutherford told me, that close-knit camaraderie was pivotal to the sense of *esprit de corps* which Telfer and his assistants had built up. The only question which remained was whether they could repel a formidable French force, whose earlier performances had left the English hooker, Peter Wheeler, describing them as 'unbeatable'. Well, the *Titanic* was talked up as being 'unsinkable'.

As it transpired, the hype in the build-up might have come to naught, but for a couple of factors. Firstly, Rutherford, all style, substance and innocent bravado, was close to his immaculate best. Secondly, France, as they were prone to do on foreign assignations, fell foul of the referee, Winston Jones of Wales, who lost his patience with 'Les Bleus' once they began imagining that the laws of the sport only applied to the other side. The French still led 6–3 at the interval, courtesy of an excellent try from Jerome Gallion, but that slender advantage could and should have been more substantial than it was. And they had committed the cardinal sin of believing that they could beat officialdom. Even the more pessimistic souls in the Murrayfield crowd, men and women who had endured all manner of false dawns and hard-luck stories in past decades, gradually began to fathom that the visitors were spending more time searching for easy targets than focusing on their prime objective in a city where they had grown accustomed to adversity. And the French, once they slip into this frame of mind, can be as volatile as the Borgias on a bad night.

Predictably, they refused to learn the error of their ways. 'Gallion went off with an injury and they just seemed a bit lost after that,' said Rutherford. Telfer, too, had been thinking on his feet and ensured that his prized stand-off received greater protection as the tussle turned in Scotland's favour. David Leslie, one of life's indefatigable warriors, became an increasingly significant figure amid the hostilities and, with Peter Dods landing two penalties, the match was tied at 9–9 and the balance shifted towards the Scots. 'Serge Blanco, the French full-back, was caught under a high ball and driven some way back downfield,' said Telfer, whose analytical skills should not be allowed to disguise how much this game mattered to him. 'The impetus that gave us was crucial and we scored from more or less the next line-out.'

His description rather ignores the frenzy and chaos which surrounded the try, with Colin Deans' put-in gathered by Paxton as the prelude to an ecstasy of fumbling before Jim

Calder seized the touchdown. But ultimately, all that really mattered was that the Scots had seized the initiative and the reliable Dods stretched the lead with his fifth penalty, despite having a badly swollen eye, to make sure that there were no twists in the tale. Scotland had won 21–12 and their personnel marched into the archives with a sinewy refusal to buckle and a Telfer-inspired controlled aggression. It was not the prettiest of victories, but this was never a day for fancy-dans.

What it *did* amount to was a resounding triumph for the leading figures in Borders rugby. Because, whether in the heroics of Dods or Keith Robertson or the cherished half-back pairing of Rutherford and Laidlaw, through to the combatants in the boiler room such as Aitken, Leslie, Colin Deans and Alastair Campbell, Scotland's first Grand Slam for 59 years was a towering affirmation of gritty resolve and collective spirit, allied to intermittent shafts of sparkle and improvisation. A dozen of the Scottish heroes were from the South, and all of the clubs which then comprised the Border League, with the exception of Langholm, had players in the mix. To be fair, there were other stalwarts from outwith the Borders who were a significant part of the success, and it is impossible to do justice to what this squad of players achieved without paying homage to the likes of Iain Milne, Bill Cuthbertson and David Johnston. Yet neither is there any doubt that this prize would not have been secured without the immense contribution of the Borderers, not least Telfer, who was surely entitled a (brief) smile or two, even while he prepared to exit the coaching scene at Murrayfield and return to the educational sector.

From Rutherford's perspective, it was a collective enterprise and this self-deprecating Selkirk man still believes there were more complete displays than those which marked the 1984 success. 'We probably needed to show that we could tough things out when it was necessary and, don't get me wrong, it was fantastic when we beat the French and the whole nation seemed to go crazy for the next few days,' recalls Rutherford. 'But there were other days where we played a lot better. I remember the Calcutta Cup match in 1986, when it was a beautiful afternoon at Murrayfield and everybody in our side – except "The Bear" [Iain Milne], who preferred the conditions to be wet and muddy – relished putting England to the sword [by a record 33–6]. That day, we produced some wonderful rugby, the opposition were overwhelmed by the finish, the crowd was going crazy, and it just made your heart race to be involved in such a spectacle. We didn't win any Grand Slams or Triple Crowns that season, because we lost in Cardiff, but I reckon we produced an awful lot of entertaining, exciting rugby. And that is important.'

This is a prevalent theme with those who were part of Telfer's tribe. Rutherford, one of his country's most stellar performers, was eventually forced to retire through injury at the inaugural World Cup in New Zealand in 1987 and one can only speculate as to the impact which somebody with his gifts would have made in professional rugby. Yet when I asked both him and Laidlaw whether they had ever wondered how their lives might have unfolded if they had been born 25 years later, the two men were typically honest.

'I've thought about quite it a bit in recent years and yes, I suppose that it would have been nice to have made some money from the sport to pass on to my family, but, on balance, the truth is that I loved my time in the game, you can still meet up with former players from all around the world and there is a real rugby family out there, and you simply can't put a value on that,' said Rutherford, while his old partner, Laidlaw, commented: 'I never thought about making money from something I loved. John and I were obsessed with rugby and the question of money never entered my head. Did I feel I missed out on anything? No, not even when I returned to

Jedburgh, after Scotland had played the French in Paris, and had to rewire the public toilets on the Monday. People think it was after Scotland had won the Grand Slam, but it wasn't. If it had been, I probably wouldn't have had to listen to so many people telling me where the Scots had gone wrong!'

That response neatly encapsulates the practical attitude of these serried performers, but there is little doubt that Rutherford, in particular, was a singular maestro, one of the few performers whose presence on the team sheet was sufficient to add a couple of hundred extra fans to the attendance at Philiphaugh, even on the filthiest of January afternoons. As somebody who grew up in an environment where the mention of Hughie McLeod or Derrick Grant or Jim Telfer elicited growls of approval from the most hard-to-please fans, he knew that he had to keep ploughing away on his private quest for perfectionism, but Rutherford has always been one of Scotland's proudest ambassadors.

In which light, it was fitting that 'Rudd' bowed out of rugby with an avalanche of tributes, including, as Allan Massie declared, some from the furthest corners of the globe:

By the middle eighties, John Rutherford was unquestionably the best fly-half in the northern hemisphere and his reputation was such that the name of Selkirk was recognised wherever rugby was played. When he retired, the former England scrum-half, Steve Smith, wrote that he bracketed him along with Barry John and Phil Bennett as the best of the British Isles fly-halves of the 1970s and 1980s.

But John was first and foremost a club man and it was fitting that, almost twenty years after his playing career was ended by injury, Selkirk should celebrate his 50th birthday [in 2005] with a dinner, attended by his old club-mates and former international team-mates and opponents. Tributes poured in from every rugby-playing country, all contributions testifying not only to his great skill and achievement on the rugby field, but also to his quality as a man. One of the best was almost a throwaway line from the New Zealand legend, Stu Wilson.

'The All Blacks knew that John Rutherford could be a big pain in the bum if you let his talent cut loose, so he was always given extra attention.' When New Zealand give an opponent 'extra attention', then you know he is really good.

Rutherford has never lost touch with his origins, nor his old allies from the Grand Slam vintage. As one of life's gentle souls, he was never going to end up taking pot-shots at patsies in a newspaper column and he still dedicates himself to spreading the gospel among the youth in his community. He might be justified in his assertion, uttered with a quiet authority, that the halcyon days of Borders rugby are in the past, because of simple arithmetic. 'The cities have the players and the universities and more and more of our youngsters are heading up there and – this is the important part – they are staying there. So they have the numbers and, in the end, you can't really compete with that.'

Perhaps not. But when this fellow was in his prime, anything seemed possible. With a twinkle and a twist of bravado, allied to the ability to unlock the most solid opposition defences and parade his full repertoire of talents in front of 750 people or 75,000, Rutherford was somebody with genius in his boots. He really was that good.

Chapter Ten

REALITY BITES AND SHARK TALES

ONE OF THE FEW consistent features of Scottish rugby through the decades has been the national team's tendency to flirt with Kipling's twin impostors on a frequent basis. There have been instances where the future has looked bright, only for a saturnine gloom to transcend the optimistic forecasts, and other times when SRU collectives have entered contests as underdogs and performed out of their skins in achieving remarkable wins. It all adds up to the sense that you never really know what to expect from the Scots, and that unpredictability has led to some giddy highs and, more often, depressing lows.

What, for instance, would any forensic analyst make of the period between 1984 and 1986, when a wondrous Grand Slam was immediately followed by a deflating wooden spoon in the following Five Nations Championship, as the prelude to a new breed of Scots casting off their inhibitions and producing some terrific displays in 1986? Or, for that matter, how does one explain the rationale behind the fashion in which a steely group of Borders players defeated the touring Australians in Hawick in 1984, only for many of these same individuals to finish up on the receiving end of an emphatic thrashing when the Wallabies confronted the hosts at Murrayfield? For Saltire-waving spectators, who had long since learned that it is better to travel in hope than expectation – unlike in England and Wales, where victories are demanded by supporters every time their national sides walk out on to the pitch – these fluctuating fortunes simply reflected that the Scots were on a white-knuckle, roller-coaster ride and most fans chose to cling on and relish the journey. But, from a coach's perspective, it must have been as frustrating as getting home early and discovering you have left your keys back in the office, 20 miles away.

During this topsy-turvy period, one could offer a variety of compelling reasons for the Scots' inconsistency. It was a serious blow when Telfer, the architect of so many positive achievements during his four-year tenure, decided to stick by his decision to stand down at the end of the 1984 campaign, while the team was weakened by the retirement of their captain and master motivator, Jim Aitken. These were massive shoes to fill and perhaps, in the circumstances, it was hardly surprising that Colin Telfer – no relation – found himself on the receiving end of some close-fought encounters, while his troops finished bottom of the heap in the championship. It was not that Scotland had suddenly become a bunch of patsies overnight, as the scores highlighted, with them losing their away matches to France and England by 11–3 and 10–7, while the two home tussles with Ireland (15–18) and Wales (21–25) were tight affairs, which could have gone either way with a bounce of the ball here or a lucky deflection there. Yet, in the final analysis, rugby union, whether some of the purists liked it or not, was increasingly becoming a results-driven business – and the inaugural World Cup was looming on the horizon – and thus there was little surprise when Derrick Grant and Ian McGeechan succeeded Telfer.

The latter individual had not been helped by Australia's overwhelming 37–12 victory at Murrayfield in the autumn of 1984. This was in the period before the Wallabies were regarded with quite the same reverence as their southern hemisphere counterparts in New Zealand and South Africa, but it was also a visit which illustrated the emergence of a new generation of wonderfully exciting, spellbinding athletes in the mould of the incomparable David Campese and Mark Ella, Michael Lynagh, Nick Farr-Jones and Matthew Burke, all of whom glistened throughout their trip to Britain. They beat all the home nations, with 19–3, 16–9 and 28–9 victories over England, Ireland and Wales respectively, before they conjured up some amazing feats in Edinburgh, with the elusive Ella, the trickster Campese and the ubiquitous Farr-Jones scoring tries. It was no disgrace for the Scots to capitulate under this onslaught, given the relentless fashion in which their opponents flourished on the power of their personnel and the mastery of Andrew Slack's leadership, they demonstrated that it was no longer the All Blacks who held the copyright to serving up mesmerising interplay between backs and forwards. But there again, Scotland had defeated the Aussies only two years previously Down Under, so it looked as if a significant gap had developed within a very short time. In which event, it is usually the coach and not his players who cops the majority of the flak.

Yet if it was a dispiriting contest in some ways, the match at least afforded an international debut to a man who subsequently became one of the most famous, and instantly recognisable, figures ever to pull on a Scotland shirt. John Jeffrey, another proud Borderer, whose face was familiar even to those who never watched a rugby match from one Five Nations to another, immediately discovered the difference between excelling for Kelso in the Border League and ascending the ladder to Test rugby. But if this was a steep learning curve, Jeffrey absorbed the message quickly and was soon marauding around opponents with the intensity which had first caught the eye of his country's selectors. He had already garnered his nickname following a trip to the West Indies, where his compatriots all developed tans in the sweltering heat, apart from one of their number. 'Everyone was black, except me, of course,' recalls Jeffrey, a fellow with roots in the Borders soil, who is also possessed of a sharp brain, quick repartee, and keen business acumen. 'We were all swimming in the sea and, when I was coming out of the water, somebody shouted out: "Hey everybody, here comes the White Shark."'

There was no need for John Williams' famous musical accompaniment whenever Jeffrey was in the vicinity – he has always been a genial, self-deprecating man away from the pitch – and, despite his torrid baptism to the Test circuit, the versatile back-row forward had thrust himself into the spotlight during the South's triumph over the Wallabies at Mansfield Park. Once again, this contest reflected the adventurous nature of the Border selectors, the majority of whom believed in the truism, 'If you're good enough, you're old enough.' They could have chosen such Grand Slam stalwarts as Iain Paxton and David Leslie to meet the tourists, but instead they plumped for a back trio of Jeffrey, Sean McGauchey and Eric Paxton, who boasted three caps between them at that stage (and the latter pair would never play for Scotland again). Yet, if it was a gamble, it never felt like that to Jeffrey, who relished the opportunity, not least because, almost incredibly, it was the only time in his senior career that he had tasted victory at the Hawick ground.

> The Aussies were reaching the climax of what had been an all-conquering tour for them and this was the only occasion they lost on a Saturday, and it showed what the South could do when they put their minds to it. It was a huge challenge, because Scotland B were playing their Irish counterparts across the water on the same afternoon, and the selectors went with a few pretty untested players, both in the front row and the back row. But it was an awful day, one of those Scottish winter afternoons where the rain keeps pelting down, and our tactics were pretty straightforward: we were to avoid any fancy stuff and launch an aerial bombardment towards [the Australian full-back] Roger Gould and see if we could put him and his team-mates under pressure. We eventually

edged it with Peter Dods kicking three penalties, in response to a couple from Gould, and I had a try disallowed because I was offside – for the first and last time in my career!

Basically, there was a tremendous sense of pride among the Scots and we kept battling all the way to the finish and you should have heard the cheers from the Borders crowd. It maybe wasn't a flamboyant performance – and I can remember one instance where Andrew Ker passed to Jim Renwick, when everybody else was screaming at him to kick it up the field. Well, Jim dropped the ball and you should have seen the look he gave Andrew. There was no more passing after that! But the game plan worked, we won the match and there was a tremendous feeling of satisfaction at the end of a contest like that, because the Australians were a terrific side, full of big powerful forwards and backs with magic in their hands and feet, and they were going flat out to beat us at the end.

So it was a pretty memorable afternoon for the team. Looking back, perhaps it seems surprising that I never won again at Mansfield Park, because Kelso were a successful side whilst I was involved with them – we won the Border League in the 1985–86 season and the Scottish championship in 1988 and 1989 – but it was always incredibly difficult for Border sides to travel to Hawick and come away with a victory, and it didn't seem to matter who was in their side, they just knew what to do to cross the winning line. That was one of the things which I admired most about them: their sheer, intense competitiveness.

Jeffrey was crafted in that same indomitable mould and despite having to battle for his international place at the outset of his Test career, the period between 1986 and 1991 yielded a string of honours, both on the domestic circuit and alongside his compatriots on the wider stage. Yet, in terms of his success with Kelso, it commenced in slightly surreal fashion when the Poynder Park organisation seized the Border League title from

under the noses of their Hawick rivals, when the latter lost a
must-win match against Melrose at the Greenyards by 18–9.
That outcome must have been singularly unexpected, because
the Green Machine had left the championship trophy back at
their own ground, which meant there was no immediate
opportunity for Jeffrey and his Kelso colleagues to get their
mitts on the prize which had eluded their club for the best part
of the previous 50 years.

Nor indeed was the handover completed until the following Monday in slightly surreal circumstances. 'Two days after
the presentation should have been made, a van drew up
outside the offices of M & J Ballantye in the Sheddon Park
Road and a man was seen carrying a large piece of silver in a
plastic bag,' reported one of the local newspapers. 'It could
have been a Co-op bag. We can now state that this was the
Border League trophy and it arrived in a way that not a single
Kelso supporter could ever have wished to see happen again.'
Wags might retort that this was not the only occasion when
Jeffrey had trouble with silverware in his time, but although
Kelso had to wait, that simply made the celebrations all the
sweeter when a clutch of the survivors from the 1936–37
squad convened with the new champions and the champagne
flowed into the night.

These were fevered, frenetic *fun* times for Scottish rugby
and, 25 years on, one can occasionally glance back and
wonder about the effervescence and spontaneity which used
to exist in the sport, prior to the arrival of professionalism and
players being sent on expensive media training courses to
learn how to send journalists to sleep. Jeffrey, for instance,
luxuriated in the sort of work schedule which would have
taxed Hercules, yet, whether toiling assiduously on his farm,
reporting for international duty at Murrayfield with a mustard-keen enthusiasm, or helping his club confrères to retain
their Border title following a hectic schedule during which

seven of their number participated in three matches (against Selkirk, Jed–Forest and Langholm) within the space of four days, there was never any talk of 'burn-out' among these fellows. Instead, it was a case of seizing life by the collar with the same devil-may-care philosophy which exemplified their performances in the boiler room of the back row. 'We had gone through a bit of a lean spell in the 1970s, but we probably peaked in the mid-1980s, when we were runners–up twice in the Scottish championship, in addition to what we achieved in the Border League, and although we eventually realised our goal of winning the national competition, we were probably reaching the end of the road by the time we managed it,' said Jeffrey.

His Kelso colleagues included fellow internationalists Andrew Ker, Alan Tait – who was shortly to depart to rugby league – and the irrepressible Gary Callander, whose dry-as-Nevada response to any difficulties obviously made a big impression on the White Shark:

Gary was one of the deepest thinkers on the game I ever met. As captain, he went on to do most of the coaching at Kelso, and he has probably forgotten more about rugby than I know. He was a big influence on me, but then, there were so many people working hard on the club circuit at that time, either as trainers, or volunteers, or the folk who gave up their Sundays to help out with the youth teams, or 100 other tasks. The players gained the glory, but we recognised that it wouldn't have happened without the efforts of so many other people and I loved that about rugby in the Borders. The supporters, in turn, relished the fact that we were scoring bucket-loads of tries at Poynder Park, but the main stumbling block for so long was, you've guessed it, Hawick. We just couldn't get the better of them, and when we finally did, it was a big weight taken off our backs.

At Scotland level, meanwhile, the new coaching partnership of Derrick Grant and Ian McGeechan presided over a significant upsurge in their team's fortunes during the 1986 Five Nations Championship, which was significant for so many reasons. The first was the dawn of a bright new generation of caps, including such luminaries as the Hastings brothers, Gavin and Scott, David Sole and Finlay Calder, who made their debuts together in the narrow victory over France at Murrayfield and who would all – with the exception of Scott – subsequently go on to captain their country. With memories of the '84 Grand Slam still fresh in the supporters' memories, the SRU's finest were not far from repeating that achievement, recording one-point victories over both the French and the Irish, and famously thrashing England by a record 33–6 margin. The only blemish was the 22–15 loss in Cardiff and even there, the visitors scored three tries to one and might have amassed more if the officials had enjoyed access to modern technology on two occasions when the relentlessly effective Sole seemed to have burrowed over the Welsh line.

It was a positive campaign, nonetheless, but, as usual with the Scots, any semblance of sustained success proved as illusory as the eponymous village in *Brigadoon*. During the next 18 months, they stuttered in the Five Nations, beating Wales and Ireland at home, but coming a cropper on their travels, albeit narrowly in a 28–22 thriller with the French, and in disappointingly anticlimactic fashion, with a poor performance against a far from vintage England side, who prevailed by 21–12. I was at the latter match, surrounded by a group of beer-swilling Sweet Charioteers, whose noisy antics may have jaundiced my memory of the contest, but one thing did shine through the fug of cigarette and pipe smoke which wafted around me, and that was the home fans' grudging admiration for the incessant work rate of Jeffrey and Calder, who sniped at their rivals and snaffled possession in the most inauspicious of circumstances, though ultimately to little avail. This set the tone for future tussles between these Auld Enemies, with both teams apparently as determined to stop the other playing, as they were concerned about their own performances. And though the English eventually tired of bumping into warriors in Jeffrey's mould and accused them of being 'scavengers', this was surely a case of pots and kettles, considering their own lumpen tactics and one-dimensionalism.

In any case, JJ did not require anybody else to appraise his qualities. An honest individual – when he was not pushing the offside law to snapping point – he refused to get carried away by the 1986 results and genuinely seemed more disappointed with the Scots' campaign in the following year's tournament. 'We never thought that we had missed out on anything, because we lost our second game [against Wales] and I think most of us knew we had been a bit lucky to beat the French, so three wins out of four was probably as much as we deserved in 1986,' said Jeffrey. 'It was a bit different in the season after that, because we believed we had it in us to win a Triple Crown. But we got our build-up wrong against England and it didn't help that we met them in April rather than January [the original fixture was cancelled, because of heavy snow]. All in all, we were frustrated with how we played, because we knew that we were better than we showed.'

It was, though, an important year for another reason: at last, the union authorities had laid the foundations for a global competition and the inaugural World Cup took place in New Zealand. Once again, frustration reigned among the Scots, as they endured a now-familiar pattern of flirting with success before being eliminated by New Zealand, who went on to lift the prize for the first and, thus far, only time in the All Blacks' history.

There were several mitigating circumstances for their problems. John Rutherford, who was still the team's pivotal influence and talismanic figure, seriously injured his knee during an unofficial tour in Bermuda, and despite recovering to start the match against France, broke down during the first quarter of an hour of that encounter and bade adieu to his Test career. Earlier in the year, John Beattie, a marauding presence whose pacy power might have been ideally suited to the hard pitches of the southern hemisphere, had been crocked amid the Twickenham debacle and several of the Scots who did make the journey to the Land of the Long White Cloud, including the illustrious Hawick duo, Colin Deans and Alan Tomes, had reached the last few miles of the long and winding road.

Yet when the Scots drew 20-apiece with France, Gavin Hastings missed a last-minute conversion from the touchline which would have avoided his side meeting the All Blacks in the quarter-finals and these hard-luck stories kept afflicting Scotland for much of the next two years: a period which saw Jeffrey and Dean Richards take the Calcutta Cup for an impromptu tour of Edinburgh, as the prelude to the Kelso man receiving a draconian six-month ban from the sport. That incident prompted much tut-tutting and tabloid titters, but it was an irrelevance in the grand scheme of things and even nowadays, when many internationalists sip mineral water at their post-match dinners, there still remain others who are not happy unless they are driving golf buggies down the wrong motorway lane. At worst, what Jeffrey and Richards did was damage an old cup. Richards, who escaped with a slap on the wrist, has gone on to commit much more serious damage to rugby's reputation amidst the 'Bloodgate' saga, whereas Jeffrey is one of the straightest arrows anybody will ever meet.

Even in the midst of the controversies and regular teddies-out-of-prams tantrums between the Auld Enemies, Borderers were at the centre of the action, for better or worse. In 1989, Keith Robertson, one of the heroes of the Grand Slam five years previously, courted headlines of a different variety when he was the only Scot to participate in a so-called 'rebel' tour of South Africa, designed to celebrate the centenary of that country's rugby governing body. Critics accused him of lining his own pockets and offering a balm to apartheid, while the player himself – and he was not the only Caledonian icon to be approached – argued that his career was approaching its end and he had never been to the Republic, so where was the harm in him joining up with a band of mostly English personnel for a few meaningless matches? Moral considerations did not matter any more to the participants than they did to Mike Gatting and his fellow England cricketers, who embarked on a similar trip, which turned into a disastrous public relations exercise for both the players and the beleaguered South African regime, whose racist policies were already beginning to disintegrate under the weight of isolation and international pressure. Interestingly, though, another Scot, who later gained iconic status as a member of the 1990 Grand Slam team, told me when the news broke about Robertson: 'Oh, the Springboks have been in touch with me as well. They offered me £35,000 to take part, but I told them it wasn't enough. They would have to double that amount or pay my mortgage to persuade me to get on the plane to South Africa.' It was another time, another place.

Jeffrey, who emphatically *was not* that person, served his ban and returned with his trademark bonnie brio mercifully intact, even as he and a string of other Border stalwarts were included in the Lions party which journeyed to Australia in 1989, under the captaincy of Finlay Calder, in what developed into another watershed experience for Scottish rugby. The squad featured nine Scots, including the precocious Borders half-back pairing, Craig Chalmers of Melrose and Gary Armstrong of Jed-Forest, and there were also places for Gala's Peter Dods and Derek White and Jeffrey, next to the Hastings siblings, Sole and Calder. Looking back through these pages, one of the refrains which struck me was how many members of the

South contingent, including some of the greatest of their or any other generation – individuals in the mould of John Rutherford and Colin Deans – had spoken about their feelings of inferiority or dearth of confidence, in comparison with their English and Welsh rivals. Yet, when I asked Jeffrey about this phenomenon, he told me matters had changed in the build-up to that Lions odyssey.

> Maybe it used to be true that the reputations of some of the great Welsh and English players meant they had an intimidating presence on those around them, who weren't as accustomed to winning all their matches and battling for Triple Crowns and Grand Slams every season. But, by the time of the '89 Lions trip, we had the two Hastings brothers and Chalmers and, believe me, these guys never felt inferior to anybody on a rugby field in their lives. When we went to Australia, with Finlay in charge, we knew we had every bit as much right to be there as anybody else from the other home nations and, if anything, the way the tour panned out, with Finlay doing a terrific job in rallying his team after they lost the first Test [30–12 in Sydney], and helping us win the next two [19–12 in Brisbane and 19–18 in Sydney] proved that the Scots were capable of succeeding at the highest level – and the Australians in 1989 were very close to being at the highest level, and they would go on to lift the World Cup just two years later. We had a debrief at the end of the campaign and we came to the conclusion that we were as good as any of the others on the tour and we probably had a better work ethic than the rest. It made us, if not confident, then certainly positive, [and we felt that] we could make an impression in the next championship.

Sensibly, there was little ballyhoo or bravado from Scotland in the build-up to the 1990 Five Nations event; the Scots, let's not forget, have always preferred the tactic of guerilla warfare to invasions. And yet, there were qualities and special ingredients mixed through the team, and the Borders influence was conspicuous, from the callow potential of the twin 21-year-olds, Chalmers and Tony Stanger, through to the 23-year-old pocket battleship in the scrum-half berth, otherwise known as Gary Armstrong, the gnarled experience of the Selkirk winger Iwan Tukalo, and the back-row brigade, in the formidable shape of Jeffrey, Derek White and Derek Turnbull. Only 16 Scots took part in the whole championship and seven of them hailed from the South of the country, with another three – Paul Burnell, Chris Gray and Damian Cronin – based in England. When you throw into the equation the return of Jim Telfer, tutoring and terrorising in equal measure, it becomes clear that this was a Grand Slam written large in Border blood.

It probably helped, as well, that the bookmakers fancied Will Carling & Co for the title in advance of the competition. As Allan Massie wrote in *The Scotsman*:

Nobody expected great things of the 1990 side. There were doubts about the quality of the front five in the scrum, although Sole was an outstanding player in the loose. Moreover, it seemed certain that England would be the team of the season. They had an immensely powerful scrum, and dangerous backs, among them Jerry Guscott, the outstanding attacking centre in Britain, and Rory Underwood, soon to become England's record try-scorer. Scotland won their first three matches [defeating Wales, France and Ireland by 13–9, 21–0 and 13–10 respectively], however two might as easily have been lost. In contrast, England seemed masterful in their three victories [and demolished Wales and Ireland 34–6 and 23–0 in the process], so they came north for the Grand Slam decider as firm favourites.

But, of course, that counted for naught once the hostilities had commenced. During the last 20 years I have spoken to all the Borderers who played their part, and what shone through was their inner conviction that they could seize the day. Armstrong, the quiet bulldozer, noticed the English players' wives being interviewed on television. 'They were just so confident that they wouldn't just win, but win easily.' Chalmers, who never lacked self-belief, observed England's pre-match preparations and noticed that, however outwardly confident they might have appeared, there were signs of jitters for those who cared to look. Jeffrey was working on his farm in the build-up and lost count of the number of people who stopped to wish him and the team good luck. 'The match definitely caught the public's imagination. But all the pressure was on England, because of the way they had hammered opponents in the previous games.' Tukalo and Stanger, the wingers, knew they would be facing men with more glittering reputations, but that merely stiffened their resolve. 'I just wanted the match to begin I was so excited,' said Stanger, whose Hawick upbringing had brought him close attention from Bill McLaren. And, as for Telfer, the contest was being staged on his 50th birthday. What better way for him to celebrate than by recording another slice of history for the chronicles, in tandem with McGeechan, his ally through thick and thin as the years rolled by?

Even at this distance, the memories are indelible of the Scots' slow, purposeful march into the frenzied Murrayfield cauldron, of the manner in which they charged at their opponents like Daniel Day-Lewis in *Gangs of New York*, of Chalmers, cool-as-you-please, pushing his side into the lead with a brace of penalties, of Guscott momentarily sparking panic in the home rearguard, of Armstrong feeding on to Gavin Hastings as the prelude to the latter hacking ahead and Stanger touching the ball down, of the frantic English efforts to retrieve the situation, of Jeffrey and Calder running themselves into the ground. By the last few moments, it was almost unbearable to keep watching and yet utterly compelling at the same time. And then, it was over; the Scots had triumphed 13–7 and the rest of the evening passed by in a blur of strangers across Edinburgh and the rest of Scotland toasting a victory which was as deserved as it was unexpected.

Ever since it happened, the revisionists have had a field day. Brian Moore, the so-called 'Pitbull', recently claimed that hatred for Margaret Thatcher and the Poll Tax had fuelled the Scottish performance, which was news to those of us who were actually there. His remarks elicited a mixture of incomprehension and laughter when I put them to the likes of Craig Chalmers, who simply described it as an exercise in straw-clutching. So too, the English duly inflicted their revenge, both in the following year's semi-final of the World Cup at Murrayfield, where Hastings missed a sitter of a short-range penalty in the closing stages, raising the question of why Chalmers was not still taking these pressure kicks, and in every meeting between the two countries for the remainder of the decade.

Surely it was more logical to scrutinise the hotbed of rugby in which men such as Chalmers, Armstrong, Jeffrey and Stanger grew up and learned their craft, and reach the conclusion that an occasion such as the 1990 Grand Slam decider was precisely the sort of environment where Border players would thrive. After all, whether they hailed from Hawick or Kelso, Gala or Melrose, these fellows had been pitched into battle with their local adversaries week in, week out, in a milieu where missing a tackle or spilling a pass could earn them the derision of their communities and their Border rivals for the rest of the season or, in a few extreme cases, the remainder of their lives. Competitiveness was in their DNA and that desire to scale fresh heights and pursue new challenges was much more relevant to their success in 1990 than any cooked-up conspiracy theories about Thatcherism or the alleged negative lyrics of 'Flower of Scotland', which preoccupied the likes of Carling, Guscott and Moore for too many years.

Telfer, a proud socialist with no particular fondness for the Scottish anthem, summed up the reason for his compatriots' victory and it essentially boiled down to the collectivism and crunching self-sacrifice of the body which they had exhibited on that manic March day, more than any non-rugby issues. 'The first thing that registered with me, and it is still a great memory, was Fin Calder taking a free kick near the halfway line, and driving straight into the English: classic position, what I called number-one position – ball gripped under the arm, legs strong, staying upright, holding off the English,' declared the seasoned coach. 'The whole Scottish pack came in behind him and they drove the English back 15 to 20 metres. And whoof! The crowd noise just lifted into the sky, the hair went up on the back of my neck, and Scotland were on the move.'

Jeffrey was similarly combative, determined not to countenance a single backward step, and the frustrations which had built up on all those unsuccessful trips to Mansfield Park with Kelso and Twickenham with Scotland simply made him doubly committed to the cause. There was never a trace of anything underhand or devious in his make-up: on the contrary, from the moment Jeffrey made his debut in 1984 to the match where he bowed out – following a hard-fought 13–6 defeat to the All Blacks in the World Cup third-place play-off in Cardiff in 1991 – he was somebody who could be relied upon to offer everything he possessed for the thistle. As a farmer, he was also acquainted with the cyclical nature of things, and appreciated that there would be more days where the Scots lost than won, so they were entitled to enjoy their triumphs all the more.

In the modern era, as Jeffrey continues to serve his country at the IRB, and rugby is in danger of becoming sterile attritional fare, it is an attitude with an added resonance.

Chapter Eleven

THE MELROSE MIRACLE-MAKERS

A T THE END OF every summer, in the first half of the 1990s, sporting affairs in Scotland settled into a familiar pattern for those of us who beavered away on the non-football beat at *Scotland on Sunday*. There would be previews to write, interviews to conduct and forecasts to make, in advance of the start of the new club rugby season, and it was always a brave person who wagered against Melrose lifting whatever silverware was on offer. This might have been predictable if we had been dealing with one of Scotland's leading city sides, bolstered by a significant catchment area, but, instead, we were highlighting the plethora of achievements of a club which was based in a small town of only 1,500 people, and yet one which churned out a string of richly-talented internationalists, with an instinctive pride in their Border origins, and a golden team spirit at the Greenyards.

The journey down to the picturesque location was always a treat, as were the regular meetings with the indefatigable club secretary, Stuart Henderson, a little buzz-bomb of energy and passion for everything in the rugby domain, but principally his beloved Melrose and how they would have to battle harder with every passing season. This was a man who remembered the days in the 1970s when they had twice suffered relegation from the top flight, and were accustomed to being trounced by Hawick and Gala whenever these derby rivals met in the Scottish championship or the Border League. Stuart, who passed away tragically young, was one of life's generous fellows who always fought his team's corner, and that industrious attitude filtered all the way through the club, from the committee room downstairs into the changing facilities, where a bunch of gifted players prepared to weave magic and forge their own historic trail.

It helped, naturally enough, that this 90s collective was coached by Jim Telfer, with Rob Moffat as his assistant, while the squad contained international stars of the past, present and future, whether it was Keith Robertson, a veteran of the 1984 Grand Slam, or Craig Chalmers, a star of David Sole's team which famously defeated England six years later, or Bryan Redpath and Carl Hogg, or Doddie Weir, Graham Shiel and Steve Brotherstone. As the winters passed, other distinguished names joined the ranks, including Peter Wright, Craig Joyner, Rowen Shepherd and Derek Stark, and there were afternoons in the little community where 15 or 16 internationalists would be battling for supremacy in front of crowds of over 5,000 supporters, in recognition of the standard of rugby on offer.

Perhaps we should strive to place their exploits in perspective, if only because it is virtually impossible to imagine that any other Scottish club will ever replicate the litany of stunning performances and consistent quality which this generation of players orchestrated over a prolonged period. The seeds of their success were sown when many of the emerging stars participated together in the Crichton Cup – which was a hotbed of youthful gusto and ferocious competition for places – as the prelude to forcing their way into the second XV and subsequently staking their claim for selection in the side which improved with every passing season after finishing third in the national championship during the 1987–88 campaign. Melrose's first major breakthrough happened when they secured the title in 1990, in what developed into a serried swansong for their veteran captain, Robertson. Then, buoyed by the realisation that they had assembled a squad which boasted oomph in the pack, panache among the backs and a burning determination and rare *esprit de corps*, Telfer and Moffat steered their charges through their halcyon period. They collected Scottish titles in 1992, 1993 and 1995, in addition to five Border League crowns, as the prelude to dominating the inaugural Tennent's Premiership in 1996 and advancing into their *annus mirabilis* in 1997, when they simply gorged on trophies, winning the Premiership, Scottish Cup, Border League and the prestigious Melrose Sevens. And all this in a Dibley-style setting, whose verdant tranquility was only disturbed when Telfer started barking out instructions to the men with union ingrained in their souls.

At the outset of their triumphal march, Melrose were forced to dig deep on a regular basis, such as during their 14–3 success over Jed-Forest in 1990, where they were pushed all the way by their Borders rivals. But gradually, as the players settled into a groove and gelled together, they acquired the knack of closing out opponents, either at home or on their travels, beating GH-K 27–16 to secure the spoils in the 1992 Scottish championship, and following that up with another nerve-shredding 16–7 success over Currie en route to their title objective in 1993. By this stage, it was evident that their initial victories were only part of a wider project, and although Melrose occasionally toiled on heavy pitches in the worst winters, they were unstoppable in pretty much every other regard.

In so many ways, Melrose were trailblazers, whose officials were rather more interested in the trail than the blazers. Their players travelled to South Africa in 1994 and visited Robben Island, where Nelson Mandela had been imprisoned for almost three decades, and several of their squad members actually sat in his cell and wondered how any human being could have maintained his spirit in such cramped confinement for so many years. A few days later, they took on Villager, the Republic's oldest club, and beat them 20–19 at Newlands in front of a crowd of over 30,000 people, with the effervescent Gary Parker landing the decisive kick in the dying moments. Even on the cusp of their team being broken up by professionalism, Melrose locked horns with Newcastle Falcons and the visiting Sir John Hall and Rob Andrew were forced to watch the action in bewilderment while the Borders contingent amassed a 26–12 lead against their rivals, before they were eventually pegged back to a still-creditable 26–26 draw. Here, surely, was compelling evidence that Scotland's clubs could adapt to the pay-for-play era. And then, almost as quickly as success had arrived, the team was cast to the wind, their personnel joining the South district or moving to England, and the opportunity to advance was gone.

Nonetheless, this is not the time for gloomy rumination, but a chance to explore how Melrose made such a fantastic impact on the Scottish game and the wider rugby community. After all, in the intervening period, several of their number have moved into coaching with auspicious consequences, not least Chalmers, who has instilled a hard-nosed professionalism in the Melrose championship-winning class of 2011, Shiel, who is currently in charge of the Scotland Sevens set-up, Redpath, who is the head coach at English Premiership giants Gloucester (where Carl Hogg mentors the forwards), and Moffat, who went on to gain further honours at Edinburgh and is now employed by the SRU. This was not some happy coincidence or a process which occurred by accident. Instead, as Chalmers, the 60-times-capped stand-off told me, it was a masterpiece of detailed planning.

We all grew up together and took part in the Crichton Cup, which was fought out between the local villages in the Borders, and there was just this tremendous sense that Melrose mattered and that rugby was at the heart of the community. You could see it in the sheer number of youngsters who came through the system at the same time; there was myself, Bryan [Redpath], Graham [Shiel], Robbie Brown, whose father and grandfather and great-grandfather had all played for the club, Carl [Hogg], Scott Aitken, Gary Parker, Steve [Brotherstone], Doddie [Weir] . . . the list just went on and on. Jim Telfer was in charge and his influence was massive. We were like sponges with him: we soaked up the knowledge and absorbed every bit of information he had to pass on, and the whole culture at the Greenyards was that we had to improve our work ethic, our mental attitude, our physical strength . . . pretty much everything, if we wanted to win.

Rob Moffat was also important and he and Jim had a 'Good Cop, Bad Cop' routine – Jim was the 'Bad Cop', by the way! – but it wasn't just about the coaching, because we wouldn't have won so many titles if we had simply trained together and then all headed off in different directions. Instead, we got to know one another, worked out what made the others tick, talked about rugby and life in general, and it helped create a situation where we could be very critical with ourselves, because we all trusted one another.

It pretty much became our lives. We used to train on Mondays and Tuesdays, and we would be given some free time on Wednesdays, but I ended up doing some kicking practice and others went to the gym, then we were back at training on Thursdays and we met up on Fridays to chat about our opponents the next day, work out how they might play and what we could do to cause them problems, and if that sounds serious, it wasn't – we would have a laugh and chat and keep in touch with what everybody was doing. After the match, we would go out for a few beers, then we would head down to the club on Sundays and Jim would have us working out and running it out of our systems.

It was a fantastic time in all our lives. There were no distractions, no mobile phones, or Playstations or Xboxes; we just loved playing rugby, and when you start winning games and chasing championship titles, your confidence builds and you believe you can achieve anything. I remember when we beat Jed-Forest to clinch our first title in 1990, it was just a few weeks before Scotland won the Grand Slam, and it was Keith Robertson's final game. There were thousands of spectators packed into the ground and they were really proud of what we had achieved and it made us more committed to doing it again. In fact, if I'm being totally honest, we should probably have won a couple more titles than we did, though you can't win every time. But we did come pretty close for a while.

Looking back, 1997 was a pretty emotional time for me, because my dad [Brian] died of a heart attack, while he was watching me play for Melrose against Hawick at Mansfield Park and it was obviously a terrible shock and you don't get over these things quickly. But he loved rugby, and he was incredibly supportive of me, and that was the final season before we all started drifting away to other clubs. I'll never forget our last game together – at the end of that championship campaign – against Watsonians where the kick-off had to be delayed by 15 or 20 minutes, because there were so many people trying to get into the stadium. Nowadays, it might sound unlikely, when you think how attendances at Scottish club matches have generally fallen significantly, but we were used to performing in front of 5,000, 6,000, even 8,000-strong crowds. There was still a genuine buzz around the Greenyards, it was a cracking game, which we eventually won by a 20-point margin. But we looked around at the finish and we pretty much knew it was goodbye.

Telfer's involvement in this process cannot be overstated. He had assumed the coaching responsibilities, at the club where he had made his name, in 1988 and between then and 1994, when he became the SRU's director of rugby, the transformation in their fortunes was extraordinary. Indeed, one estimate has it that Telfer's winning record during his six-year stint added up to a tally of 150 victories and three draws in 182 matches, culminating in a success rate of 80 per cent, which is the sort of achievement coveted by any coach in any sport. There were few pleasantries involved in his methodology and woe betide any of the players who imagined that they could go on a bender and escape the dominie's beady eye. Yet the litany of exploits and their cumulative effect testified to how impressively his charges responded to Telfer. The Melrose and Scotland scrum-half, Bryan Redpath, explained it succinctly:

I will never forget when he used to take us for training on Sunday mornings. There would always be somebody or other throwing up, having taken a bit too much beer the night before. Jim would lay into him about standards and, more than once, he was asked to tone down his language, as people left the church beside the ground [at the Greenyards]. But I knew that his sole motivation was to make me and my team-mates better, to keep pushing us to discover new levels, and ultimately to win.

I remember on the day Scotland were leaving for the World Cup [in 2003], I first went along to a birthday party with my son, Cameron. It was for his friend, Harvey Ferguson, the son of Jason and grandson of Sir Alex Ferguson. Alex told me he remembered hearing Jim Telfer had once said to his players: 'You are not just doing this for your team-mates, you are doing this for your country.' He said that he really liked that quote and I can remember thinking: 'You are just like him.' Two great Scotland coaches.

It was one thing to expect discipline and focus on the international stage. But the most notable feature of the manner in which Melrose responded to their newly-acquired status as Scotland's leading club in the early 1990s was the lofty standards the players set for themselves, both on and off the pitch. They were a diverse group: Chalmers, chirpily confident, in-your-face, and blessed with a steely streak, was never going to win any popularity contests, and cheerfully admitted as much to his interrogators, but when we used to turn up at the Greenyards in the middle of winter with a last-minute interview request, he would stand patiently, answering all manner of inquiries and responding to the phalanx of photographers' great lie – 'Just one more . . .!' – with a commendable patience and appreciation of what the media required, whereas his football counterparts at Rangers and Celtic would have flounced away with a show of petulance inside a few minutes. Basically, Chalmers is a winner, a hard taskmaster, with what Scots tend to describe as a 'guid conceit' of his abilities, but he never asks his players to do anything which he did not once do himself. He had this to say on the subject:

Whether I am popular or not isn't going to change my approach. I have made mistakes and I have learned. I have changed as a coach and I will always be learning, because that is part of life.

But I am passionate about the game and want the best for me, my team, my club, and tend to say it as I see it. I am not always right, of course I'm not, but as long as you listen to other people's opinions, you are entitled to have a view of your own. Growing up in the Borders, I know what it is like to suffer abuse from rival teams, but you just use it to motivate yourself and your team. The diehards, who call me names during a match, often come up to me in the bar afterwards, say hello, and slap me on the back. That's the way it has always

been in the Borders and, whether you are connected to
Melrose, Gala, Hawick or the other clubs, I hope that passion
for the game never disappears.

There is a soupçon of Derrick Grant and a touch of Telfer in
this philosophy. Redpath, for his part, was tough as old boots,
somebody whose unshirking approach appealed to his mentors, and a character who always exuded the impression that
he would make a good coach in the future. Shiel, modest to a
fault, seemed almost embarrassed to be the subject of any press
attention, while Doddie Weir revelled in the spotlight and
never replied with one word where he could fit an exhilarating chapter into the conversation. As for Gary Parker, the
former Heart of Midlothian footballer who later turned out in
American football for the Scottish Claymores, those successful
seasons in the spotlight at the Greenyards were among the
most priceless in his life, as he explained to me.

I can remember having a chat with Stuart Henderson after we
had won our third or fourth championship title and he turned
to me and remarked: 'I don't think you boys realise what you
are doing – but you are making history!' And he was right. It
was a magic time, and it wasn't just at Melrose, but whenever
we travelled to Boroughmuir or Dundee HSFP or Stirling
County, the crowds were there in their thousands and it was
inspiring. They wanted to beat us, of course, but because we
had grown up in these atmospheres in the Border League, the
hostility usually made us play better.

Jim was a big part of the success, and I was very fortunate
because, wherever I went in sport, I found myself working
with excellent coaches, whether it was Sandy Jardine in
football or Jim Criner in gridiron. I actually believe there
are a lot of similarities between Alex Ferguson and Jim Telfer,
because both men had the ability to educate their players and

it's no surprise to me that a lot of the guys Alex worked with at Aberdeen, such as Alex McLeish, Eric Black and Mark McGhee, have become good coaches, while it has been the same with the Melrose players who were mentored by Jim Telfer.

Yet my abiding memory from that period is how well we all got on. We could argue, we could fall out, we could fling punches at one another in the heat of the moment, and then it would all blow over, and we would be good mates again in a few seconds. I think any good side has to have that streak of nastiness . . . no, that's the wrong word, ruthlessness, and there was also a fierce amount of competition among the boys. We battled for everything: if somebody threw an apple core into the bucket and it missed and fell on the floor, there would be seven of us rushing to pick it up and be the first to get it in the bin. And that had started from the days when we were all kids, so it was just how we were, who we were, and something else that shouldn't be forgotten is how well Melrose was run in those days, between the slick organisation of the annual Sevens and the way that nothing was left to chance by the committee people and men such as Stuart Henderson. When we nearly beat Newcastle in 1996, I heard Sir John Hall asking Rob Andrew: 'How can amateurs get the better of professionals?' But, to be honest, I never thought of Melrose as being in any way an amateurish club: you would never have used that word in connection with Jim Telfer or Rob Moffat and I am convinced that the same remarks apply to Chick [Chalmers], Basil [Redpath] and the rest of the squad in the 1990s.

The regret is that we headed down the wrong [district] route in 1997 and thereafter and I sometimes wonder what might have happened if the Scottish clubs had taken the bull by the horns. Because, it's all very well for the critics to say that the likes of Melrose didn't have the money to become a professional club, but we never gave it a chance and that is the model which has worked almost everywhere else in the northern hemisphere. In fact, if we had done down the club route, I personally think we would be talking about live Scottish games being screened on Sky at the moment. But it didn't happen, we headed in a different direction and I can't say that it has worked for many in our game.

It remains one of the more perplexing ironies of the Melrose saga that Telfer, the same man who masterminded most of their successes, was also the individual who fought the hardest to prevent them from embracing professionalism when the IRB sanctioned the latter principle in 1995. He argued that he was acting from the best of motives, believing that there simply was not the money for clubs such as Melrose, Boroughmuir, Stirling County and Glasgow Hawks to contemplate searching for potential sponsors and philanthropic backers to fund the pay-for-play era. And yet, the consequence of his alternative strategy – the creation of a centrally-controlled district policy, which has thus far cost the SRU more than £100m, and which nearly bankrupted the governing body a decade ago – has patently disillusioned the majority of Scottish rugby supporters, and pulled the rug from under the feet of the clubs, who were never properly consulted during the union's rush to hand out contracts to scores of players in the late 1990s.

Certainly, as Parker observed, it was hardly as if the grass roots game at the height of Melrose's heroics was in poor health. If anything, it was flourishing in the South more than at any time since the boom of the 1950s, and it was difficult to believe that a Borders club select could have fared any worse than the South ensemble who were thrashed to within an inch of their lives by the All Blacks in 1993. Parker continued:

When we came up against Watsonians in 1997, and secured a 37–17 victory in a really tough match, we had seven or eight Scotland internationalists and they had guys like Jamie Mayer, Jason White, Derrick Lee and Tom Smith, so it was scarcely as if the fans were being served up second-rate rugby. The crowds were still trying to get into the Greenyards five and ten minutes after the scheduled kick-off and that told you a lot about the demand and the atmosphere was fantastic. That is what I remember about my time at Melrose; a load of brilliant matches, where we were pushed all the way, but we had this genuine belief that, whatever the scoreline, we would find somebody who would turn things round for us. It didn't always work in our favour, but it was a terrific adventure and the depth of talent around the club at that stage was remarkable.

In the end, whatever the rights and wrongs of the matter, Doddie Weir moved to Newcastle Falcons, Redpath agreed terms with Sale Sharks and Chalmers shone with Harlequins, Worcester and Pertemps Bees, while the majority of the others from their town with aspirations to playing professional rugby hitched their stars to the Scottish district wagon train, which was soon careering towards a sporting Grand Canyon. Yet, while the ensuing years were painful for some people, there was no faulting the decisions of men such as Weir, who told me they had livelihoods and careers to think about.

Obviously, it was a wrench to leave Melrose, because the club had been part of my life for so long and we were such a close-knit bunch of lads. My father and brother actually played for Gala, but I used to go horse-riding with a boy called Sandy Fairbairn, who invited me along to a youth training night at the Greenyards and the rest, as they say, is history. When professionalism first arrived, I have the feeling Scotland's clubs initially believed they could make the transition and hang on to us, but when it became clear that wasn't going to happen, we had to look wherever we could to find a new challenge.

And personally, going to Newcastle was great experience. One of the things which always struck you about playing for Melrose was how there were internationalists scattered throughout the team, but making the switch to Kingston Park put that in perspective. When I was down there, we had the likes of George Graham and Pat Lam, Dean Ryan and Peter Walton in our pack and when you looked at the talent in the backs . . . well, it was different class. There was Gary Armstrong at No 9, Rob Andrew at stand-off, and some youngster called Jonny Wilkinson – I don't know what happened to him! – hot on his heels, whilst you had men of the calibre of Alan Tait, Tim Stimpson, Va'aiga Tuigamala and Tony Underwood waiting to do their stuff out wide. It was fantastic and the atmosphere around the Falcons was incredible at the time. We won the championship, the Tetley Bitter Cup, and the crowds flocked along in their thousands. So it was definitely an experience which I wouldn't have missed for the world.

None of which means I wasn't sad about leaving Melrose, given how much I owed to Jim [Telfer] and Rob [Moffat] and the buzz we got from going on the trophy-winning run in the nineties. And, even today, regardless of how much rugby has changed, I still get a thrill whenever I go along to the Melrose Sevens and meet up with the old gang. None of us has really changed, we can still exchange banter, and show our kids the photographs from the days when we used to be slim young athletes! There were friendships formed at that time which will never be broken and that was one of the most positive things about the old days: you knew everybody at the club and you were all in the same boat as them, doing it for the sheer love of the sport, and nothing else. But rugby has moved on.

Stuart Henderson, with typical candour, remarked to me, shortly before his death in 2004, that he was 'immensely saddened' by what had happened to his club – at that stage, attendances had plummeted dramatically from the zenith of the mid-1990s – but it was a measure of the pride which men in his mould derived from their team's glorious spell in the spotlight that, pretty soon, Stuart was purring again at the memory of Weir embarking on one of his coruscating forays through opponents as if they were not there. Or Redpath was shipping the ball wide to Chalmers, and the latter passing on to Shiel, Joyner or Derek Stark, all of whom were capable of rousing the Greenyards' fans to ecstasy.

That was how he wanted to remember the halcyon days when rivals used to quake in their boots at the prospect of confronting Telfer and Moffat's hungry horde and when those of us who were sitting in the press box, who were always better treated at this venue than anywhere else in Scotland, used to wonder whether there was not something faintly miraculous happening in our midst as Melrose conjured up unlikely feats, including one special afternoon when they shoved a century of points past the hapless Stirling County and another when they amassed 89 against West of Scotland, both of whom were bewildered by the hosts' pace and power and stamina, whatever the conditions. 'It was always one of the things about Melrose: we were fitter than most of the opponents we came up against and that was purely down to the fact we trained harder and longer than they did,' said Parker. 'It meant that if things were tight and we were going into the final 20 minutes, we always fancied our chances of getting past the winning post.'

These were the kinds of exhibitions which elicited delirious approval from the home supporters and there was a clinical edge to most of Melrose's displays which proved that they were professional in everything but name. Some questioned whether, in fact, their star recruits, such as Peter Wright, Rowen Shepherd and Derek Stark had all moved to the Borders for the sake of the scenery, the friendly welcome and the quality of the sport on offer. Yet, in the absence of any evidence of wrongdoing, we should view these comments simply as a by-product of envy and it could not have been the worst move to parade one's skills where the likes of Telfer was watching on the periphery.

Ultimately, this was a team whose exploits merited lavish acclaim and, just as we celebrate the Green Machine and salute the methods which inspired the Teris to record-breaking achievements, so we should doff our caps to the players, coaches and officials who transformed Melrose from perennial 'Britain in Bloom' candidates to a community which was known all over the globe for the quality of its rugby.

It may never happen again. But it was wonderful while it lasted.

Chapter Twelve

GLORY DAYS AND GORY DAYS IN THE BORDERS

THE LAMBING SEASON was in full flow when I caught up with Jim Currie, the energetic farmer who was one of the pivotal figures behind Peebles being granted admission to the Border League in 1996. But this stalwart figure at the Gytes has long been accustomed to wearing as many hats as Audrey Hepburn and, whether starring in the front row on the pitch, carrying out his duties as club president, or coaching the youths on Sundays, rugby is in his blood. Thus it was, in the course of a wide-ranging conversation, that I discovered how Peebles had become the first organisation since Kelso joined the event in 1912 to receive the opportunity to lock horns with the giants of Hawick, Gala and Melrose on a regular basis in league competition. Currie and his colleagues had responded to that challenge with the sort of indomitable attitude which justified their inclusion alongside the other seven teams. Indeed, even if one accepts that the standard of the competition is no longer at the exalted heights it reached when the Green Machine was one of the country's most feared institutions, Peebles have tasted glory on a frequent enough basis, whether defeating Gala, who fielded a young Chris Paterson at stand-off, in their maiden season, or prevailing on a fairly regular basis against their opponents while also unleashing some exhilarating displays in various cup tournaments.

On the evidence of Currie's brisk, no-nonsense response to a variety of questions, he is cut in the traditional Borders mould of somebody who bows to nobody and treats people as he finds them, which helps explain why he was never daunted when Peebles embarked on their odyssey in 1996. They slipped to a 28–20 defeat in their first match against Selkirk, but responded to falling behind with a scintillating late surge which forced the Souters on to the defensive, and highlighted that they belonged in this company, not that their skipper had ever doubted it. 'We had a good group of players, our coach, David Kilshaw, had worked his socks off behind the scenes, and was instrumental in getting us fit and ready for Border League action, and we were so excited about the prospect of being involved in the competition that there wasn't any time for nerves,' said Currie, who flitted between the front and second rows, and established an efficacious partnership with the Scotland A prop, Stephen Ferguson, who was a paradigm of solidity in the Peebles cause. Currie continued:

We were also driven by the fact that some of the senior clubs struggled to accept we were on a par with them, and there were a few sarky comments flying around at some clubs, which simply motivated us all the more to make them eat their words. I suppose we had been brought up with chips on our shoulders – in the 1970s, the club had been in the East section of Division 5, at one point – and we also discovered that the bigger clubs tended to have more of the big [refereeing] decisions going in their favour. It's similar to Hearts in football: they get accused of complaining too much about officials, but then you look at how many decisions go against them and how many seem to work to the Old Firm's benefit. It occasionally made us a bit frustrated, and I still believe that Stevie [Ferguson] would have won 15 or 18 international caps if he had left us and joined another club, because he was a really talented player, but although we might have complained about some things, it was both fantastic to be involved in the Border League and even better when we recorded out first victory at the Gytes.

That materialised on a typically dreich evening in late autumn when Currie's men tackled Gala, in what turned into a magnificently pugnacious contest, with the balance shifting one way then the other as the combatants searched for the winning gambit. Such a close–fought encounter had appeared improbable during the opening 40 minutes, with the hosts dominating and bossing their rivals, scoring tries through Colin Kerr, Steven Brockie and the unstinting Currie, who crashed over from close range for a touchdown, which enabled his team to advance to an imposing 19–0 lead at the interval and the cheers of the home faithful were no more than the Peebles effort had merited.

Yet if Gala seemed marooned, the club which had already defeated Hawick and Jed-Forest in the campaign were a different proposition upon the resumption, orchestrating a string of fine tries from Richie Scott, Craig Townsend, Alan Bell and David Changleng. Peebles' sole response was a penalty from their prolific kicker, Paul Rutherford, which meant they trailed 24–22 as the game advanced towards its denouement. For a spell, it looked as if Currie's personnel were staring at another honourable loss, but their skipper urged his men to launch one last offensive and his unstinting aggression paid dividends. He recalled:

We just kept pushing forward and we pegged the Gala boys back and they attempted to run the ball from out of their own territory, but only succeeded in conceding a penalty in injury time. The place fell silent and Paul had to keep his nerve, because there are no easy kicks in these circumstances, but he struck the ball sweetly, the cheers from our fans told their own story, and we had beaten the mighty Gala by 25–24. It was a fantastic evening thereafter, as you might imagine, and it was the first time I kissed my girlfriend, Fiona, who is now my wife, and that match will never be forgotten by anybody who was there. It was the spark which we needed and we played 14 games in the league that season and also got the better of Selkirk, Hawick and Langholm, so nobody could possibly argue that we hadn't proved we deserved to be in the competition. We kept it going in the next few years, with victories over Kelso, Langholm and Gala again, before we headed to Mansfield Park and beat Hawick in the Millennium Cup and if they were making sarcastic remarks at the start, the ground was pretty quiet by the finish!

These boisterous, bellicose Border tussles offered a reminder of why rugby continued to flourish in the South, even when the Scottish club game suffered a slump in attendances and a crisis of confidence on either side of the start of the 21st century. Quite simply, even at the same time as Scotland were parachuting in 'Kilted Kiwis' such as Brendan Laney – 'I used to go to all the Murrayfield internationals, but that started the rot,' said Currie with a resolve which suggested that he will not be easily swayed back to the stadium – the likes of Peebles were revelling in the exploits of ordinary heroes. And while fellows such as Jim Currie knew they were never going to be bracketed in the same company as a John Rutherford or a Gary Armstrong, so what! What mattered was that Jim and Stevie and David Kilshaw, allied to the enterprise of a batch of talented youngsters including Murray Blackstock, Chris Shaw and Steven Clapperton, offered their all for Peebles, and so nearly beat Heriot's in the Scottish Cup, prior to the inter-national stand-off, Gordon Ross, landing a last-ditch penalty to save the Edinburgh side from embarrassment.

The Scottish Cup tournament was a terrific innovation for the grass roots circuit, not least because the original sponsors,

Tennent's, marketed the event so successfully that even rugby agnostics found themselves glancing at the faces of participating players on the sides of Edinburgh buses. Better still, from a historical perspective, Hawick, whose ruthless efficiency of the 1970s and 1980s had ground to a halt while they struggled to keep pace with Jim Telfer's Melrose maestri, viewed the radical new competition as an opportunity to reassert their traditional authority and duly set in motion the campaign which eventually conveyed them to Murrayfield, in the company of thousands of their townsfolk, for a lip-smacking showdown with Watsonians in the spring of 1996.

Quite simply, this was one of the grandest occasions in the history of Scottish club rugby and those of us who witnessed the arrival of a seemingly endless cavalcade of buses could detect that something special was in the air. The Green Machine's progress had been clamped for a significant period, but that had simply heightened their determination to demonstrate they were still the premier force in the country and, as their long-time secretary, John Thorburn, told me: 'Hawick had a proud record to maintain. We had been the first team to win the Border League, the first to win the Scottish championship [in 1974] and we wanted to be the first club to win the cup as well. But, even so, I don't think anybody could have imagined how it would capture the town's imagination.'

In many respects, it was reminiscent of the cricketing village Freuchie's triumphant visit to Lord's in 1985, when the population decamped to London en masse and left a solitary local bobby to look after the place, while they won the National Village Cup. In Hawick's case, this maiden campaign soon turned into a crusade, and especially following the Teris' impressive victory over Melrose at the penultimate stage which set them on a collision course with a star-studded Watsonians line-up, featuring such Test luminaries as Tom

Smith, Scott Hastings, Duncan Hodge, Cammy Mather, Derrick Lee and Stuart Grimes. On paper at least, Hawick looked hopelessly outgunned, even if they were able to call on the services of Grand Slam hero Tony Stanger. And yet, even while the Borderers set about the task of composing special anthems and prepared to bring a marching band to Murray-field – oblivious to whether it contravened any health and safety regulations relating to spectators lugging musical in-struments into the ground with them – the feeling grew that this match might be settled as much by pride in the com-munity as it was by the impressive cap tallies on the CVs of the Watsonians line-up.

As for the travelling hordes, the cup might have been a new phenomenon, but such was their faith in Hawick's ability to traverse any barriers or obstacles that they made up their minds that the visit to Edinburgh would not simply be a sporting occasion; it would be an impromptu mini festival of raucous songs, bands in full swing, and poetry readings. And, as the Mansfield Park's chronicle of the day related, what a swell party it was!

> The build-up to the final involved the whole town, as shops carried displays of the team colours and memorabilia of past successes, and the club's own shop opened on demand to make available jerseys, hats, scarves and strips for supporters to identify themselves on the day. There was desperation to find tickets, which would place the holder in the Teri section of the crowd, yet a main talking point was where the large number of buses, required to carry all those supporters to Murrayfield, was going to be found.
>
> Much was made by the Scottish Rugby Union of the great contribution which Hawick made to the atmosphere on Finals day. The Saxhorn Band's contribution throughout the afternoon was immense; Hawick's Poet Laureate, Ian

Landles, led the singing in the tents; and the excitement in the crowd seemed tangible. In the Scottish tradition of supporting the underdog, the neutrals also seemed to be backing Hawick, just as they had done at Netherdale [in the semi-final, where the Green Machine had prevailed over their Melrose rivals by 28–15]. The stage was set! It was said by some people that Hawick had enjoyed the easier path to the Final [they defeated East Kilbride 46–6, Duns 22–3, Biggar 52–17 and Preston Lodge 26–11 in the earlier stages of the competition], but, at the end of the day, they had to beat both the fancied teams and earned the applause.

All the same, not even the 28 busloads of supporters and factory's worth of cars which departed from the Borders on the morning of May 11 – some wag stuck a sign on a lamp post at the exit to the town, which read: 'Would the last person to leave Hawick turn out the lights?' – could have countenanced the fashion in which their heroes were left clutching at shadows in the early stages of the match. Indeed, Watsonians looked capable of humiliating their rivals when they raced into a 15–0 advantage, with Hodge providing a try, a penalty and the conversion of Scott Hastings' touchdown. At that juncture, it felt as if the Myreside club were simply too powerful and purposeful to be denied. But, as had happened so often before, the Borderers knuckled down and gradually began to make inroads through the towering performances of their unsung front row, Jim McDonnell, Jim Hay and Andrew Johnstone, and when Alistair Imray surged over for a try out on the wing, shortly before the interval, the decibel level cranked up around the ground.

In itself, the attendance – which was in excess of 22,000 – was remarkable, considering that this was greater than the entire population of Hawick, while Watsonians were not exactly renowned for filling up their own stadium, let alone anywhere else. But the more the fans chanted and screamed their backing, the better the Border team rallied and thrived. Entering the last quarter, the Hawick No 15, Colin Turnbull, came into the line and Scott Welsh converted to reduce the deficit to only 15–12. Then, as the racket from the bandsmen and their aficionados swelled up to ear-shattering proportions – and the din reached rock-concert proportions when the band launched into a lusty rendition of 'Up wi' the Banner High' – the ubiquitous Welsh took a quick tap penalty inside his opponents' 22, and forced his way over. His team led and although Watsonians huffed and puffed in the climactic moments and did their utmost to engineer a drop-goal position for Hodge, they were blown away by the dynamism, the collective will and the physical exertions of the Hawick pack, who never budged an inch amid the denouement.

Even those of us who were not Borderers could empathise with the swirl of emotions which reverberated throughout Murrayfield at the death, as the victors and their effervescent captain, Brian Renwick, lapped up the delirious adulation of the crowd. Written off in some quarters in advance, this was not a million miles removed from the 1990 Grand Slam decider at the same venue, though one shudders to think how Will Carling's side might have fared if they had gone three scores clear in the first half an hour. 'There was a lot of pressure on our shoulders. No other club in Scotland has a history like ours,' said Renwick when (a semblance of) normal service had been restored. 'But today, a lot of young players came through and made their own history.'

There was no disputing that assessment, nor the skipper's praise for the wholehearted, Musketeer-style commitment displayed by Hawick, while they rallied from their initial setbacks and rose to the challenge magnificently the longer that the proceedings continued. Watsonians, in contrast, seemed to be dwelling under the delusion that 20 minutes of quality was enough. before they took their feet off the accelerator and duly paid the price.

Understandably, that Saturday evening was marked by exultant revelries from the new cup holders. On the journey back home, the team bus passed by hastily-prepared banners of welcome at Newton Farm and on Wilton Hill. The decision was taken to go round, via Wilton, to deliver the club's ex-president Barrie Laidlaw direct to his door, and the mood was euphoric as the festivities stretched on until heaven knows when the following morning. Yet, having savoured the triumph, the next task for men such as John Thorburn was to ensure that the team's success gained due recognition from their community. And the manner in which they went about their task was typically practical and sensible.

We decided that it would be a terrific idea to have an open-top bus parade around Hawick with the players and the cup on the Sunday, but we had to work out how many people would show up and how quickly we could spread the message round the town. So we phoned up a few of the local ministers and asked them if they would announce what we were planning and they did so from their pulpits. Time was short and you can't just arrange something like this without consulting the police, the council and health and safety, but everything moved smoothly and, in the space of a few hours, word got round that the townsfolk would have the chance to acknowledge the fantastic job that the boys had done. This was in the middle of May, so we weren't sure how many people had gone away for the day, or organised other things, but we needn't have worried on that score. More than 5,000 people, including men, women and children of all ages, turned up for the celebration and it showed yet again what rugby meant to so many folk in the town.

Overall, it was a phenomenal achievement, because the

billboards in Edinburgh had been full of pictures of the Watsonians stars, and they were perceived as being clear favourites, but I think that just geed up our own lads. It also helped that, after knocking Melrose out in the semis, we sat down and drew up a plan and part of that was to get our local town band involved and make sure our supporters were sitting next to them, and it all helped to create a tremendous atmosphere, which definitely boosted the team.

There must have been a feeling around Mansfield Park that these resplendent occasions would carry on indefinitely, especially when Hawick continued their impressive march by claiming consecutive championship titles in the 2000–01 and 2001–02 campaigns, the latter of which yielded a treble success with the Teris also lifting another Border League title and repeating their earlier heroics in the Scottish Cup, sealing the latter with a nail-biting 20–17 victory over Glasgow Hawks after extra time. Yet, amid a mounting financial crisis in the Scottish game, the next few years saw a shift in the power base away from the Borders with the Premiership being shared between Glasgow Hawks, Currie, Boroughmuir and Ayr. In itself, this development was bad enough to inspire complaints from the traditionally hard-to-please Hawick fraternity, but they were suffering more than a minor blip as became evident when the spectre of relegation started to hover over a club which would once have laughed at the notion of not feasting with the elite.

Yet, by the time it was confirmed in December 2008 that the Borderers had sacked their coach, Jim Hay, after their president, Donald McLeod, and director of rugby, Doug Jackson, made it clear to the former Scotland hooker that they were not prepared to countenance the club dropping out of the highest echelon for the first time in their existence, Hawick were already on such a slippery slope that no quick search for scapegoats was going to rectify the situation. In the bigger picture, those responsible for dismissing Hay, a man almost as closely associated with the town, whether in the role of player, captain or coach, as the greatest figures in the Green firmament, were entitled to demand why a community with such an apparently vibrant structure, including three more adult clubs, and a network of age-group sides and links with local schools, was faring so poorly on the Scottish circuit.

But Hay, who has never shirked a tackle in his career, was equally robust in fighting his corner and doing so in the public domain:

> I have not been sacked because of my coaching ability. A new person [McLeod] came in to run the club and the results were just an excuse to get rid of me. I am a realist and the person at the top of the tree takes the rap, but you have to ask why a club like Hawick couldn't find anybody else when I wanted to step down last year.
>
> There is too much politics in Hawick rugby and that makes it very difficult for this club. But I'm not bitter with Hawick rugby. It has been my life and it is a wonderful club, and I have done the best I can to help us move forward. Now I am looking forward to spending more time with my family and watching my son playing in the local park.

If the blame had rested solely with Hay, his former employers might still have escaped the trapdoor to ignominy. But, on the contrary, I visited the community in March 2009, as the team slid closer to the precipice and it was obvious that they were suffering from a variety of problems, whether in the migration of several of their best young talents and coaches to rivals in Edinburgh or further afield, or the fashion in which the supply lines, which used to churn out an apparently inexhaustible supply of world-class players, were in urgent need of restructuring. In their defence, Hawick had already started to address these problems and their officials spoke defiantly as the axe loomed, but nevertheless, it was sad to behold the apathy of many of the youngsters on that brief visit and even more dismal to behold the fashion in which they duly plummeted into the second tier following a 29–18 defeat at home to Stirling County, who suffered the same fate.

'The flags aren't at half mast, but there is a real sense of disappointment about the town and the worry has to be that we will struggle to improve from here,' said Jim Renwick, more in sorrow than anger, and that was another common thread among the customers at bars such as Callaghan's, where one long-term supporter told me: 'We're hurting about this, of course we are. But this has been coming for a number of years and the biggest problem is that young kids these days want to go to Glasgow or Edinburgh – or England – and sign a professional contract when they are 19 or 20. They don't care that Hawick helped them reach the standard they are. All they want is to get out of here and when you look at the unemployment level in the Borders, you can't really blame them.'

The last rites were duly performed by Watsonians, in a contest which was a mirror image of these sides' classic confrontation 13 years earlier. Here, it was Hawick who came roaring out of the blocks, all pace, passion and pent-up frustration, and mighty impressive in building a 17–0 lead through tries from Craig Neish, Dan Landels and Neil Renwick. Yet, once the visitors' initial fizz had vanished, they were routinely swatted aside in a flurry of touchdowns from the Myreside men, in the guise of Michael Fedo, Ben Di Rollo, Richard Minto, Dougie Brown and Andrew Skeen. There was an anticlimactic air at the finish, if for no other reason than Hawick had offered lashings of perspiration and their veteran captain, Kevin Reid, deserved better than to be inextricably linked with the team that got Hawick relegated. But sport can be a cruel business sometimes.

On a positive note, there was not anybody stupid enough to argue that Hawick were 'too good to go down'; a line which has been trotted out by a string of (usually doomed) managers, mentors and coaches within every team sport since time immemorial. Instead, the evidence from these meetings with Stirling and Watsonians was that the Border giants might benefit from a season in Premiership Two, just as long as they came back up immediately. In the event, they achieved this objective, before ditching Gerry McGuinness, the man who had piloted their path out of Premiership Two, and attained a degree of solidity and respectability in the 2010–11 campaign, though the use of these latter words will probably induce apoplexy among the Hawick traditionalists. But, for the moment, the Green Machine has stalled in second gear and while one would never write them off, they have slipped significantly behind Melrose, just as they did in the 1990s, and their priority must lie in closing the gap through their home-grown players over a period of years, not months. But they have done it before and the fashion in which these organisations have plotted regeneration has been an abiding feature of Borders lore.

At least Hawick's difficulties were restricted to rugby-related matters. Selkirk, on the other hand, suffered a crisis of almost biblical proportions in 2003 when the town was struck by a torrential deluge of rain, accompanied by thunder and hailstones (at the end of May!) during a four-hour period, which deposited massive torrents of foaming water down the hillsides, engulfing not only the rugby field and the adjacent club rooms, but also the nearby properties in Ettrickhaugh Road, Bannerfield and the Yarrow Valley. This was a serious matter for the whole town, and Philiphaugh had been in the eye of the storm, to the extent that the whole pitch was flooded, while more than £350,000 worth of damage was caused to the club's facilities. The situation would have been serious enough for a senior football club, and rugby has always had to deal in smaller budgets. Yet their president, John Smail, is one of life's resourceful chaps and the manner in which he and his fellow officials (and their townsfolk, many of whom had suffered their own privations) acted was an object lesson in the values of communities rallying together in adversity. Smail described the operation thus:

> Players, officials and supporters were quick to volunteer their services in the post-flood clean-up, with local contractor, Elliot Henderson, and chartered surveyor, Chris Highton, both members of Selkirk's general committee, at the forefront of efforts to co-ordinate the mopping up and rebuilding efforts. Offers of help from fellow Border rugby clubs and other sporting organisations were greatly appreciated, as was the financial assistance pledged by Selkirk's Common Good Fund, Ettrick and Lauderdale District Sports Council and the Scottish Rugby Union. Interest-free loans and donations were also forthcoming from club members and supporters and, within ten days of the flood, the water covering the main pitch had been drained off and, shortly afterwards, the pitch's contaminated surface was mechanically stripped, verti-drained, injected with sand and reseeded. Meanwhile the changing rooms, toilets and shower area, under the stand, were given a complete facelift and replaced by a magnificent new elevated clubhouse. This structure was designed by Chris Highton and Jim Harold of Allied Surveyors, whose initial ideas were sketched out on the backs of beer mats over a drink in the Town Arms Inn. The new clubhouse continues to win plaudits for its style and character.

However, if Selkirk imagined their problems were over, they were dealt a further grievous blow only 16 months later when history repeated itself, this time with flood water from the nearby Long Philip Burn sweeping through the club's premises following days of persistent rainfall in the midst of another saturated summer. On this occasion, only the rugby club bore the brunt of the elements, and it was asking a lot of people to dig deep into their pockets for a second time in as many years. But, lo and behold, they again rose to the challenge. 'When news of Selkirk RFC's predicament spread around the town, members, players, supporters and the local public were soon turning up at Philiphaugh to lend a hand,' added Smail, who was typically reticent about his own unstinting efforts to enable the beleaguered Souters to transcend these tempestuous times. He went on:

> The offer of two pumps from Scottish Borders Council was immediately accepted, and retained fire-fighters from Selkirk also lent a hand. Meanwhile, a squad of volunteers set about rescuing items from under the stand and transferring them to the new lounge, with ex-club captain, Scott Tomlinson, removing doors to facilitate the sweeping of water from the building, while prop, Steven Renwick, brought a tractor and bowser down from his family's Craig Douglas farm and began sucking up the flood water from the back pitch. The success of the clean-up operation could be seen eight days later when Selkirk took on a touring side, Thurrock, on the main pitch, which appeared to be in perfect condition. Because flood insurance had been withdrawn [after the 2003 deluge], Selkirk RFC was faced with repair bills running into many thousands of pounds. But once again, the Common Good Fund kindly offered financial support, which was matched by Scottish Borders Council. The club had once again lived to fight another day.

These words epitomised the never-say-die spirit which kept these clubs afloat in periods of turbulence. They also highlighted the fact that while the various Border towns retained their keen rivalry, they were quick to help others out when a genuine emergency came along. It was a tangible illustration of the merits of the 'Big Society' years before any politicians used the phrase and it is surely worth recording in these pages.

Yet, if there was a concerted effort to rescue Selkirk from their plight, one team in the region started to stride away from the others as the decade continued and how the rest of the Borders must envy the resources and expertise which are currently available to Craig Chalmers at the Greenyards. For the last five seasons, the former talismanic Test star has steadily, impressively, moulded a squad, which has engaged in a series of Herculean struggles with the likes of Ayr, Currie and Glasgow Hawks. Chalmers, as has been mentioned elsewhere in these pages, is unlikely to receive an excess of Christmas cards from his peers anytime soon, and, absurdly, the Melrose stalwart was not even nominated in the 'Coach of the Year' category at the SRU awards in the spring, but he is one of life's winners, a restless perfectionist, whose constant striving for new standards might occasionally create rifts, and yet who has created a team in his own image.

Certainly, as far as the 2010–11 campaign was concerned, the absorbing battle between Chalmers and the Ayr coach, Kenny Murray, possessed all the necessary ingredients to suggest that these ambitious little coiled springs of boundless industry will be vying for the major prizes on the club circuit for some considerable time. In the Scottish Cup, it was the Ayr men who were flying slightly higher, en route to a 25–21 triumph, courtesy of a brace of tries from the gifted teenager Mark Bennett, who has now departed Scotland to join the Clermont-Auvergne Academy, while there were other touchdowns from Steven Manning and Damien Kelly, the latter of whom will also not be at Millbrae for the 2011–12 season, following the Australian's extended stay in Burns country.

Chalmers, who paced the touchline with a mixture of angst, aggression and admiration, saw his charges score two tries from Nick Beavon and Hayden Mitchell, with Scott Wight – another to leave the club circuit, en route to Glasgow Warriors – adding another 11 points. But, although Chalmers embraced Murray at the end and was civil enough in the aftermath, it was evident that he was churning inside in the wake of another Murrayfield defeat. Make no mistake, this fellow utterly detests losing – and I can recall bumping into him following a thrilling try-fest against Heriot's at Golden-acre when his side lost 44–38 and he responded with one four-letter word – 'Crap!' – to my suggestion that it had been a great advert for the Scottish club game. To his credit, he walked up, a few moments later, and could not have been more affable in discussing what we had just witnessed. But that was only after – or so I learned later – he had gone through his players like a dodgy curry. And what's wrong with that? It is this burning desire to iron out mistakes and persuade his players to be the best they can be which fuels his passion and when Melrose are good, they are very, very good, as they demonstrated while triumphing in the Premiership, the Border League and beating South African rivals in the final of the Melrose Sevens.

The first of these prizes was only secured at the climax of one of the most engrossing title pursuits in recent memory, with the outcome in doubt until the last day of the campaign, when Melrose renewed hostilities with Ayr, only a week after their cup disappointment. In the build-up, Chalmers talked up the qualities of his opponents, as if determined to release the pressure on his club, who had not won the championship since 1997 when the 28-year-old No 10 was still at the height of his powers. But, privately, he was preparing them to launch a ferocious onslaught and the game duly developed into another stirring, red-blooded exchange between two meaty packs and some coruscating backs.

The hosts had identified Kelly as a major threat, but they could not prevent the rampaging lock putting Ayr in front with a try, converted by Ross Curle. Yet if that incident exasperated Chalmers, his men regrouped and advanced into a 12–7 lead at the interval with four penalties from Wight. It was still too close to call, and the one-man wrecking ball, Kelly, crossed for another try, even as a deluge of rain descended from the skies in the South of Scotland, but, in circumstances where many other teams would have panicked, the Greenyards collective kept nagging away at their opponents like a persistent itch and eventually gained their reward when Gary Elder and Ross Miller seized touchdowns, and Wight added another seven points to establish a decisive lead. Even then, Chalmers refused to allow any hint of complacency to creep into his ensemble and still seemed agitated when Ross Curle notched a penalty and try. But the latter only arrived in injury time, and there had been no way back for a while for Ayr, whose lengthy season had caught up with them. Melrose emerged with a deserved 29–20 win, the prelude to an explosion of champagne corks popping through the town.

This result should have been applauded elsewhere in the Borders – although one doubts that it was – because it was the first championship success by one of their number since 2002 and arrived at a time when Selkirk were being relegated from the top flight, the likes of Jed-Forest and Kelso were growing used to life outwith the highest tier and Langholm had virtually slipped off the radar altogether. In which light, Chalmers was entitled to proclaim it as a vital outcome for his region. 'This is a great result for Melrose and the Borders. We kept our heads and kicked our kicks. I think Scott Wight controlled the game and the referee was very strong. There were a lot of shenanigans going on last week and we didn't let them get away with it again,' said Chalmers. 'I'm a greedy so-and-so and I wanted to win the cup final as well, but this was the title we really needed to win and this is the one that we have been working towards. It evoked all sorts of memories of 1997, and it was nice to win in front of our home crowd.'

In so many respects, this was a throwback to the halcyon period when Chalmers, Redpath and their compatriots regularly enjoyed demolishing their domestic adversaries. After all, 20 of the 22 players involved in their title achievement were Scottish, while Telfer is still doing his bit by encouraging the Melrose Wasps under-18s, who will doubtless present their country with some gifted talents in the future. And that 'greedy' word used by Chalmers was similar to the mentality espoused by Telfer in his prime. Most of the best coaches have this voracious appetite for prizes, and one suspects that Chalmers, who is still only 42, will not hang around in Scotland forever if, at some stage, the chance to fight for the right to coach his country does not become a genuine possibility.

Yet, for the moment, he and his charges are on a substantial upward curve, whether in the 15-a-side or the abbreviated version of the sport. Occasionally, the Melrose Sevens can feel more akin to a social event – albeit a distinctly pleasant one – than a genuine test of sporting mettle. But the 2011 contest belonged firmly in the latter category, most notably when the hosts secured the famous Ladies Centenary Cup for the first time in 13 years by overcoming the powerful South African guest side, Hamilton, by 31–26. There was little love lost between the teams as the climax raged on, with the visitors taking the lead through Terry Jacobs, prior to the elusive Wight replying with a break of his own.

That ebb and flow continued with a Jeffrey Williams score

being countered by a brace of tries from Calum Anderson, which were cheered to the rafters by the usual packed crowd, who were treated to something distinctly unusual from a Scottish team — a tough-as-teak ruthlessness in exploiting opposition weaknesses — and the Scots were indebted to the lung-bursting exertions of the rugged veteran John Dalziel and the spontaneity of Jamie Murray for allowing Wight to establish a decisive advantage. All that remained was for Hamilton's Jandre du Plessis to be yellow-carded and for Alshaun Bock and Allan Dodds to swap tries before Janno van Zyl scored again, but too late to influence the outcome. Once again, a Scottish contingent had proved they could flourish against southern hemisphere rivals. And once again, Chalmers was the architect of that success. Perhaps it is overdue for his qualities to be properly acknowledged. The best coaches do not need to be loved; they need to be respected and, to some extent, feared. And if the choice lies between glory days, inspired by a streak of arrogance and some forward thinking, or gory days, hamstrung by the 'Aye-been' philosophy, it should not take long to decide which option is more required by Scotland at the moment.

Chapter Thirteen

THE BORDER REIVERS FIASCO

ON A LATE Tuesday morning in March 2007, the media were invited to Murrayfield for what was described as an important policy announcement by the Scottish Rugby Union. It was one of those instances when nobody was entirely sure what might be about to unfold, although there had been reports for weeks in advance that the governing body was poised to implement drastic action to reduce costs in their three professional teams, Edinburgh, Glasgow and the Border Reivers, which were losing significant amounts of money and failing to hit any kind of heights in the Magners League Cup and Heineken Cup.

Once the various press and broadcasting outlets had arrived at the stadium, the ashen faces, fidgety shuffling and slightly embarrassed demeanours of the SRU chief executive, Gordon McKie, and the union's chairman, Allan Munro, indicated that good news was off the agenda. Instead, and despite their best efforts to focus the Fourth Estate's minds on the fact that they intended to increase investment in the Glasgow Warriors, the only item which mattered in their press release was the adjoining confirmation that the Reivers were being closed down at the end of the season. And though these gloomy tidings might not have been wholly unexpected when one examined the mediocre results and paltry attendances which the Netherdale-based team had been attracting in previous months, there was still a sense of anger as the implications became clear. This, after all, was not the first occasion when the Borders had been hung out to dry by the SRU.

Munro, for his part, argued that it was unrealistic to carry on ploughing capital into a failing business and yet the caution with which he picked his words underlined his realisation that he was treading through a sporting minefield, the more so, given the number of Border-based journalists and broadcasters who were in the same room.

'The decision has not been an easy one. But we believe the Reivers' closure and strengthening Glasgow will go some way towards improving high-performance rugby in Scotland,' he told the throng, several of whom were waiting to vent their anger, and duly flung piles of ordure in the administration's faces the following morning. 'We recognise the contribution which Border coaches and players have made, and their determination to succeed against the odds. But it was quite clear that we could not continue as we were, and something had to be done if we were to maintain professional rugby in Scotland.'

Within the next few days, the backlash was in full spate. McKie, rightly or wrongly, was perceived as a 'bloody bean-counter', attacked as being somebody who knew the cost of everything and the value of nothing, and was further casti-gated for his alleged paucity of rugby knowledge and back-ground in the sport. On the following Thursday, 29 March, the Scottish Borders Council approved an emergency motion, arguing that the sport was integral to the region's identity and culture. 'Rugby is woven into the social fabric of the Borders. It is a generator of trade and income. It attracts tourists and visitors to the Borders from across the world and it is part of what creates the worldwide affinity with the Scottish Borders and, through rugby, it has contributed hugely to Scottish life.'

None of this was in question, but the problem was that all the subsequent sound and fury added up to precious little in terms of providing potential solutions: in which sense, it was a microcosm of the dismal fashion in which Scotland had reacted to the challenge of moving away from the amateur era and getting to grips with professionalism. A decade earlier, the SRU, spurred on by their director of rugby, Jim Telfer, and his former Scotland team-mate, Duncan Paterson, had pressed the case for districts as the best way forward and, even while some of the country's leading clubs protested that they should be allowed to enter the Heineken Cup, the union seized the initiative by placing around 120 players on contracts and setting up four provincial teams in Edinburgh, Glasgow, the Border Reivers and the Caledonia Reds (formerly the North and Midlands). This policy provoked a mixture of fury and consternation from some quarters, with officials at Melrose, for example, asking why rugby's governing body had chosen to fund professionalism, when there would have been an almighty ruckus if their SFA counterparts had gone down a similar route in bankrolling Rangers and Celtic. It was a rational contention, but the trouble was that the SRU had a plan and were primed to act, while their opponents did not and procrastinated. And although there was a small sprinkling of clubs who talked about mergers or discussed following the path adopted by Glasgow Hawks, the majority were either too frightened or too complacent to threaten the sort of breakaway from the SRU which was mooted at various stages of the argument. Instead, they resorted to leaking selective pieces of information to various newspapers, which made a few rugby hacks feel akin to Woodward and Bernstein for a period, but whose appeal soon palled when it was clear that these men (they were all men!) were expecting us to do their dirty work for them by waging war against the SRU.

The next few years brought predictable confusion and resentment to Scottish rugby at exactly the time when the administrators should have been striving for consensus and building bridges. Waffle proliferated on both sides. Paterson predicted that the four district selects would soon convert the sceptics and he forecast that they would be drawing crowds of 15,000 within the space of three years, which was at best wildly optimistic, and at worst a naked diversionary tactic. Telfer, so astute and inspirational in devising tactics to beat opponents on the field, suddenly appeared out of touch, apparently hell-bent on importing a New Zealand-style structure to his homeland despite the obvious differences between the two nations. But the clubs, too, were stricken by internal dissent and their actions were often a consequence of narrow self-interest, while the more progressive elements, who mentioned such ideas as club co-operatives or the grass roots organisations creating a rugby version of the SPL, were drowned out by the nay-sayers, who disagreed with the SRU, but could not come up with an alternative.

Even when four of Scotland's biggest names – Finlay Calder, Jim Aitken, David Sole and Gavin Hastings – launched a well-publicised crusade, calling for the scrapping of the new district structure in early 1997 and subsequently issuing a searing condemnation of the SRU's stewardship of the game, they discovered that all their kudos in Test rugby mattered for little when it came to gathering votes at the annual general meeting. 'We are four belligerent individuals and maybe that is why we have not been invited to give our views in an official capacity at Murrayfield,' said Calder. 'But this isn't about personalities. It is about the future of the Scottish game and if the SRU wins, that game will die.'

In these circumstances, it was hardly surprising that the club circuit nearly collapsed in a slagheap of apathy – they had been deprived of the services of nearly all their leading luminaries and the public found alternative sources of entertainment. I can remember going to Myreside one Saturday in 1997 and there were police traffic cones and a posse of stewards inside and outside the ground – and the 'crowd' was no more than 150. Even in the Borders, the spectators began to pick and choose their fixtures and, as one might have anticipated, they tended to plump for their local derbies in the Border League which meant that, in less than two years, an organisation such as Melrose had to deal with up to half their support base going AWOL when it came to championship matches.

If the hope was that the districts would turn things around with results on the pitch, that proved equally misguided. Glasgow travelled down to Leicester and conceded more than 90 points at Welford Road and such was the ease with which the Tigers mauled their Scottish opponents that Dean Richards, who had been complaining of an upset stomach, strolled off the pitch at one stage, relieved himself in the lavatory, and returned to the fray without his team bothering to replace him in the interim period. The SRU's finances, meanwhile, were equally going down the toilet, and, to almost nobody's surprise, their debt level soared to the extent where even the likes of Telfer and Paterson recognised the need for 'retrenchment'. The original four teams were re-duced to two, with the merger of Glasgow and Caledonia and Edinburgh and the Borders; a move which led to many players losing their jobs and relocating to England, France, or roles outwith rugby.

If this short-term pain had been the catalyst for increased success on the international stage, the Murrayfield hierarchy might just about have been able to survive the crescendo of criticism from those who proclaimed that they were letting the sport wither on the vine. But, if anything, the opposite was true. In 1998, the Scots endured a demoralising sequence of comprehensive defeats after Jim Telfer returned to the coaching job in place of David Johnston and Richie Dixon, who had been peremptorily sacked in January. However, if anything, the slide intensified with Telfer's charges being thrashed 51–26 by Fiji in Suva and demolished 45–3 by the Australians in Sydney. Even more damningly, they had earlier subsided to an emphatic 51–16 loss against the French at Murrayfield, where the sight of significant numbers of supporters heading for the exits long before the climax spoke volumes for the disenchantment which had permeated the game less than a decade after David Sole had slow-marched his troops to Grand Slam glory over England at the same venue. Eventually, Paterson resigned in December of that year, but the bickering carried on unabated. And while it did, the SRU's debt level reached crisis levels and led some to speculate that the banks were effectively in control.

At that juncture, only the most dewy-eyed Micawberish sprite would have predicted that the Scots would rally to win the last Five Nations Championship a few months later, bolstered by the tremendous efforts of such Borders stalwarts at Gary Armstrong, Gregor Townsend and Alan Tait, whose return from the rugby league ranks was one of the few positive developments amid the mounting gloom. Yet, if anybody envisaged that the Scottish public would suddenly transfer their allegiance to the so-called 'super-districts' on the back on the national team's heroics, it was to prove a forlorn hope. By the turn of the millennium, even as the internecine warfare continued, many fans had found other diversions. Stuart Henderson, the Melrose secretary, rang me on the Friday before a tussle with Boroughmuir and told me: 'We are dealing in hundreds [of fans] down here rather than thousands these days. They still take an interest in the Sevens and they might still come along to the Border League matches with Hawick and Gala, but they're all really disillusioned. Where is this going to end, Neil? Where is it going to end?'

To be honest, it was a question which remains unanswered, despite the strategic reviews, such as the one conducted by Lord Mackay of Clashfern in 1999, the incessant sabre-rattling at AGMs, and the appointment of high-profile figures such as Andy Irvine and the current incumbent, Ian MacLauchlan. There was a window of opportunity to make genuine progress following another bout of committee-room carnage in 2005, which led to the resignations of the respected chairman of the SRU's executive board, David Mackay, and the governing body's innovative chief executive, Phil Anderton, as the prelude to Murrayfield finally scrapping their discredited general committee. Yet, when one travels around the country, whether it is to Melrose, where Craig Chalmers and his charges have recently sparked a renaissance, or such forward-looking clubs as Ayr and Currie, any optimism tends to be tempered by continuing dissatisfaction, especially in the grass roots environs with the way the SRU justifies spending between £8m and £10m a year on their two professional entities when both are still struggling to draw crowds in excess of 3,000, and whose recent performances against their Celtic League rivals have been mired in mediocrity.

It is in this context that one should consider the ham-fisted fashion by which the SRU's initial four regions were trimmed to two, then upped to three again with the restoration of the Borders in 2002, prior to the latter's disbandment five years later. It must have been obvious, given the dearth of support for what were widely perceived to be centrally-controlled marionettes, forever in thrall to the Murrayfield puppet masters, that these regional sides badly needed to be granted autonomy to run their own affairs and thrive or die in the free markets. But the process never ever happened. Indeed, one wonders whether Telfer, who has been widely praised in these pages, but whose talents as a player and coach scarcely extended to administrative excellence, actually wanted the Reivers to be resuscitated in the first place.

After all, as he wrote in his autobiography: 'I was delighted when we saw the light at the end of the tunnel in the push for a third professional team.' But then, on the next page, he added:

> Of all the areas, when the four-team scenario was created, Caledonia was the one which really grasped it with enthusiasm. They played at football grounds and youngsters got right in behind it and there remains a very positive approach to the game.
>
> What people at some Border clubs have not yet grasped is that their enemy is not the professional team. If there is an enemy, it is the city teams, because of the natural and increasing drift of young people to cities . . . The pendulum of strength in club rugby has swung towards the central Lowlands, especially in Edinburgh and Glasgow. There are many reasons for this, but chief among them are the increasing opportunities in tertiary education, employment and worldwide travel, and the Borders has struggled to compete. Even though the sport is uniquely a way of life here, *I don't think Border teams will ever dominate Scottish rugby again* [my italics] – but if they were to use the professional team to their advantage, then they could rediscover success.

It is difficult to know where to begin in highlighting the inherent flaws in this argument. Firstly, where on earth is the sense in handing money to football clubs when Scottish rugby is in such financial dire straits? Next, if Telfer was so impressed with the Caledonian set-up, why did he not propose they were the ones who were brought back to life in 2002? Thirdly, where is the recognition that no Borders team was ever going to succeed while every decision about its affairs was signed, sealed and delivered with the Murrayfield imprimatur? Yet that latter factor was one of the major reasons why people in the South were so lukewarm about the Reivers organisation which landed on their doorstep. One of their former officials told me as much, on a confidential basis, the gist of which was as follows: 'If anybody had sat down and talked to us, we would have advised the SRU it was best to take matches around the region, some to Netherdale, others to Mansfield Park and the Greenyards, and we would have built up the brand by liaising with the Border League clubs and ensuring there were no clashes between the Magners League fixtures and the Sevens tournaments down here. It's only common sense that you speak to all the relevant parties and make them feel they are valued. But Jim effectively told us that it was the Reivers or nothing and that our local clubs would no longer be able to compete with the big city teams, and that was the end of the matter. Border people don't like being presented with these sorts of arrangements and they reacted accordingly. You would have imagined that Jim might have known that, given his background, but there was a blind spot with him when it came to the pro sides.'

These reservations, which ranged from mild scepticism to outright hostility, explained why the South, for all the enterprise of such coaches as Tony Gilbert, Rob Moffat and Steve Bates and the progressive attitude of their chief executive, Alastair Cranston, were always climbing up Everest with a piano on their backs. It was one thing for massed ranks of Borderers to get collectively behind a team featuring 15 home-grown players in the mould of Chalmers and Armstrong, Tait and Townsend, but quite another thing for them to have a composite squad foisted on them. They could support the former, whether they were beating the Australians or being trounced by the All Blacks, but there was no particular affinity with the disparate personnel who pitched up at Netherdale. Yes, they worked hard, yes they were wholehearted competitors, but any connection between them and the proud South ensembles of the past was purely coincidental. And when the team's crowds regularly slipped below 2,000, even though this was proportionally far superior to the modest numbers who turned up to watch Glasgow and Edinburgh, it sent out a clear signal to the SRU that the Reivers were heading on an expensive road to nowhere.

Hence, the media's summons to that conference at Murrayfield in March 2007, followed by the slightly absurd scenes thereafter of Border politicians getting whipped up into a frenzy of righteous indignation, approximately five years too late. There were the usual Internet-inspired campaigns to launch demonstrations and take the fight to the SRU, but, in the event, the breast-beating simply presaged a rather low-key finale for the Borders when they hosted the Ospreys in Galashiels on May 13. *The Scotsman* reported:

> The curtain finally came down on the Reivers in an emo-tional night at Netherdale. Despite the fact their fate had been determined a few weeks ago, the Reivers played with a professionalism which belied their league status and it was not until James Hook's penalty in injury time that the Ospreys put daylight between them, the new Magners League cham-pions, and the disbanded Reivers. It was almost surreal as the fireworks lit up the evening sky, the ticker tape littered the pitch, and the champagne popped. To their credit, the home supporters stayed and applauded as they had done when Gregor Townsend left the field, where he made his senior debut, to a standing ovation.
>
> There was satisfaction that Kelly Brown, who is expected to join Glasgow [which he did] was named man of the match and there were equal measures of contentment that the Borders had bowed out with dignity and passion. They were not overawed, but seemed inspired by the occasion, in front of the 1,837 crowd, a good number in view of the popular Jed-Forest Sevens, which were being played 18 miles down the road.

Yet, it can now be revealed that the decision to swing the axe on the Borders was not some hastily-reached judgement made by the SRU's committee in a few days or weeks prior to the announcement on 27 March. On the contrary – and this information came from a high-ranking former Murrayfield official – their death knell was sounded on the afternoon of 9 December in the previous year when they entertained the European giants of Biarritz at Netherdale, in what was supposed be a high-profile clash, and only 1,373 supporters could be bothered to pay their admission money. 'It was a non-event, on and off the pitch, because the Borders were beaten heavily [25–0], but the match was being shown on Sky and the pundits could find nothing to talk about at the end, except that there was nobody watching in what was supposed to be a rugby-mad region,' intimated my contact. 'It was clear, that afternoon, it just couldn't go on.'

My source, who requested anonymity, added that he has attended several meetings, both before and after the confirmation of the Reivers closure, and these had convinced him of three things. Firstly, that while there was a lot of noisy protest in the immediate aftermath of the SRU's action, this merely reflected the opinions of a 'very small' number of people and that their anger was not even shared by the majority of club members when the likes of the then SRU president Andy Irvine, chairman Allan Munro and chief executive Gordon McKie travelled down to the Borders to spell out why they had implemented the closure of the professional side. They arrived expecting a firestorm, but instead were greeted with a few glum faces and shrugs of the shoulders. Secondly, that a group of that Borders squad, 'including two or three experienced internationalists', were themselves so disenchanted with the side's long-term failure to capture the imagination of the public in the South of the country that they had already intimated to Murrayfield that they wanted to leave the club at the end of the 2006–07 campaign. Thirdly, and probably most significantly in the bigger picture, the SRU had attempted to discuss entering into partnerships with a number of investors, and there were people prepared to talk about sponsoring Glasgow and Edinburgh, but absolutely nobody came forward when similar overtures were made in the Borders. This, of course, is very difficult to refute or confirm, especially given the confidentiality agreements which seem to be installed in the contracts of most sports administrators these days, but if it is true, it adds up to a bleak scenario where the Reivers' fate was sealed, long before the story hit the press.

At any rate, it brought down the curtain on what had been a pretty poor show. One can blame the SRU for their control freakery, condemn those who focused more on budgets than being flexible in their strategies, and launch facile potshots at the Murrayfield panjandrums who steered Scotland down the dreaded district route in the first place. But there again, let's think about it a minute. The architects of that 'master plan' from the 1990s were Telfer and Paterson, who were born in Melrose and Galashiels respectively. The chief executive of the Reivers, when they sprang back to life, was Cranston, one of the proudest names in the Border firmament, while such stellar talents as Ross Ford, Gregor Townsend and Bruce Douglas were involved in the underwhelming Biarritz defeat.

So there should have been no shortage of Border passion or supporters. Yet, as Simon Turnbull wrote in the *Independent* the following day:

The bright midday sunshine could have been transported from home, but the chill from the morning frost offered a sharp reminder that this was the Borders of Scotland, not Biarritz. Still, the surreal sight of Serge Blanco getting stuck into a burger, against the backdrop of the Eildon Hills, suggested that the rugby aristocrats from the Atlantic coast of south-west France might not be lacking in appetite against the artisans from the foot of the Magners League.

Biarritz might have blown their last Heineken Cup match on British soil, their four-point loss to Munster in last season's final in Cardiff, but in Galashiels, there was no [Paul] O'Connell, [Donncha] O'Callaghan or [Ronan] O'Gara in the opposition ranks – and no 16th man to face in the form of 50,000 opposition fans. Instead, there were huge gaps around the ground, although the presence of Blanco and several Santa-hatted Basques took the attendance up to all of 1,373, and, on the pitch, there were far too many visiting players who were capable of punching holes in the home guard. Still, at least the gulf on the scoreboard stopped short of entering humiliation territory . . .

The whole tone of this report spells out why the Reivers were sacrificed. When there is no atmosphere, when once-packed stadiums are pitifully empty, and there were even rumours that many people were more interested in attending the opening of a new supermarket in Jedburgh than watching high-class European rugby that afternoon, it was probably time to call a halt on the whole creaking edifice. It might, of course, have been more sensible if the SRU had actually delivered this message at the time rather than accentuating their commitment to the Glasgow Warriors, but there again, the production of Scotland's approach to professionalism has been in the grand tradition of slapstick and farce and this is one pantomime where there is no immediate end to the run. That will only materialise if and when the other teams are allowed to live or die by the tenets of the free market and are permitted to escape the stifling constraints of state ownership.

The only bright spot in this dismal narrative has been the re-emergence of Scotland's club organisations, who have picked themselves up, dusted themselves down, and started to generate their own revenue streams, while encouraging significantly more supporters to come through the turnstiles than was the case a decade ago when several officials at the grass roots spoke gloomily about the imminent demise of the sport and their consternation was clearly sincere. Mercifully, though, matters have improved, with Melrose, as usual, at the forefront of the developments, winning a raft of prizes in 2011, and even though it may be difficult to orchestrate a return to the glory days of the early 1990s, they are being pursued by Ayr, Currie and Glasgow Hawks, and several other well-organised teams who have displayed the requisite gumption and gallus attitude to transcend their difficulties and emerge from their travails with the approach that nobody owes them any favours. Ultimately, given the knowledge that there is no spare cash in the SRU coffers and that people have to be persuaded to reconnect with the club circuit, the only means of guaranteeing their survival and preparing for the future is via their own efforts.

In which light, there should not be an excess of lamentations for the demise of the Reivers and certainly not the team which struggled to make any significant impact between 2002 and 2007. Better, surely, for the other sides in the South to hunt down Melrose afresh than fling good money after bad. And the signs are that the clubs are finally working in unison and collaborating on joint ventures. It is just a pity that it did not happen 15 years ago.

Chapter Fourteen

THE BEST EVER BORDERS TEAM?

WHENEVER SPORTING politics threatens to dominate the landscape of any pursuit, it is usually sensible to remind the audience that these games are meant to be fun, not an exercise in masochistic torture. What better way, therefore, to follow a chapter on the woes which have bedevilled Scotland since the IRB eventually opened the door to professionalism, than by drawing up a list of the best ever XV to have played for the Borders?

Such exercises, of course, are essentially frivolous. Who is to say how the best from 1920 would fare against their counterparts from 2010? And how does one weigh up the merits of an athlete from 50 years ago, who combined a day job with training to represent their country, against the modern generation of professional competitors who have access to video analysis, specially-tailored fitness programmes, advice from sports psychologists, personal nutritionists and the latest in sports science at their nearest institute?

And yet, I might be one of the old school, but I suspect that the majority of great sporting personalities from the past would still have thrived if their gifts had been transported to the present day. Thus, Rod Laver would continue to be the epitome of grace and effortless precision on a tennis court, Pelé or Jimmy Johnstone would carry on weaving and shimmying their way beyond would-be defenders in the 21st century, and even if Sir Garfield Sobers might not dominate cricket with bat and ball as effortlessly as when he was in his pomp, well the old fellow has just turned 75, so let's give him a break!

In that light, the mission which I laid down to half a dozen of Scotland's leading rugby journalists was, ahem, fairly simple. Namely, which players would they select for their imaginary best ever Borders team? I was not overly pedantic about whether the writers in question had actually witnessed all their selections, although there was an immediate response from one or two in their ranks, to the effect: 'Please make sure you make it absolutely clear that I haven't missed out Hughie McLeod on purpose, it's just that I never saw him play!' On another tack, I elected not to be too pernickety when it came to a player's origins, because there are plenty of instances of non-Borderers who turned out for clubs in the South, yet nobody in Selkirk ever complained that Iain Paxton was actually born in Fife, while Gala were indebted to the indefatigable David Leslie whenever he shone for the Maroons, despite his roots being on Tayside.

Given the fact that we started this book with a tribute to the late Bill McLaren, it seems only appropriate that we should begin with the choices of his nephew, the broadcaster and journalist Bill Johnstone, who knuckled down to the task with the sort of careful attention to detail which used to be a hallmark of his uncle's preparations for his peerless commentaries. His team reads as follows:

15) Chris Paterson (Gala).
14) Tony Stanger (Hawick).
13) Jim Renwick (Hawick).
12) Jock Turner (Gala).
11) Ronnie Cowan (Selkirk).
10) John Rutherford (Selkirk).
9) Gary Armstrong (Jed-Forest).

1) Hugh McLeod (Hawick).
2) Colin Deans (Hawick).
3) Tom Elliot (Gala).
4) Alan Tomes (Hawick).
5) Peter Brown (Gala).
6) Derrick Grant (Hawick).
7) David Leslie (Gala).
8) Jim Telfer (Melrose).

There are plenty of familiar faces in this attractive side, although the mellifluous Bill was the only person to plump for Cowan, who was a star on the wing at Philiphaugh before he switched codes to rugby league, while his inclusion of the Netherdale prop, Elliot, was only shared by one of the other journalists.

But there again, it was not surprising that nobody picked exactly the same ensemble, and one suspects that we could go into 50 different hostelries, scattered throughout the Borders and emerge with 50 different line-ups (and a sore head!), even if several positions were unanimous choices. The most obvious was John Rutherford, who could have walked into any club anywhere in the world at his peak, while Colin Deans is widely acknowledged as the best hooker who has ever played for Scotland and not just the Borders. There was similar unanimity when it came to Gary Armstrong, who must be one of the toughest little fighters who ever pulled on the No 9 jersey, although the symbiosis which existed between Rutherford and Roy Laidlaw was such an abiding feature of their partnership that it is difficult to think of one without the other.

Next up, we have the selections of David Ferguson, the rugby correspondent of *The Scotsman* and the man who worked with Jim Telfer on the latter's autobiography, *Looking Back . . . For Once*. As somebody who grew up in the Borders,

David has been obsessed with oval-ball matters since he was at school, and this is his XV.

15) Chris Paterson (Gala).
14) Tony Stanger (Hawick).
13) Keith Robertson (Melrose).
12) Jim Renwick (Hawick).
11) Roger Baird (Kelso).
10) John Rutherford (Selkirk).
9) Gary Armstrong (Jed-Forest).
1) Hugh McLeod (Hawick).
2) Colin Deans (Hawick).
3) Norman Pender (Hawick).
4) Alan Tomes (Hawick).
5) Doddie Weir (Melrose).
6) David Leslie (Gala).
7) Derrick Grant (Hawick).
8) Derek White (Gala).

Once again, the spine of the side almost picks itself, and although few of the present crop of rugby scribes are old enough to recall McLeod, one only has to speak to some of the older supporters at Mansfield Park to recognise that he was something special. David added the following: 'In the back row, Leslie and White are not Borderers, but were players who opened my eyes to rugby, as a youngster in Gala, in the late 1970s/early 1980s. I would pick John Jeffrey and Jim Telfer if you wanted real Borderers.' We will have them sitting on the bench, then, waiting to take out their frustrations on the opposition in the final quarter.

Paterson, the quiet achiever, who has amassed more than 100 caps and has turned out in a variety of positions, or sat on the bench for a significant spell without ever throwing a Kris Boyd-style strop, also featured on the roster chosen by

Alasdair Reid, the rugby correspondent of the *Sunday Herald*. This ran as follows:

15) Chris Paterson (Gala).
14) Tony Stanger (Hawick).
13) Alan Tait (Kelso).
12) Jim Renwick (Hawick).
11) Roger Baird (Kelso).
10) John Rutherford (Selkirk).
9) Gary Armstrong (Jed-Forest).
1) Hugh McLeod (Hawick).
2) Colin Deans (Hawick).
3) Tom Elliot (Gala).
4) Alan Tomes (Hawick).
5) Nathan Hines (Gala).
6) John Jeffrey (Kelso).
7) David Leslie (Gala).
8) Jim Telfer (Melrose).

As many people might have recognised by this stage, there were more variations among the backs than in the forwards and the power of the ferocious Green Machine was understandably well to the fore in the panel's deliberations. Alasdair added: 'I've limited myself to players I've actually seen . . . apart from the props, where I'm going on their (lofty) reputations.' As for those people who are inclined to argue that if Hines is Scottish, then they are Dame Edna Everage, one does not recall too many of the home fans quibbling with his Aussie background in 2006 and 2008 when the big forward was performing heroics in the Scottish cause while they beat England at Murrayfield.

Some of my respondents approached their task with rather more zeal than others. The most conscientious of the lot, which will surprise nobody who has ever witnessed him filling pages of the Edinburgh *Evening News* with the energy which springs from a man who truly loves his sport, was that newspaper's rugby correspondent, Bill Lothian, who not only took care with his choices, but provided a detailed brief on the rationale behind them. First up, let's have a look at his best ever Borders XV:

15) Chris Paterson (Gala).
14) Keith Robertson (Melrose).
13) Jock Turner (Gala).
12) Jim Renwick (Hawick).
11) Alan Tait (Kelso).
10) John Rutherford (Selkirk).
9) Gary Armstrong (Jed-Forest).
1) Hugh McLeod (Hawick).
2) Colin Deans (Hawick).
3) Jock Wemyss (Gala).
4) Jock Beattie (Hawick).
5) Billy Hunter (Hawick).
6) John Jeffrey (Kelso).
7) David Leslie (Gala).
8) Jim Telfer (Melrose).

This was certainly a more eclectic line-up than some of the others in this chapter, but Bill added the following comments, which shed light on his reasons for his second-row picks, neither of whom appeared on any the other lists.

I make no apologies for starting with two players who never made a Lions tour, because they unquestionably should have done and, in the case of the full-back, there is hopefully still time. I sat a few feet away from the slightly-built Robertson when he was immediately put under pressure on his Scotland debut by the All Blacks and he passed with flying colours, going on to show great ball skills throughout his Test career.

Jim Renwick would be the first name down on any team sheet of mine and Alan Tait is a league/union legend. Jock Turner was class. John Rutherford is synonymous with time on the ball and he worked so hard on his kicking to become world-class. Gary Armstrong was extraordinarily brave and skilful enough to edge Roy Laidlaw, Bryan Redpath and a particular favourite player of mine, the ultra-competitive Duncan Paterson.

I'm fortunate to have a had a dad from the Borders (Redpath, outside Earlston), who knew his rugby and regaled me with tales of players/characters like Charlie Farmer and Wull Purdie of Jed, Willie Welsh of Hawick, Happy Wilson of Kelso and others.

But the reverence in which my dad talked of Hugh McLeod and Jock Beattie, in particular, convince me that they must be worth their place, along with Deans, who seemed to get such a raw deal from the '83 Lions Test side in New Zealand. Jock Wemyss was capped on either side of the First World War, which was some feat and, having been taken around various Edinburgh club grounds whenever a Border side was in town, an abiding memory for me, as a youngster, was the sheer size (back then) of Hawick's Billy Hunter. He would be tiny by today's standards, of course.

Telfer walks in because of his work rate and sheer commitment and some of my ex-club-mates tell of playing Melrose and him standing tall in a tackle, shouting: 'C'mon lads, they dinnae ken what a ruck be!' Leslie, the ultimate hunting dog of a flanker, qualifies from his time at Gala (and strong-mindedness to pick his games, so as to be fresh and the star of the 1984 Grand Slam), while Jeffrey was always perpetual motion.

Bill's choices spanned the period between 1914 and the present day, but he was fulsome in his praise for Alan Tait and that view was echoed by Kevin Ferrie, the chief rugby writer at the *Herald*, who sang the praises of the man who excelled in both rugby codes. Asking me to stress that this XV only includes players he has watched in the flesh – which explains the omission of Hugh McLeod – Kevin's team reads thus:

15) Peter Dods (Gala).
14) Chris Paterson (Gala).
13) Alan Tait (Kelso).
12) Jim Renwick (Hawick).
11) Roger Baird (Kelso).
10) John Rutherford (Selkirk).
9) Gary Armstrong (Jed-Forest).
1) Jim Aitken (Gala).
2) Colin Deans (Hawick).
3) Geoff Cross (Border Reivers).
4) Alan Tomes (Hawick).
5) Iain Paxton (Selkirk).
6) John Jeffrey (Kelso).
7) David Leslie (Gala).
8) Derek White (Gala).

Straight away, this strikes one as a team with plenty of oomph, with the versatile Paxton able to slot into the second row, while it was perhaps surprising that Kevin was one of only two people to choose the redoubtable Aitken, who was one of the cornerstones of the Scottish front row at the same time as he was leading his country to Grand Slam glory in the late winter of 1984.

The last of our part-time selectors is William Paul, who used to be a colleague of mine on *Scotland on Sunday* and who

can remember the days when our then editor, Andrew Jaspan
– a Mancunian, incidentally – decided that his newspaper
should fling caution to the wind and prepare a pull-out for
publication on the day after the 1990 Scotland–England clash.
If the match had progressed as anticipated, climaxing in Will
Carling's visitors lifting the Grand Slam, Triple Crown and
Calcutta Cup, this might have precipitated one of the biggest
acts of mass littering ever witnessed in Scotland, but mercifully, the editor's faith was vindicated and the paper, which
came out on Sunday 18 March, duly sold more copies than
any edition since the launch issue. Willie's line-up is:

15) Chris Paterson (Gala).
14) Tony Stanger (Hawick).
13) Jim Renwick (Hawick).
12) Gregor Townsend (Gala).
11) Keith Robertson (Melrose).
10) John Rutherford (Selkirk).
9) Gary Armstrong (Jed-Forest).
1) Jim Aitken (Gala).
2) Colin Deans (Hawick).
3) Hugh McLeod (Hawick).
4) Alan Tomes (Hawick).
5) Peter Brown (Gala).
6) John Jeffrey (Kelso).
7) David Leslie (Gala).
8) Jim Telfer (Melrose).

On first inspection, the only major quibble lies in the inclusion of the mercurial but inconsistent Townsend, and yet that
ignores the fact that he dazzled during the 1999 Five Nations
Championship, even if one suspects that he would be better
paired with somebody like Tait. Yet, on the other hand, this is
the only side which finds room for both Aitken and McLeod

who, together with Deans, would surely have comprised a fearsome front row. Willie added: 'There was no place for Roy Laidlaw and Craig Chalmers, which seems wrong almost. It was also a toss-up between Derek White and David Leslie, while Tony Stanger gets in on the back of his famous Grand Slam try which cheered a nation.'

Many Border aficionados will have their own views on this subject, so it seemed a decent notion to draw up two lists of the best players the Borders have produced in the last 100 years and invite readers of this book to suggest their own formations and offer their opinions on how the contest might have unfolded. These are my selections, and, hopefully, they reflect the massive amount of international-class performers who have paraded their talents in the South and also glittered on the global stage, whether for their homeland or as part of various Lions parties in the southern hemisphere. And, in order to put together two fine partnerships, I have reunited Rutherford and Laidlaw in one of the sides and matched up the more recent duo of Chalmers and Armstrong in the other.

In the spirit of the occasion, one team is called 'The Borders' and the other 'The South'. And, who knows, perhaps, at some stage in the future, some Internet wizard can turn this contest into a 'virtual' match, light the touch-paper and await the sparks. At any rate, one can offer two confident predictions. Firstly, that no matter the victors, they would know they had been in the mother of all scraps by the conclusion. And secondly, that a massive number of spectators would willingly turn out to watch these warriors do battle.

THE BORDERS
15) Chris Paterson (Gala).
14) Tony Stanger (Hawick).
13) Jim Renwick (Hawick).
12) Jock Turner (Gala).

11) Roger Baird (Kelso).
10) Craig Chalmers (Melrose).
9) Gary Armstrong (Jed-Forest).
1) Jim Aitken (Gala).
2) Ross Ford (Border Reivers).
3) Tom Elliot (Gala).
4) Alan Tomes (Hawick).
5) Doddie Weir (Melrose).
6) John Jeffrey (Kelso).
7) David Leslie (Gala).
8) Derek White (Gala).

THE SOUTH
15) Peter Dods (Gala).
14) Keith Robertson (Melrose).
13) Alan Tait (Kelso).
12) Gregor Townsend (Gala).
11) Iwan Tukalo (Selkirk).
10) John Rutherford (Selkirk).
9) Roy Laidlaw (Jed-Forest).
1) Hugh McLeod (Hawick).
2) Colin Deans (Hawick).
3) Jock Wemyss (Gala).
4) Peter Brown (Gala).
5) Iain Paxton (Selkirk).
6) Kelly Brown (Border Reivers).
7) Derrick Grant (Hawick).
8) Jim Telfer (Melrose).

Chapter Fifteen

A Hero for the 21st Century

HOW DOES ONE define professionalism? Is it a case of strutting into the spotlight, playing a starring role for a small club, and automatically aspiring to move elsewhere for better terms and conditions, in a winning team, as soon as the opportunity arises? Or is it a state of mind, a relentless quest for self-improvement and constant practice on the filthiest of nights, even when the rest of your peers have decamped to the comfort of the changing room or the bar? It cannot simply be the former, otherwise a teenage David Beckham, dreadfully homesick, but nonetheless determined to make his mark in football, would never have persisted with working incessantly on his free kicks, even as he held back the tears in Manchester. But it cannot solely be the latter either because, if it was, then anybody with enough guts and commitment would have the wherewithal to forge a successful career in sport when reality dictates that only a tiny percentage actually achieve that ambition.

I ask these questions because I have just been talking to Chris Paterson about his rise to the highest ranks of Scottish rugby and, as we flicked back to the 1980s when the youngster was growing up in Galashiels, the thought occurred: has there ever been a more self-effacing, down-to-earth customer in his nation's sporting history than this 33-year-old, who has created his own piece of fame by becoming the first Scotsman to gain 100 international caps in rugby? Given his litany of record-breaking exploits, his surpassing of the points tallies accrued by such legends as Andy Irvine and Gavin Hastings, and the fashion in which he became, for a lengthy period, the most prolific kicker on the planet, Paterson could surely be forgiven a trace of hauteur, or a tinge of solipsism, following a career which has been replete with honours. But no! He may have become a poster boy for Scott's Porage Oats and modelled new Scotland kit, but his feet have never left terra firma, even as he has travelled to the southern hemisphere, South America and Europe, either with Scotland or Edinburgh (or briefly at Gloucester), or in his early days as a teenager, turning out for his local club in Galashiels. All that has mattered is rugby and doing his utmost for his team. Personal glory has never entered the equation, not even when he was being messed around by a variety of Scotland coaches in a tempestuous decade which saw Paterson placed on the wing, or at full-back, relegated to the bench or left out of some squads altogether . . . and this without him ever thinking about following Kris Boyd's example and walking out on his country in the huff.

Perhaps his background in the Borders shaped and moulded him to the most significant degree. Or maybe it was his family and their encouragement in the early days. At the outset, there were bounce games with his elder brother, Davie, while the fledgling Chris heeded the quiet advice passed on by his uncle, Duncan, who was an altogether more aggressive and voluble presence in the Scotland stand-off berth during his ten-cap career in the late 1960s and 1970s. So too, he joined Gala and became a regular on the periphery of the action, patrolling the sidelines, as he told me, and learning from the greats.

> When I was growing up, the attitude in the Borders was that you looked after your own first, so I went to Netherdale and I was a ball-boy at league matches and, soon enough, I was being inspired by different players; Peter Dods, Derek White,

Ian Corcoran [who won just one cap, but made a big impression on Paterson] and the great thing was that you weren't just close to the Gala players, but you also got to see the stars from the other clubs as well. I remember being impressed by John Jeffrey and saw, at first hand, how much work he put in, and that showed me what you had to do to succeed in rugby.

My brother was always keen on the game and I just joined in when I was old enough. Everybody played in those days, and that was another terrific thing about the Borders; the sense that everybody you met was keen on the sport and there were always places to play, chances to practise and people who wanted to help, whether it was at school, or in the park, or whenever I went down to the Gala club. You never actually thought twice about it. It was just natural that I should play rugby, because I was surrounded by it. It is part of the Borders culture and it always will be. There was just this tradition, this awareness, that a lot of people had come from these small towns and they had gone on to play at Murrayfield and Twickenham and all those places. That made it real for me, the same as being a ball-boy did: you saw all these high-profile players a few yards away from you, and you could relate to rugby in a way that you never could with football.

These were the days, in the late 1980s and early 1990s when it was simply taken for granted that the Borders was *the* place to make your name in rugby. The national team won more matches than they lost, the Scots were on the brink of a Grand Slam in 1990 and a semi-final place at the World Cup 18 months later; Melrose were poised to commence a sustained period of dominance, following on from Kelso's success on the club championship circuit; and even at school, Paterson received coaching from the likes of Rob Moffat, and occasional tips and motivational speeches from Jim Telfer. Of course, these figures belonged to another generation, but Chris was also in thrall at Galashiels Academy to one of the senior boys, a teenager whose burgeoning talent and instinctive skills were already the talk of the town. The name was Townsend, Gregor Townsend, and he had a licence to thrill on his meteoric rise from Netherdale into his country's ranks in 1993, during which period the normally matter-of-fact Paterson began to regard him with a sort of hero worship. 'He was an icon to me, and he couldn't have been nicer,' said Paterson, adding the important rider: 'People will always have opinions about Gregor because of the way he played the game, but he was brilliant to me.'

Basically, Townsend, on any given afternoon, could dazzle and dismay spectators in the space of a few moments. Much of what he did was off-the-cuff, sublimely spontaneous, and the thought often occurred that if he did not know what he was going to do next, how on earth could the opposition possibly twig what was passing through his mind? The downside was that when his improvisation unravelled, so did his poise and, too often, the genius was accompanied by a gaffe or two, which cost his side dearly. In Paris in 1995, for instance, people marvelled at the 'Toony Flip', which allowed Gavin Hastings to run, unmolested, under the French posts in the last minute. They tended to forget that it was Townsend's erratic kicking which had gifted his opponents a way back into the match in the first place.

Yet, from Paterson's perspective, his Galashiels confrère was a rugby-style Lochinvar, a lustrous knight of the oval ball milieu, and although people nowadays might associate Chris more with metronomic kicking, fantastic cover tackling such as the efforts which repulsed Ben Foden and Luke McLean during the 2011 Six Nations Championship, and all-round steadiness, we are inclined to forget that he, too, was a master of the unexpected when he started weaving his magic for

Gala, such as when they marched to the final of the Scottish Cup at Murrayfield and beat their Border rivals, Kelso, 8–3 in 1999.

Indeed, if ever there was an illustration of the fashion in which Paterson clung to his roots and retained his allegiance to the Borders, it happened on that afternoon when his inspirational solo try and drop goal were the only points his side mustered, and yet they proved sufficient to guarantee victory. Even now, as he told me, the recollection of that special occasion obviously has a resonance for Paterson, because, although he had already made a positive impact with Scotland's under-18, under-19 and under-21 sides, some of them as captain, that final was different. This one was for Galashiels.

It perhaps sounds a little bit twee, but that was a fantastic day and one of the reasons was the fact that the whole town was behind us and thousands of them came to Edinburgh to cheer us on. The game itself was tense, and, predictably enough, Kelso made us fight for our win, but a lot of our former players were in the crowd and we weren't just doing it for ourselves, we were doing it for the whole community, and that has always been part of the key to the success of rugby in the Borders. Basically, you realised that when the club was going well and the results were positive, the town felt better about itself.

I can remember driving down the A7 back to Galashiels later that night and some of the supporters' buses had stopped at various pubs on the journey, and you could barely believe your eyes. Our fans had got right into the fancy dress lark and the A7 was lined with penguins, parrots, whatever you care to mention. It was quite surreal, but it summed up the emotions which were flying about at the end. I will never ever forget that day.

If these were precious memories, Paterson experienced mixed fortunes during the next decade, as did Scotland, whose infernal and protracted difficulties in coming to terms with professionalism hardly helped. When he made his debut, against Spain in the 1999 World Cup, it was in the full-back position, and his side romped to a 48–0 victory in Edinburgh. But that was the 21-year-old's only appearance in a tournament which finished, like so many others, in defeat to New Zealand. That climaxed a year where the Scots had produced some wonderfully compelling displays, most notably in burying the French in Paris, but life was rarely to taste as sweet again for a long time. Part of the problem was that the selectors were never really sure what to do with Paterson and the player himself scarcely made their task any easier, because he was so damned versatile. Townsend, an effective and dynamic attacking threat in 1999 when partnered by two quality midfield enforcers in the shape of Alan Tait and John Leslie, cut a much less menacing figure in the 2000 championship, not least as a consequence of the tough-as-teak Tait having retired at the conclusion of the World Cup campaign. But when Ian McGeechan could have handed Paterson his opportunity in the No 10 berth, instead, he persevered with Townsend in the role during the losses to Italy (34–20) and France (16–28) before switching him to centre and picking Duncan Hodge in the ensuing three matches. These brought further reverses against Wales and Ireland before, against all the odds, the Scots regained the winning habit against previously all-conquering England on a filthy day in Edinburgh with Hodge proving the hero of the hour in his team's 19–13 success.

Perhaps, with hindsight, that victory was something of a mixed blessing. If the Scots had landed the wooden spoon, one doubts if McGeechan could have stayed so loyal to his troops and he might have been forced to tear up the script and begin afresh. Whereas, with the RFU's finest despatched back to London with their tails between their legs, the Scottish coaching team acted as if the rest of the Six Nations had been a series of aberrations, rather than acknowledge the more plausible explanation that a complacent English line-up had sauntered into Murrayfield and their overconfidence had been exposed in conditions which were a great leveller. McGeechan had plenty of time to reflect on the matter in the build-up to the summer tour of New Zealand, but it was evident to the majority of us who had watched the Six Nations that Scotland were a pale shadow of the side which had dazzled briefly in the spring of 1999. And all their deficiencies were brutally exposed when they were thrashed by the All Blacks over the course of two Tests, which highlighted the fact that life had moved on in leaps and bounds since the Scots used to acquit themselves well on these torrid southern hemisphere trips.

Paterson was involved in both matches and, despite scoring his maiden international try, was as shell-shocked as anybody by the scale of the 69–20 trouncing in Dunedin and subsequent 48–14 pummelling in Auckland. But although he turned out at stand-off in one of the midweek fixtures on the tour, it did not signal his belated move to No 10. Instead, and this was at the point where some of us seriously began to question whether McGeechan was losing the plot, the need to fit Paterson and Glenn Metcalfe into the same team saw the Borderer moved to the wing in 2001, where he applied himself as manfully as ever, but was patently not in his best position. Yet, conscientious as ever, and simply thankful that he was gaining the chance to wear the thistle, Paterson rolled with the punches, kept his head down and practised relentlessly on improving his goal-kicking. There was something quietly heroic about the manner in which he transcended the rising clamour among many supporters and sections of the media for him to be picked at stand-off. If he had been more of a prima donna, he might have won the argument. But if he had been more of a prima donna, he would not have been Chris Paterson.

However, this did not mean that he was not thinking about the question. As a teetotal non-smoker with a consummately professional attitude, he was ready to wear any number on his back, but Paterson later admitted that he had indulged in thoughts of what might have been. 'In all honesty, I do wonder how I would have developed as a stand-off. If I played consistently at international level, looking back, there's a "what if" scenario in the back of my mind,' said Paterson last year. 'On the other side of that, I wouldn't have had as many caps, probably wouldn't have had as long a career. But yes, there is a "what if". There are some unanswered questions in my own mind, but I don't feel as if I have played in the position long enough to compare myself to the guys that are there.'

Perhaps we should merely consider the most telling piece of evidence, which arrived in the midst of an otherwise depressingly pedestrian display from Scotland at the World Cup in Australia in 2003, where there were rumours of dressing room unrest, allied to some pretty awful performances in the early stages. Paterson grabbed a brace of tries during the otherwise drab 32–11 victory over Japan, and kicked all their points in the dismally one-sided 51–9 loss to the French at the Telstra Stadium in Sydney, and these results meant that Scotland needed to beat Fiji to avoid missing out on the quarter-finals for the first time in their history. By this stage, it was pretty clear that Townsend's old ability to serve up champagne rugby had gone flat and thus, in what was a make-or-break situation, Paterson was asked to take over in the No 10 berth, oblivious to the fact that he had played in that position only three times since turning professional in 1999. With other individuals this would have constituted a massive gamble, but not with Chris, whose steely resolve was one of the few positives to emerge from that World Cup of woes.

Quite simply, he was outstanding, both in his defensive chores and in marshalling his troops round about him. For a while, the Fijian sledgehammer, Rupeni Caucaunibuca, threatened to beat the Scots on his own, scoring two barn-storming tries, and giving his side a potentially crucial advantage. And yet time after time, Paterson kept kicking the Scots back into contention. He scored five penalties, which meant they only trailed by a few points when the Pacific Islanders might already have been out of sight. As the climax arrived, his team were still in arrears, but eventually, the redoubtable Tom Smith managed to score a try in the dying moments and Paterson slotted the conversion for a 22–20 victory which had been as fraught as it sounds. Surely now, the debate could cease, and the Gala man could settle into his new berth on an extended basis?

Er, that would be a no. Or at least, not any longer than it took Matt Williams, the coach who was tasked with orchestrating a revival at Murrayfield in the aftermath of that miserable World Cup – the Scots were swatted aside 33–16 by the Australians in the quarter-finals – to find somebody else who could step into the breach during one of the most turbulent and troublesome periods in Scotland's recent history. In his defence, the Australian mentor could probably counter that Paterson did not exactly set the heather on fire in 2004, but nor did anybody else for that matter during Williams' ill-starred tenure. Then, of course, there was another vocal critic of Paterson's displays at No 10.

And that man was Paterson himself, as he told Alasdair Reid in the *Sunday Times*.

It's nice when people say good things about you, but during the World Cup, I wasn't really noticing such things. To be honest, I wasn't very happy with the way that I played against Australia and I made a lot of mistakes against Fiji and a lot of mistakes all the way through the tournament. In any case, what you read and what you believe are two entirely different things. It's flattering to know now that good things were being said about me, but that can all change so quickly, so you know you shouldn't dwell on it. At the end, I actually found the talk of disarray in the squad to be quite ironic because the only effect of it was to bring us all closer together.

In many ways, these remarks embodied Paterson's inner being and his outlook on life. He fully understood how swiftly bouquets could turn to brickbats and it was his misfortune to be appointed Scotland captain for the following season of what turned into a winter of unrelenting gloom. I use the word 'misfortune', but he would never describe it in these terms. On the contrary, and regardless of the fashion in which 2004 developed into a long season in hell and the hapless Williams proved to be the opposite of King Midas in that everything he touched turned to dross, Paterson kept putting on a brave face amid the wreckage. His debut as skipper yielded a 23–10 defeat at the Millennium Stadium in Cardiff, and there were subsequent heavy losses to England (who won 35–13 at Murrayfield) and Ireland (who breezed to a 37–16 success in Dublin). The French waltzed into Edinburgh and won 31–0 and the Italians triumphed 20–14 in Rome, which did not simply earn the Scots a wooden spoon, but highlighted so many problems that it was painful to quiz Williams about these results. Paterson, in contrast, kept his head held high, refused to be dragged into talk of despair, sought positives from the worst of these displays – even the English and French debacles which left supporters in urgent need of antidepressants – and although there was to be no swift recovery, or not until

Williams had finally been put out of his misery, this was a Borderer, bloodied but unbowed.

That image has stuck with me for the last seven years. In the interim period, Paterson has been involved in some excellent victories – including the wins over France and England in 2006 and the Scots regaining the Calcutta Cup, as well as beating Argentina in 2008 – and he came off the bench to land a splendid drop goal, which helped his compatriots defeat Australia for the first time in 27 years in the autumn of 2009. Nobody could possibly quibble with his kicking record; he converted a remarkable sequence of 36 consecutive goals for Scotland between August 2007 and June 2008 – not missing a single attempt during the 2007 World Cup or the 2008 Six Nations Championship – and he has continued in that vein while overtaking all the old records held by Gavin Hastings. But it was a sign of his refusal to swagger or glory in these milestones which made him as much of a hero with the supporters as it left him uncomfortable in the spotlight.

Nonetheless, by the stage that Paterson prepared to gain his 100th cap – against the Welsh in Cardiff last year – nobody could question his commitment, nor training zeal, nor un-stinting desire to make the most of his qualities and keep pushing himself harder. Indeed, one of the most welcome sights in Scottish rugby throughout the previous decade had been the spectacle of 'Mossy' preparing to add to his tally of Test match points. There has never been anything flash in his approach, but his marksmanship, composure and appetite for constant practice had reaped a fantastic dividend and yet there was still the nagging issue of whether Scotland had got the very best out of him. Having started 33 matches at full-back, 45 on the wing and only 11 at stand-off – he had come off the bench on the other occasions – Paterson had remained stoical about this chopping and changing and done his nation proud, whether in his kicking, or robust tackling and effective attacking. He had led the Scots during two stints, firstly during the Williams fiasco, and secondly after the incumbent skipper, Jason White, was ruled out of the 2007 Six Nations with injury. Yet, despite his heroics at Edinburgh, where he had grafted tirelessly to nurture a winning mentality among his younger charges, or in the thick of battle with Scotland, where his exertions had shone like a beacon through a largely lacklustre decade, it was a reflection of the dilemma which surrounded Paterson that, even on the eve of his 100th cap, many people asked whether he had been messed around.

The player himself could do little about that speculation. But his preparation for the Welsh contest explained a lot about his longevity and sustained hunger for the fray.

> I have never, ever, looked back and been happy with what I have done. I think that is the main reason why I am still here. In my own mind, I have never reached anywhere near where I have wanted to reach in my own performance. I have been massively lucky, but I don't feel as if I have got these many caps. I feel that I want another one, and another one, and I want to keep going. Yes, there will come a point where I will get to the end, and my major aim is that when I get there, I can sit back and say I am proud of what I have achieved, really proud, and I couldn't have done any more. But I am almost embarrassed that I have been lucky enough to amass this many. I feel really quite uncomfortable talking about it. Every time there is a new Six Nations Championship, I feel as if I am starting from square one. I am getting older and everybody is expecting me to drop off a bit, but that knowledge drives me on. I want to be the fittest in training. That sounds like a physical thing, but mentally, it is probably more important.

This incessant drive was admirable, but it could not prevent his 100th cap from unravelling into a traumatic experience which was nearly ruined by tragedy. In pure sporting terms, the Scots threw away an excellent position to lose 31–24 after leading by ten points with as many minutes remaining. But that was rendered almost superfluous when their winger, Thom Evans, sustained a life-threatening injury which forced him to be stretchered from the pitch, as the prelude to having major surgery on his neck during two operations. Within a few minutes of the match finishing, a former Scotland great – whose column I was ghosting – phoned to tell me, 'I've heard that Thom's neck is broken', and suddenly, the details of who had won or lost, missed a penalty or been yellow-carded, seemed very trivial. Paterson, too, had finished up in Cardiff's University Hospital after sustaining painful bruising to his kidney. Mercifully, there was no permanent damage to either man, although Evans, to nobody's surprise, later announced that his rugby career was over.

For months afterwards, as the Scotland coach, Andy Robinson, led his charges to some impressive results, including a first ever southern hemisphere series win in Argentina and a 21–17 win against South Africa at Murrayfield, it appeared that Paterson, too, might not gain many further opportunities to illuminate the Test stage, although he did make a brief appearance as a replacement in that latter triumph.

But nobody should have been in any doubt about the severity of his problems in Wales. He expanded:

Now I know that I am a hell of a lot better, I am able to look back and it was touch and go. The rugby medics hadn't come across anything like that before, but when they got me to hospital, they explained it was an injury that was quite common in car crashes. It looked at first as if I was going to have to lose my kidney, because it was torn in two places. So I was lucky the way it healed. That first night in hospital, there were a lot of tests and, fortunately, there were signs that it was healing. So, looking back, there was a high possibility that my career could have been over, but I was well looked after. Playing professional rugby with one kidney is maybe something you could have done if you had grown up with it, but losing it at 31 would have been different.

By this juncture, one began to suspect that Andy Robinson was preparing to let Paterson slip quietly into retirement without an excess of fuss or sentiment, because there was no sign of the Gala man when the Scots marched into the 2011 Six Nations Championship, with what now seems like a remarkable degree of misplaced confidence. The visitors, bolstered by a spectacular individual display from Richie Gray, produced some moments of genuine class despite slipping to a 34–21 loss at the Stade de France and, in the build-up to the next tussle with Wales at Murrayfield, there was an incredible amount of confidence in Robinson's charges gaining revenge for their late collapse of 12 months earlier. This was another problem with Scotland – the fashion in which the team swithered between lumbering pedestrianism and occasional shafts of spark and splendour – but that late afternoon turned into one of the most anticlimactic showings from the Scots in recent memory and the optimism vanished like the air in a burst balloon as the Welsh, no great shakes themselves, sauntered to a comfortable 24–6 victory. That night, as I walked back from Roseburn to Haymarket, I heard the same refrain a dozen times, albeit in differing stages of sobriety, from the Saltire-clad throng. 'Why are they still playing [Dan] Parks? Where has Chris Paterson gone? Christ, we need him back.'

The answer, of course, was that Paterson had gone nowhere, and was continuing to apply himself for Edinburgh, kicking points and tackling rivals with the juddering intensity of a man who knew that he might be required if Hugo Southwell or Rory Lamont – or both – suffered injuries, which is precisely what materialised. A month before his 33rd birthday, he was as desperate to add to his cap tally as ever, and offered a further explanation of his approach to these contests by spelling out that what his country needed in rugby was a solid base and gradual improvements rather than dramatic switches between one set of tactics and another. Indeed, he did this with such clarity it reinforced the impression that Paterson will become a pretty decent coach when he finally hangs up his boots.

He was, after all, speaking from experience and the knowledge that the Scots had only scored 61 tries during the previous decade of Six Nations activity. Predictably, England and France had fared substantially better, with 169 and 138 touchdowns respectively, while Ireland were on 133 and Wales on 107. But the statistic which really provided food for thought was the one which confirmed that the Italians, so often perceived as a one-dimensional unit with scant ability to break down rival defences, had managed 62 tries, despite losing the majority of their fixtures and often by heavy margins. Surely, in these circumstances, there was a mental block in the Scots' collective psyche? Yet, typically down to earth, Paterson responded that he and his compatriots could not control what had already happened, but they could resolve to improve on their execution, sharpen up their killer instinct, and master their basic professionalism in the future. This, he added patiently, would not be achieved by flinging the ball around like headless chickens, but by making sure there were support runners if somebody orchestrated a break, and that players were trusted to make the correct decisions in the heat of the moment. 'You don't go from 0 to 100, you go from 0 to 10, to 20, to 50,' he told the excellent writer, Tom English, in *Scotland on Sunday*, prior to adding: 'You do it in blocks. Wales and Ireland did it the last two years. I've played against these guys and I have known them for years and I am jealous. It's not about ambition or glory, it's just wanting to have that experience. I would love to be involved in scoring tries. And you almost envy those teams who run in a lot of them. We can do it too. But we just haven't proved it.'

The words underlined a couple of important points which Paterson had always stressed throughout his own career. Firstly, you do not gain any sustained success or lay the foundations for the future by indulging in quick fixes. Even as a pupil at Galashiels Academy, the teenager had watched and learned from the fashion in which the best coaches persevered with the boys who had talent; one or two mistakes at that embryonic stage of their development were never going to make or break a career. Secondly, there was no value in the Scots attempting to copy anybody else, whether it was the All Blacks or the Argentinians; they had to develop their own rhythm, and settle into a pattern which suited their personalities. This was what had happened in Paterson's early days at Netherdale and the lessons from that auspicious period had never been forgotten.

> We had the core of a good squad and we worked really hard for each other. Gary Parker was coaching at the time and he had this great confidence, which just rubbed off on everybody else. We developed a style of play where we just enjoyed what we were doing, having a go, scoring tries and winning games. Playing with Edinburgh, I have gone through some bad spells, when the harder we tried, the harder it seemed to be to have success. Sometimes, it makes sense to step back a little, and take things a little easier, because the more tension there is, the harder it is to perform to your best.

More than a decade later, Paterson was ready for the call and Robinson duly summoned him back into the Scotland squad for their third match of the 2011 campaign against Ireland at Murrayfield. This eventually yielded a close-fought 21–18 defeat – against opponents who subsequently played England off the pitch in Dublin – and it was as if Paterson had never been away, whether in the precision of his kicking or the solidity which he brought to an otherwise creaky defensive performance from the Scots, who lost three ties to nil, and continued to create openings without making opponents pay. Still, the afternoon illustrated that the 'P' words – Paterson, passion and professionalism – were still inextricably linked. And although there was to be no joy once again when he and his compatriots ventured to Twickenham in March, the visitors at least battled hard before succumbing 22–16 and one of the most memorable incidents in the contest occurred when Paterson, somehow or other, tracked back to thwart what appeared a gilt-wrapped try-scoring opportunity for his English counterpart, Ben Foden, who felt the full weight of a slab of Borders beef while being bundled into touch. This vignette was screened repeatedly in the aftermath, and yet, to his credit, Paterson refused to focus on an isolated act of derring-do. Instead, there was visible frustration that the Scots had been edged out in another close Six Nations fixture and, once again, were reduced to scrapping with the Italians to avoid the unsought wooden spoon. It was a script which had become wearily familiar and especially to somebody such as Paterson, who had made his international debut before the Azzurri had even entered the European tournament.

In the event, with the Borderer winning his 104th cap and frequently demonstrating that his powers had not diminished, allied to the Scots finally breaking their drought at Murray-field with tries from Nick De Luca and Nikki Walker, Italy were repelled 21–8 and could have few complaints about finishing bottom of the heap after squandering a glorious opportunity to beat the Irish in Rome earlier in the tournament. They might have run the Scots closer but for another piece of defensive brilliance from the senior man of the back line, with Paterson crunching into Luke McLean when the latter looked destined to cross for a try. And even if, in the final analysis, this was another mediocre crusade by Scotland, whose professional teams had equally struggled to make any serious impact on either the Magners League or Heineken Cup in the 2010-11 season, there remained a few reasons to be cheerful, whether in the powerful showings of warriors such as Gray, Al Kellock and Kelly Brown, or the attacking threat of Max Evans and youthful vim of Ruaridh Jackson, allied to the knowledge that Duncan Weir was sparkling in the wings and awaiting his chance.

However, any optimism had to be tempered by results; the only currency which counted for those who plied their trade on the professional rugby circuit. Anybody who has ever encountered Paterson would swiftly appreciate that he has no interest in stats for stats' sake – even though he has now accumulated an incredible haul of 783 points and will be confident of passing the 800 mark at the 2011 World Cup in New Zealand. Yet he has the requisite dedication, relish for training and ability to roll with the punches to suggest that he could become the rugby equivalent of Ryan Giggs or David Weir and continue his career at the highest level even as he approaches his fifth decade.

And that was the message which resoundingly came across when Paterson looked forward at the climax of another season. In May 2011 he had this to say:

I have no plans to stop playing. Your body dictates a lot, of course, but at the moment, I feel good, I want to improve, and I am as enthusiastic as ever. I'm a great believer in dealing with what is in front of you. Other people than me have adapted successfully. Take Jim Telfer, who has been involved in 40 years of rugby coaching and think of the developments that there have been there, particularly in the sport developing from an amateur to a professional game. Plenty of others played for Scotland and I came in, right at the end of the amateur era, although I was first capped, effectively, out of Gala. You have to adapt and be flexible and one of the ways of doing that is by using the advice of people around you.

This talk of Telfer and Gala and of Paterson's continuing pursuit of excellence brings us right back to where we started, in celebrating the constant ability of men (and women) in the South of Scotland to nurture and nourish generations of rugby talent. In which light, it seemed appropriate that I should ask Chris about the future for the region whence he originated, and also his message to youngsters who might want to try rugby.

I think it is as brilliant a game now as when I was first picking up a rugby ball at primary school and we were watching Gala every weekend and listening to the commentaries of Bill McLaren whenever the Five Nations Championship came around every year. Rugby teaches you about competition, about playing as part of a team and, basically, you get out of it what you put into it. So if you train hard and show a bit of discipline, you will learn the basics and you'll come to realise how much fun the game can be.

The top players are also still accessible to their communities. I know that I always want to hear how Gala have done and you can come to Murrayfield and we'll be glad to say hello and pass on a few tips, because that is how I started, when I was a ball-boy and people like Rob [Moffat] and Jim [Telfer] came along to Galashiels Academy and made it clear to us that they were interested in anybody who wanted to learn about rugby.

As for the Borders, well, there will always be rugby at the core of these towns, because there are too many people who care about the game for it to be otherwise. I have been to a lot of different countries, and I have seen how much rugby matters to people in New Zealand, for instance, but I also know, from my own experience, how much it means to people in the South of Scotland. And that isn't going to change any time soon.

The rest of Scotland might be fixated with football, and remain preoccupied by a pursuit which has, in the last few months, brought shame to Scotland's reputation, amid lurid stories, in banner headlines, of a manager being sent bullets in the post and being attacked during a game; and of the Old Firm being dragged along to Holyrood to explain exactly what they proposed to do to tackle the cancer of sectarianism. Rugby, in contrast, has never been more accessible to communities, to both genders, and to people of all ages, and while the sport has problems, it also has achievements to celebrate.

Much of this is down to the vision and the dedication of so many people in the Borders, for whom rugby continues to be an activity of beautiful noise and passionate intensity, and who have passed that message on from one generation to another. One trembles to think where the sport would be without that special distillation of Southern Comfort.

BORDERS TOWN-BY-TOWN GUIDE

GALASHIELS

This is the second largest town in the Scottish Borders, with a population of 12,367, according to the 2001 census. It is a major commercial centre in the region and the community is acknowledged for the quality of its textile manufacturing and is also the location of Heriot-Watt University's School of Textiles and Design.

To the west of Galashiels, there is an ancient site, known as the Picts' Work Ditch or Catrail, which extends many miles south. There is another ancient site in the north-west edge of the town, Torwoodlee, an Iron Age hill fort, which included a broch, which was built in the western quarter of the fort. However, the Romans destroyed this in AD 140, shortly after it had been completed. In 1599, Galashiels received its Burgh Charter, an event whose memory has been celebrated every summer since the 1930s by the 'Braw Lads Gathering', with riders on horseback parading through the town.

Robert Burns wrote two poems about Galashiels, 'Sae Fair Her Hair' and 'Braw Lads', while Sir Walter Scott built his famous home, Abbotsford, just across the River Tweed from the town. There remains some largely good-natured rivalry and banter between sections of the Galashiels townsfolk and those from the other Border communities, particularly their Hawick counterparts. The Galashiels citizens often refer to their fellow Borderers as 'dirty Teris', whilst the Hawick folk retort that Galashiels people are 'pail merks', supposedly because their town was the last to be plumbed into the main water system, and, as a consequence, residents had to rely on buckets for toilets!

In the east of the town, Netherdale is home to Gala RFC, and Gala Fairydean football club. The rugby organisation has produced a string of Scotland internationalists, including current star, Chris Paterson, who became the first man from his country to gain 100 test caps, against Wales in the 2010 Six Nations Championship. Other leading luminaries include the former British and Irish Lions duo, Gregor Townsend and Peter Dods, and the Maroons won the Scottish Cup when they defeated their Border opponents, Kelso, by 8-3 at Murrayfield in 1999. The former Scotland, Celtic and Hibs footballer, John Collins, was also born in the town

HAWICK

This is the largest town in the Borders, with a resident population of 14,801. A tributary of the River Teviot, the Slitrig Water, runs through the community, whose architecture is distinctive in that it features many sandstone buildings with slate roofs. The town is best-known for its annual Common Riding festival, which was described by the tourism *Rough Guide* as one of the best parties in the world, and for producing a greater number of rugby internationalists – 58 – in the modern era than anywhere else in Scotland. (It should be noted that Glasgow and Edinburgh Academicals accumulated a string of international honours before any other Scottish clubs sprung into existence). It was also the home of the late broadcaster, Bill McLaren, who famously declared that a day out of Hawick was a day wasted and who became universally known as the Voice of Rugby. He used to carry around with him a variety of mint sweets, called Hawick Balls, which were passed out by McLaren on his travels around the world.

The town is also renowned for its quality knitwear production, carried out by such well-known companies as Hawick Cashmere, Lyle and Scott, and Pringle of Scotland. The first knitting machine was brought to the town by an officer of the law, known as 'Baillie' John Hardie, who established his business with four hand-worked frames, producing linen stockings, and subsequently pioneering the use of lamb's wool.

People in Hawick call themselves 'Teris' after a traditional song, which includes the line 'Teribus ye teri odin.' Many residents also speak the local dialect of their community, which is informally known as 'Teri Talk'. This is similar, but not identical by any means, to the idioms spoken in surrounding towns, especially Jedburgh, Langholm and Selkirk. The Hawick tongue retains elements of Old English, together with particular vocabulary, grammar and pronunciation and its distinctiveness arose from the relative isolation of the town – it is one of the furthest communities from the sea anywhere in Scotland, and there was concerted, but ultimately futile, opposition to the decision to close the local railway station in 1969, one of the many victims of the notorious Beeching axe.

Some of the famous people to hail from Hawick include Sir Chay Blyth, Dame Isobel Baillie, and the motorsport trio, Steve Hislop, Stuart Easton and Jimmy Guthrie. The town has also produced three Scotland rugby internationalists who have won more than 50 caps: Colin Deans, Jim Renwick and Tony Stanger, the latter of whom scored the winning try in the famous 1990 Grand Slam-winning match against England.

JEDBURGH

This is a town and former royal burgh in the south of Scotland with a population of 4,090. The community lies in the Jed Water, a tributary of the River Teviot, and it is only a matter of 10 miles from the border with England. It boasts several historic buildings, including the substantial remains of Jedburgh Abbey, Mary, Queen of Scots' House, and Jedburgh Castle Jail, which is now a museum.

The town's close proximity to England made Jedburgh traditionally vulnerable to raids and skirmishes from south of the Border and, in 1745, the Jacobite army, led by Prince Charles Edward Stuart, passed through the town, en route to England. The expression 'Jeddart justice' or 'Jethart justice', where a man was hanged and tried afterwards, seems to have arisen from one summary execution of a gang of villains.

The town has produced several well-known people, including James Thomson, who wrote 'Rule Britannia' and was educated in Jedburgh, the Conservative MP, Michael Ancram, and the international scrum-half duo, Roy Laidlaw and Gary Armstrong, both of whom performed for Scotland and the British and Irish Lions with distinction.

Among the local specialities are Jethart Snails, which are brown, mint-flavoured sweets. The recipe is thought to have been brought to the town by French prisoners of the Napoleonic Wars and the boiled confectionery remains popular to this day.

KELSO

This is a market town and civil parish in the Borders, located where the rivers Tweed and Teviot have their confluence. The community has a population of 6,385, and is regarded as one of the most charming and quaint places in the south of

Scotland, with cobbled streets, elegant Georgian buildings and a French-style market square. The other main tourist attractions are the ruined Kelso Abbey, and Floors Castle, a William Adam designed house which was completed in 1726. The bridge was designed by John Rennie, who was subsequently pivotal in the construction of London's Waterloo Bridge.

Sir Walter Scott attended Kelso Grammar School in 1783 and said of the town: 'It is the most beautiful, if not the most romantic village in Scotland.' The aforementioned bridge was the cause of local rioting in 1854 when the Kelso townsfolk objected to paying tolls after the construction costs had been covered. Famous people from the community have included Sir William Fairbairn, the engineer who built the first iron-hulled steamship, the *Lord Dundas*, and constructed over 1000 bridges, using the tubular steel method which he pioneered, and Sir James Brunlees, who constructed many railways in the United Kingdom, in addition to designing the docks at Avonmouth and Whitehaven. On the sporting circuit, John Jeffrey was a member of the 1990 Scotland Grand Slam team and became famous throughout the game as the White Shark, whilst other internationalists from the club have included Roger Baird, Gary Callander, Andrew Ker, Adam Roxburgh and Ross Ford. Every year in July, the town celebrates the Border tradition of Common Riding, which is known in this case as Kelso Civic Week. The town has ample sporting and recreational pursuits to commend it, including two 18-hole golf courses and a National Hunt horse racing track, while the River Tweed is renowned for the quality of its salmon fishing.

LANGHOLM

This is known, colloquially, as the 'Muckle Toon' and is a burgh in Dumfries and Galloway, on the River Esk, with a

population of 2,311. The community grew around the textile
industry, but Langholm is probably best known as being the
birthplace of the poet and author, Hugh MacDiarmid, and the
engineer, Thomas Telford, and for the fact that the first man
to walk on the moon, Neil Armstrong, became the town's
first freeman of the burgh in 1972. The American, of Scottish
ancestry, was delighted to accept the honour and declared at
the time: 'My pleasure is not only that this is the land of
Johnnie Armstrong, rather that my pleasure is in knowing that
this is my home town and in the genuine feeling I have among
these hills, among these people.'

Langholm is surrounded by four hills, the highest being
the 300m Whita Hill, on which stands an impressive
obelisk, commemorating the life and achievements of Sir
John Malcolm, the distinguished soldier, statesman and
historian. The others are Warblaw, Meikleholmhill and
the Castle Hill. The community's local newspaper, *The
Eskdale and Liddesdale Advertiser*, which is known locally
as *The Squeak*, was established in 1848 and became the first
penny paper in Scotland.

In rugby terms, Langholm RFC is the oldest club in the
Borders, having come into being in 1871, although they have
only won the Border League on one occasion in the 1958-59
season when they were inspired by the presence of British and
Irish Lion, Ernie Michie.

MELROSE

This is one of the most picturesque locales in the Borders, a
town with a population of 1671. The community's name, in
its earliest form, was 'Mailros' ('the bare peninsula'), referring
to the original site of the monastery, which was recorded by
the Venerable Bede. This was later mentioned in the *Anglo-*

Saxon Chronicle with the name 'Magilros' (at which time, the town was part of Northumbria). It is a place which is steeped in history; with the resplendent Melrose Abbey surviving as one of the most beautiful monastic ruins in the country, and the burial site of the heart of the Scottish king, Robert the Bruce. The remains of the Abbey are cared for by Historic Scotland and the Roman fort of Trimontium stands nearby, close to Dryburgh Abbey. Melrose is also surrounded by a string of scenic villages such as Darnick, Gattonside, Newstead and Bowden.

Melrose is the home of Sevens rugby, with the abbreviated version of the sport, which has now been granted Olympic Games status, being invented by Ned Haig. The club has produced a significant number of Scotland internationalists, including Jim Telfer, who also coached the British and Irish Lions to success in South Africa in 1997; Keith Robertson and Craig Chalmers, who were members of the 1984 and 1990 Grand Slam-winning sides; and other such luminaries as scrum-half and former Scotland captain, Bryan Redpath, Doddie Weir, Robbie Brown and Graham Shiel.

The nearby Eildon Hills offer stunning vistas of the region and, if rumour is to be believed, King Arthur is supposedly buried there. Whatever the truth or otherwise of that statement, the community has much to recommend it to tourists and other visitors.

PEEBLES

This is a burgh in Tweeddale in the Borders, with a population of 8,159. Initially a market town, it also played a role in the woollen industry up until the 1960s, but the industrial composition of the community has changed in recent decades and it now home to many people, who commute to and from Edinburgh, as well as being a popular tourist destination. In the mid-19th century, this included health tourism, revolving around hydropathic establishments, which gradually developed into hotels, with the famous Peebles Hydro being one of the few survivors of that era. Notable buildings in the town include the old Parish Church, and Neidpath Castle, while Kailzie Gardens is another focal point. On a quirky note, Peebles has the highest shoe-shop-to-population ratio of anywhere in Britain, and the High Street features a diverse range of stores.

The community's annual local festival is called the Beltane and involves – as in many other Border towns – a Common riding and a pageant, which culminates in the crowning of the Beltane Queen, flanked by her court, on the steps of the parish church.

Traditionally, a person who was born in Peebles was called a 'gutterbluid', although precious few can lay claim to that distinction any longer, because the community no longer has a hospital. However, some of the famous people connected with Peebles include the explorer, Mungo Park, who practiced medicine in the town; the author, John Buchan, who practiced law; and the folk musician, Eric Bogle.

In rugby terms, Peebles RFC were only recently invited to join the Border League in 1996 and, before then, had participated in friendly matches with their Border rivals, since being founded in the 19th century. They have recorded a number of positive victories in the last 15 years and more than justified the decision to grant them entry. In football, meanwhile, the Scotland player, Kevin Thomson, became the first Borderer to appear in a European final when he played for Rangers in the UEFA Cup final of 2008.

SELKIRK

This Royal Burgh lies on the Ettrick Water, a tributary of the River Tweed, and has a population of 5,839. The people of the town are commonly knows as 'Souters', meaning cobblers, shoe makers and menders. Selkirk was formerly the county town of Selkirkshire and is the site of the first Border Abbey, while William Wallace was declared guardian of Scotland in this community, which also has connections to Bonnie Prince Charlie and the Marquess of Montrose. Selkirk's population swelled, because of the woollen industry, although that has virtually vanished in the Borders, and the town is better known in the 21st century for its Common Riding, the production of bannocks (dry fruit cakes) and tourism, containing as it does many spots of natural beauty. It boasts a museum, an art gallery, and strong associations with the explorer, Mungo Park, the poet and writer, James Hogg ('The Ettrick Shepherd') and the fabled Sir Walter Scott, as well as being the home of the contemporary author and journalist, Allan Massie. It also boasts Scotland's oldest horse racing track, the Gala Rig, on the town's outskirts.

Selkirk men fought with Wallace at Stirling Brig and Falkirk, and also with Robert the Bruce at Bannockburn, but it their connection with the battle of Flodden in 1513, when all but one of their number perished, which has provided the most poignant memories. That lone survivor, 'Fletcher', brought back with him a blood-stained English standard, which belonged to the Macclesfield regiment, and cast the captured standard round his head to indicate that all his compatriots from Selkirk had died on Flodden's fields.

The *Selkirk Grace*, a staple of every Burns Supper, has no connections with the town, beyond its name, originating as it did in the west of Scotland. Although attributed to Burns, it was already known in the 17th century as the *Galloway Grace* or the *Covenanters' Grace*, but came to be called the *Selkirk Grace*, because the Ayrshire poet was said to have delivered it at a dinner, hosted by the Earl of Selkirk.

It reads as follows:

> Some hae meat and canna eat,
> And some wad eat that want it,
> But we hae meat, and we can eat,
> Sae let the Lord be thankit.

Rugby has played a proud role in the history of the community, with the peerless Scotland and Lions stand-off, John Rutherford, only one of a clutch of Philiphaugh-based performers to have represented their country. The town's cricket club, which was founded in 1851, has gone on to win the Border League on more than 20 occasions. And Selkirk also has links with a number of Scottish footballers, including Bobby Johnstone – one of the Hibs' 'Famous Five' – and Celtic's Sandy McMahon.

Index